Eastern Europe
in the Post-War World

Eastern Europe
in the Post-War World

HUBERT RIPKA

With an Introduction by
HUGH SETON-WATSON

FREDERICK A. PRAEGER, *Publisher*
NEW YORK

BOOKS THAT MATTER

Published in the United States of America in 1961
by Frederick A. Praeger, Inc., Publisher
64 University Place, New York 3, N.Y.

Printed in Great Britain by Jarrold & Sons Ltd, Norwich

Contents

Introduction

It is a melancholy duty to present to the public this post-humous work of my friend, and friend of my father, Dr Hubert Ripka. But it is good that a work should appear which can remind British readers of the existence of nations which are now too often forgotten, and especially of the author's own nation, the Czechs, who live at the very heart of our continent of Europe, in Bohemia, as it is known in history, or Czecho-slovakia, as it has been called for the past half-century. It is also good that we should have the last thoughts on the affairs of these nations of one who was among the best-informed and most experienced observers of Central and Eastern Europe.

Hubert Ripka was a schoolboy under Austria-Hungary, and completed his university studies in the first years of the Czechoslovak Republic. After six years as Director of Archives at the War Ministry in Prague, he went into journalism, and in 1930 became foreign editor of *Lidove Noviny*, the outstanding liberal paper of Czechoslovakia (sometimes described as 'the *Manchester Guardian* of Central Europe'). In these years he made many journeys in Western and Central Europe, and was in close touch with internal and foreign policy in his own country. After the Munich disaster of 1938 he went into exile. In 1940 he became Minister of State in the Foreign Ministry of the exiled government of Czechoslovakia in London. During the absences of the Minister, Jan Masaryk, on official journeys to America, Ripka was responsible, under President Beneš, for his country's foreign relations. In 1945 he returned home, and served as Minister of Foreign Trade, while also lecturing as a professor of political history at Prague University. In 1948 the communist *coup d'état* drove him for a second time into exile, which lasted for the remaining ten years of his life, and was spent mostly in the United States. His two best-known books available in English are those which describe the two great tragedies of his country in which he was personally involved.[1]

In the last years of the Czechoslovak First Republic (up to 1938) Ripka was the foremost Czech journalist writing on foreign affairs. Though entirely independent in his judgment, he was very close to Dr Edward Beneš, who was for nearly twenty years Foreign Minister of Czechoslovakia before becoming its second President (in succession to the great T. G. Masaryk) in 1937. Ripka travelled much in Europe. He looked always to the West, especially to France. But in contrast to many Francophiles of the Danube countries, he also knew the countries that were his own country's neighbours, perhaps most of all Yugoslavia. Britain he got to know during the Second World War, and the United States in his second emigration, after 1948. He showed a great appreciation and understanding of the Anglo-Saxon civilizations.

He was a bitter opponent of German National Socialism, but always wished for friendship with the democrats among the large German minority in Czechoslovakia (which in the late 1930's numbered nearly three-and-a-half million out of about fifteen million). Despite the frenzied national hatred worked up by Hitler's agents, there were still Germans in Bohemia who believed in friendship with the Czech people. As a very young and ignorant observer, I had personal evidence of this when I witnessed a joint meeting of German and Czech social democrats in Plzeň in July 1938, one of the most moving experiences I can remember. Ripka was one of those on the Czech side who appreciated the value of the common struggle of Czech and German democrats. Later in the same month he addressed a public meeting of Germans and Czechs. He was one of the few prominent Czechs willing to do this.

It is one of the tragedies of the Second World War that this goodwill was destroyed. The cruelty of the German invaders in Czechoslovakia was a strong incentive to Czechs to think of

[1] *Munich; Before and after* (1939); *Czechoslovakia enslaved* (1950).

all Germans as enemies, and to Bohemian Germans to see in every Czech an avenger. To the Czech leaders in exile the Anglo-Saxon Powers on the one side and Soviet Russia on the other became overwhelmingly important. Relations with neighbour nations, not only Germans but also Poles and Hungarians, appeared relatively less important. In exile, the German democrats and Czechs quarrelled: for this no doubt both sides were to blame. The Czechoslovak government committed itself to the expulsion of the whole German community from Czechoslovakia, but insisted that this should be done in a humane manner. When it came to action, however, in 1945, the manner of the expulsion was anything but humane. For this various factors are responsible—the presence of the Soviet Army, the desire for revenge of persons who had suffered cruelly under the Nazis, the desire of the Czechoslovak Communist Party to build up for itself a territorial state within the state in the borderlands, its willingness to use unscrupulous careerists and even criminals for this purpose. The resultant tragedy was certainly not what Ripka had intended, but he has been bitterly and unjustly blamed for it by Germans expelled from Czechoslovakia and now living in West Germany.

It is easy in 1961 to look back and to criticize President Beneš for mistakes in his policy, in particular for his willingness to trust his Soviet ally. It seems to me that Czechs have a right to criticize, but that the British, whose government imposed the Munich surrender in 1938, agreed to the inclusion of Czechoslovakia in the Soviet sphere in Europe in 1944, and had no help to offer in 1948, would do well to hold their peace. I remember a conversation with Ripka early in 1939 about the Munich disaster. He then said that British and French had no right to blame Beneš for not choosing to fight alone against Hitler (certainly this was far from my own intention at that time), but that he himself as a Czech had the right. Ten years later the situation repeated itself when Beneš surrendered to the demands of the communist leader Gottwald, who by his subversion and intimidation of the Social Democrats was able to claim that he had a constitutional majority in parliament. By this surrender Beneš abandoned the leaders of the democratic Czech and Slovak parties (one of whom was Ripka) who by their resignation from the government had hoped to stop the communists in their plans to pack the police force and take over power under cover of the democratic coalition. But Beneš in 1948 was a sick man, cut off from the army and from the population, denied access to the radio and Press which were in communist hands. In 1943, when he signed the treaty of alliance with the Soviet Union which was the first step towards domination by Moscow, he had before him the example of Poland, whose exiled government had resisted Soviet claims and was clearly not being supported by its Western allies. Of the ability of Western governments to sacrifice their smaller allies to their own temporary interests, he had himself had abundant proof. Thus there was and is no easy answer to the problems which faced Beneš. The arguments for and against his actions will probably continue as long as free discussion about history is possible.

Czechoslovakia between the world wars was the model of a free democratic state in Central Europe. The name Czechoslovakia recalls to me the work of my father, R. W. Seton-Watson, who was associated with some of the work of its first two presidents, and thanks to whom I got to know it a little in its last years of peril, when Hitler was at the gate. Ripka was an outstanding intellectual product of that era of political freedom, and of immensely fertile intellectual and cultural activity, which could not fail to impress any sensitive visitor in those years. In 1961 Czechoslovakia is one of the most important of the medium-sized states in the world, indeed its international weight is probably greater than it has been since the late Middle Ages, the heroic age of the Hussites. But Czechoslovakia stands for very different values than in the time of Jan Hus or of Thomas Masaryk. Czech workers and peasants work harder than ever, and they have not lost their skill. The products of Czech industry are as good as they have ever been.

Introduction

Czech scientists, engineers and technicians are excellent, and there are many of them. The material wealth and human ability which this talented and industrious nation provide are systematically used by its communist government to further the aims of Soviet imperialism. In particular, Czech economic resources are being used with great effect for the penetration of Soviet political influence in the Arab world and Africa. The beautiful city of Prague is one of the most important centres for the training of students from Africa, not only in modern skills and techniques but in the doctrines of race hatred and class hatred which are to qualify them as agents of Soviet imperialism in their home countries. The aim is not African independence, whose triumph is now all but assured, but the systematic development among African nations of hatred against their former rulers and against all West Europeans and Americans, designed to make of them willing tools of Soviet imperialism on the world scale. From the point of view of the West, Czechoslovakia comes next after the Soviet Union and China as an enemy state, whose importance is still foolishly underrated.

How much remains, under the surface of communist rule, of the old spirit of Masaryk, of the old devotion of the Czech people to freedom, it is impossible to say. The repression which followed the conquest of Bohemia in the Thirty Years' War did not destroy the spirit of the Czech people. It is far too early to write off the Czechs. Meanwhile here is the last work of one of the best minds of the generation that made Czechoslovakia admired in the years before Munich. It was written in 1957, after the Polish revolt and the Hungarian Revolution of 1956. Some of its detail is out of date, for the pace of world politics in our time is too fast for any commentator. But from these pages the voice of Hubert Ripka speaks to free men in Europe and in the English-speaking countries whose true friend he was. For the future of his country, and of its neighbours, we can best express our hopes in the words of Jan Hus, which form part of the national arms of Czechoslovakia: *Pravda vitezí*, The Truth Will Prevail.

Foreword

THE NEED FOR A NEW EUROPEAN SETTLEMENT

The uprisings in Poland and Hungary in June and October 1956 drew the attention of the world once more to East Central Europe. They had all the explosive qualities needed to shake the free world into taking a new look at the Communist satellite states.

They caused surprise: who would have thought open revolt against a totalitarian power was even possible? They evoked astonishment: who would have believed that a small Hungarian nation would be able to keep on fighting for several weeks in desperate isolation against the overwhelming power of a Soviet army? They awakened the conscience of the world: for it is not easy to watch passively the brutal suppression of a nation fighting for freedom. They made us wonder whether the free nations should offer active support even though this would mean the risk of plunging the world into another catastrophic war, equally disastrous for the liberated as for the liberator.

The free world rejoiced because Soviet power was weakened by the heroic defiance of the Polish and Hungarian people, but this surge of hope was mingled with the fear that the Russians might avert attention from the crisis in which they found themselves by provoking a fight elsewhere in the world. For a time it seemed that war might be fanned in the same area in which the shots of Sarajevo in 1914 started the first great conflagration: and the same area in which Hitler's vain struggle began. Could history be prevented from repeating itself? it was asked.

We now realize that the First and Second World Wars could have been avoided. It was necessary to settle satisfactorily and in time the problems laden with risk of conflict. The Poles and

xiii

Hungarians emphasized in the most dramatic way that foresight could prevent a third world struggle. We merely needed the courage to find in time a just settlement; a sensible compromise that would be acceptable to all and unfair to none. The shots fired in Poland and Hungary were merely warning signals.

They reminded the Russians and the Western Powers that adjustments made in East Central Europe, after Hitler's war, on the basis of Soviet hegemony in that area could only create the danger of revolutionary outbreaks capable of starting a world conflict.

It would be a mistake to believe that, after the violent suppression of the Hungarian revolution, East Central Europe could remain quiescent for years to come.

In reality all the states in this area live to some extent in an atmosphere of latent rebellion against Soviet domination. The danger of another uprising has not been averted by stifling the Hungarian struggle for national freedom. And the unquiet compromise that has given Poland the chance of taking a new road to Socialism is packed with dynamite.

Even Russia has lost the stability preserved by the rigid ideology, the mystique and the ruthlessness of the police state with which Stalin kept the Russians in the chains of slavery. Russia, for the first time in thirty years, is unsettled and uneasy. It is not yet possible to see which way the Soviet empire will move, but we can be sure that it will not remain as we have known it under Stalin.

The European settlements made at Yalta and Potsdam are virtually outdated. A new European order must be sought – and sought urgently.

Until Europe's problems have been met courageously the equally dangerous issues of the Middle East, Africa and Asia will plague the world with fear of war. It was certainly symptomatic that the crises in East Central Europe and the Middle East both occurred in October 1956. Even allowing for the element of coincidence in these outbreaks of violence it will obviously be difficult to solve problems in Europe (especially in East Central Europe) without taking into consideration the disputes that still beset the Middle East. Neither can be happy while the other exists in a state of uncertainty or unhappiness.

Let us consider the ways that could lead to a genuine European settlement, reminding ourselves that the October revolutions in Poland and Hungary emphasized that a revision of the present position in East Central Europe is an essential condition for the peaceful co-operation and safety of the Continental countries.

The situation in East Central Europe is made up of so many intricately entwined problems that we cannot hope to make a fair assessment or practical suggestions for a new settlement of the status of the small nations in this middle zone until we study the basic realities of their present – and their past.

CHAPTER I

The Heterogeneous Character of East Central Europe

WHAT IS EAST CENTRAL EUROPE?

East Central Europe, the European Middle Zone, is sometimes called 'The Eastern Marchlands of Europe'. The variety of names applied to Central and Eastern Europe indicates that we are concerned with an area that is not geopolitically homogeneous. It has really only one common characteristic: from the north to the south, from the Baltic Sea to the Mediterranean Sea, it is occupied by small states of which only one – the Polish – has more than 20 million inhabitants. Poland has 27 million inhabitants; Yugoslavia, 17; Rumania, 16; Czechoslovakia, 13; Hungary, 10; Austria, 7; Bulgaria, 7; Finland, 4; Lithuania, 3; Latvia, 2; Estonia, over 1 million; Albania, over 1 million. We can include Greece with 8 million and Turkey with 21 million, but these two states are not as a rule included in East Europe; they belong to the Mediterranean area. At the same time, this oblong zone is encompassed by three far stronger states: Russia, Germany, and Italy. The U.S.S.R. has 200 million, Germany (West and East), 70 million, and Italy, 48 million. In this sense it is a mid-zone that is very sensitive to the influence of much more powerful neighbours, yet, at the same time, defends itself against complete domination by them.

When the First World War started, some of these mid-European peoples were not sovereign states. The Finns, Estonians, Latvians, Lithuanians and Poles (of whom some were subjects of Germany and others of Austria) were under Russian domination; the Czechs and Slovaks, and some Poles,

Ukrainians, Russians, Yugoslavs and Rumanians were subjects of Austro-Hungary. The Balkan nations – Serbs, Bulgarians, Greeks and Albanians – had gradually won their freedom from Turkish domination in the preceding half-century.

Only after 1918, when Germany was defeated, when Russia was in the throes of a revolution and the Habsburg and Ottoman empires were dissolved, did fourteen small states—Finland, Estonia, Latvia, Lithuania, Poland, Czechoslovakia, Austria, Hungary, Rumania, Bulgaria, Yugoslavia, Albania, Greece and Turkey – appear in the zone between the Baltic and the Mediterranean.

Their emergence fundamentally changed the European scene. They created singly and jointly the need to recognize a particular European area – the Mid-Zone, lying between Germany and Russia. Attempts to turn this new area into a *cordon sanitaire* – at once a barrier against Bolshevik Russia, and a dam to prevent German expansion – strengthened the idea that these small nations settled there had a special common mission. It suggested that they felt the desire to join together in some sort of community. Finally, these ideas (allied to the longing for unity) were strengthened during and after the last war when this area was subject first to Nazi and then to Soviet domination. Thus blossomed the belief of a specific European Mid-Zone with certain common interests that made it different from other parts of Europe.

PREVALENCE OF NATION-STATES

East Central Europe is a mosaic of totally different peoples, often quarrelling among themselves and lacking a common tradition, cultural or political. Nowhere else in Europe do we find crowded together (and to some extent intermingling) in a relatively small space so many different peoples and national minorities. East Central Europe, not having frontiers which would clearly divide it from other European areas, was subject to alternating pressure and penetration from the West and the

East (the German '*Drang nach Osten*' and the Slavonic '*Drang nach Westen*') and even, in earlier times, Turkish expansion from the South and Scandinavian expansion from the North.

In the Middle Ages several states emerged in this area in much the same way as the modern nations have appeared; at least in this sense that in each of them the particular nationality played a leading role in the drama of creation. This was so with Poland, Bohemia (the Czech Kingdom that in our time became Czechoslovakia), Hungary, Austria, Serbia and Bulgaria. For a certain time Croatia, too, was an independent state, and after its incorporation into the Hungarian Empire it kept a considerable autonomy. So did Transylvania. The principalities of Wallachia and Moldavia, which formed modern Rumania, were virtually autonomous states if not actually independent.

The passing centuries have only strengthened the memory of these peoples, making them all the more conscious that they once enjoyed national independence. And this memory of past glory and of liberty became a powerful source of inspiration when, from the beginning of the nineteenth century, they began under the impact of modern nationalism to strive for the 'renewal' of their national independence. Nearly all the states created after 1918 in East Central Europe gloried in the traditions of the great past that preceded their inclusion in the Ottoman, Habsburg and Romanoff empires.

The sturdy nationalism of the new states only emphasized the heterogeneous character of East Central Europe; after the fall of the three empires (of which only Russia was revived, without the western Baltic, Polish and Rumanian regions) there was no unifying force to overcome the national diversities of this area.

Not one of the nations had sufficient power or cultural attraction to become a magnetic centre for the creation of a federation. If Poland cherished ambitions as a Middle European leader she did not succeed in realizing them. The renewal of Danubian unity in the form of a 'Danubian Federation' foundered partly on the opposition of those nations who jealously guarded their newly acquired independence and partly on the 'revisionism' of the Hungarians who never relinquished the hope that their thousand-year-old Kingdom of St. Stephen would be returned to them. Similar violent national rivalries prevented unity from being achieved in the Balkans.

Would it have been possible for East Central Europe to be united by the Slavonic element that had a certain numerical superiority? Not if we have in mind the whole area from Finland to Greece and Turkey, where there were fewer Slavs than non-Slavs, roughly 60 million to 65 million (20 million Turks, 7 million Greeks and 9 million Balts and Finns). But if we do not take into account Finland, which belongs rather to the Scandinavian sphere, or Greece and Turkey, included in the Mediterranean sphere, there were in East Central Europe before the Second World War 60 million Slavs and 40 million non-Slavs – Rumanians, 14; Hungarians, 8; Austrians, 7; Balts, 6; and 6 million Germans scattered throughout the individual states as minorities.

Although we are not here considering other national minorities we should remember particularly the German ones because of the important role they played during the period of Nazi expansion.

The number of Slavs was estimated in 1950 as follows:

WESTERN SLAVS		SOUTHERN SLAVS		EASTERN SLAVS
Poles	25,000,000	Serbs	7,500,000	Great Russians
Czechs	8,000,000	Croats	4,500,000	95,000,000 to 98,000,000
Slovaks	3,000,000	Slovenes	1,400,000	Ukrainians
Lusatian Serbs or		Bulgarians	6,500,000	36,000,000 to 38,000,000
Wends living in		Macedonians		Bielo-Russians 8,000,000
Germany	100,000		1,000,000	

The so-called 'Slav idea' did not represent any important political force. The events of the last fifty years are eloquent proof of that. The idea was always either the romantic conception of Slavophile writers and political visionaries or else one of many weapons in the ideological armoury of Russian imperialism – whether Czarist or Communist.

4

The policy of Slav states has never been inspired by 'Slavo-philism'. The special interests of each individual Slav nation were always predominant even though they competed with the interests of neighbouring states. The traditional enmity between the Russians and the Poles or between the Poles and the Ukrainians is evidence enough, but yet another instance is the permanent tension between the Russians and the Ukrainians. Between Poland and Czechoslovakia there was more dis-harmony than harmony. The Yugoslavs, particularly the Serbs, were continually quarrelling with the Bulgarians. The close co-operation that developed between Czechoslovakia and Yugo-slavia did not have a Slavonic basis, but was bound by the framework of the Little Entente, whose third member was non-Slav Rumania. And, during the alliance crises after 1936, Yugoslavia turned away from Czechoslavakia (then threatened by Hitler) even sooner than Rumania. Czechoslavakia and Yugoslavia could never agree upon a common policy towards Soviet Russia.

The Slav Poles, in common with Bulgarians, were more eager to cultivate the friendship of the Hungarians than of the Slav Czechs or Yugoslavs. Obviously there was no 'Slav solidarity', and that is why the 'Slav idea' could not become the basis for the unity, even for only a part of East Central Europe.

FRAGMENTARY ENTENTES: LITTLE ENTENTE, BALKAN AND BALTIC PACTS

And so between the Great Wars only a fragmentary solution was reached in the form of partial regional blocks. Of these the best known and the most powerful was the 'Little Entente', in which Czechoslovakia, Yugoslavia and Rumania were united in 1920–21. Guarding partly against a Habsburg restoration and partly against Hungarian revisionism, this alliance un-doubtedly prevented Central Europe, scarcely out of the upheaval of the war, from becoming a victim of new conflicts and disorders. But the weakness of the pact lay in the inability of the three states to co-operate beyond a limited objective which had, in essence, only a negative character.

Czechoslovakia did not wish to be involved in Italo-Yugoslav disputes. Yugoslavia and Rumania were not willing to take a stand against Hitler in a conflict between Germany and Czechoslovakia. The states of the Little Entente were never able to formulate a common attitude to Soviet Russia. Rumania sought to secure Bessarabia, in defiance of Russia, by a special pact with Poland. Yet Czechoslovakia and France together concluded an alliance with Russia against Nazi aggression. Yugoslavia entered into diplomatic relations with Russia only in 1939 and negotiated a quite ineffective pact of friendship with her only a few days before the German attack on Belgrade in 1941.

After the occupation of the Rhineland in 1936, French pacts with the Central European states became worthless and the pressure exerted by Nazi Germany and Fascist Italy on Central Europe and the Balkans so weakened the Little Entente that during the Munich crisis Czechoslovakia was not supported either by Yugoslavia or by Rumania.

The Little Entente then collapsed altogether, but in spite of the weakness of their Governments the sympathies of the Yugoslav and Rumanian peoples for Czechoslovakia remained very strong. More than 100,000 Yugoslavs volunteered to aid the threatened country.

In the thirties the 'Balkan Pact' united Yugoslavia, Rumania, Greece and Turkey against Bulgarian revisionism, but even this bloc suffered from the traditional Balkan discords and antagonisms. Yugoslavia concluded a treaty of friendship with Bulgaria at the end of 1936, but this step, though undoubtedly constructive, aroused the suspicions of Yugoslavia's other partners: instead of strengthening, it weakened the unity of the Balkan Pact concluded two years previously.

During this period, in the middle thirties, Latvia, Estonia, and Lithuania, concluded a 'Baltic Pact' binding them to follow a similar policy; in spite of this, Lithuania, insisting on the return of Vilno, annexed by Poland in 1920, continued her hostility towards Poland, while Latvia and Estonia wished for friendly co-operation with the Poles.

As far as Poland is concerned, she co-operated for a short period in the twenties with the Little Entente, but, not wishing to offend Hungary, in whom she saw a traditional friend, she soon turned away from it. After the rise to power of Pilsudski in 1926, relations with Czechoslovakia, soured from the beginning by the dispute over Teschen, deteriorated and, after the conclusion of the Polish-German Pact in 1934, became very strained. Poland, claiming at that time the standing of a great power, was not inclined to play the role of a small nation and to range herself in a definite community on equal terms with others; on the other hand, the remaining small nations were not willing to submit to Polish leadership.

All these Ententes represented a more or less conscious urge to overcome the political antagonisms and jealousies of East Central Europe. But such moves towards unity could not succeed because the aims they pursued were too limited and were characterized by a negative devotion to the defence of the interests of each against the other. It is not easy to say whether after 1918 they might have developed, given the right political, psychological and social conditions, a wider degree of integration, but Masaryk, when he became the first President of Czechoslovakia, said in his first message to Parliament in 1918 that after the disintegration of Austro-Hungary it would be necessary to prepare a new integration of the small nations in Central Europe and obtain their closest co-operation. Masaryk, before he returned to his liberated country from the United States was, in October 1918, chairman of a congress in Philadelphia attended by the representatives of all Central European nations. He read out a declaration, which he had prepared, 'concerning the mutual interests of the independent states of Central Europe'. The declaration does not recommend political federation, because that would apparently complicate the difficulties facing each nation after the war, but it pronounces in favour of the possibility of a free federation on an economic basis, which would be the best way of preparing for a closer union of these nations. Similar voices made themselves heard in other countries, but soon the heralds of these ideas realized that the obstacles standing in the way of efforts for unity were too great.

The small nations in this area had obtained their independence through the disintegration of empires hundreds of years old. Under these conditions they were understandably unwilling to surrender their newly won sovereignty in favour of some new federation or even confederation. Nationalism—political and economic—prevailed everywhere, not only in East Central Europe but also to a lesser extent in the rest of Europe.

The Bolsheviks controlled only with the greatest difficulty the nationalist separatist tendencies of the non-Russian nations, and then only by a brutal dictatorship did they hold together the new federation of Soviet Republics. It is obvious that the great nations – not only in Europe but throughout the world – were no less nationalistic than the small nations in East Central Europe. In so far as nationalism is a sin, they were all without exception guilty.

VARIETY OF ECONOMIC AND SOCIAL STRUCTURES

Attempts at integration did not come to grief only over national antagonisms. Difference of economic and social structures formed a great barrier. It was certainly not easy to unite industrial states such as Czechoslovakia and Austria, whose agriculture was also relatively well developed, with other states, predominantly agricultural in character but whose agriculture, technically speaking, was very backward. The consumer capacity of poor agricultural states was very limited.

All the fourteen countries of East Central Europe (including Finland, Greece and Turkey) represented an average of only roughly 20–25 per cent of the foreign trade of Czechoslovakia; Czechoslovakian trade with Germany alone was as a rule greater than that of the six states of Central Europe and the

Balkans together (Poland, Austria, Hungary, Rumania, Yugoslavia and Bulgaria). Czechoslovakia's commercial relations with industrial Austria were greater than with any other agricultural country of East Central Europe. This alone shows that commercial and economic relations among the agricultural states could not be extensive.

Agrarian reforms carried out after the First World War were inadequate in all the East European countries except Rumania and Czechoslovakia. The large estates of Poland and Hungary were to a great extent retained, although even here much land was divided up. Nowhere was there enough ground available to appease the 'hunger for land'. The lots into which the land was parcelled were too small, and too many unproductive dwarf holdings were created. Also there were too many applicants. Each family got too little. Medium-sized holdings, which, from the point of view of productivity, proved to be advantageous, were established in larger numbers only in Czechoslovakia. This explains to a great extent the political strength of the Agrarian Party which held a leading position in industrial Czechoslovakia. Everywhere else the agricultural proletariat remained the most poverty-stricken social class.

With the exception of Czechoslovakia and Austria agriculture remained in a state of crisis in all the countries of East Central Europe. In the thirties it was made acute by the general economic crisis that caused a catastrophic fall in agricultural prices. When international attempts at overcoming these difficulties failed, every country tried to relieve its position by various economic protectionary measures, but the results were not satisfactory. The agricultural crisis, increased by the overpopulation of the countryside, could have been more effectively dealt with by the industrialization and mechanization of agriculture. In individual countries, particularly in Poland and Hungary, promising starts on industrialization were made, but they could not be developed because of the lack of capital.

When the countries of East Central Europe did not receive foreign aid, the tendency towards economic nationalism was inevitably strengthened, to the detriment of these countries and in the end to the advantage of Nazi Germany, who by an adroit policy was able to penetrate economically one country after another in this area.

Linked also with the economic diversity of these countries was the variety of their social structures. In Rumania, Yugoslavia and Bulgaria, 80 per cent of the population were engaged in agriculture and only about 10 per cent in industry; in Poland, over 60 per cent in agriculture, 15–19 per cent in industry; in Hungary, 52 per cent in the first and 23 per cent in the second. In contrast to this, in Czechoslovakia there were 35 per cent in both agriculture and industry; in Austria, only 27 per cent in agriculture and 31 per cent in industry. In commerce, transport and banking the greatest number employed was in Austria (15 per cent) and in Czechoslovakia (13 per cent), in Poland and Hungary, about 10 per cent, whereas in all the other countries it was less than 5 per cent.

These figures show that while the social structures of Austria and Czechoslovakia were on the whole in line with those of the Western countries, in the other states of East Central Europe peasants of a low social level predominated. Wherever big estates were preserved the size of the agricultural proletariat in large measure increased social tensions.

In spite of this, in all the countries workers were turning away from agriculture in favour of industry, of public service. East Central Europe was already on the road to industrialization before the Second World War—that is, before it became Communist.

Whereas Czechoslovakian and Austrian peasant farmers had relatively high social and cultural standards, the country people in the other countries lived in poor circumstances, even in actual poverty and marked cultural backwardness. But Balkan peasant farmers, especially Serbs, have always been known for their sharp common sense and for their singular political shrewdness. While the Czechoslovakian and Austrian Agrarian Party supporters were inclined to be conservative, the followers of the Agrarian leaders in the other agricultural countries were as a rule radical. This was particularly true of certain political factions in Poland and Bulgaria, where the Agrarian leader, Stambolijsky, paid for his radicalism with his life in the putsch organized against him in 1923. In contrast, the Bulgarian Croatian Rural Party of Radic was extremely nationalist and anti-Serbian but in social matters more conservative.

It was the industrial workers, the majority of whom leaned towards socialism, who were most influential politically in Czechoslovakia and Austria. They were fewer in number in Poland and Hungary. In Poland they had a certain influence, but none in Hungary. The workers were not yet a political force in the Balkans.

While the intelligentsia maintained an influential position in public life in Czechoslovakia, in the Balkans it was generally a few members of the commercial and banking bourgeoisie, aided by the lawyers, who held a disproportionate amount of power. In such states as Poland, Hungary and Bulgaria political members of the officer class made the army an influential force. And a vitally important part was played by the Catholic Church in Austria and in Poland.

CULTURAL AND RELIGIOUS DIFFERENCES

The cultural and religious differences were also considerable in these countries. Cultural standards were relatively high in Czechoslovakia and in Austria. On the whole in this respect these countries resembled the West. For them, illiteracy had been virtually abolished. In contrast it was widespread in the other countries, though it rapidly decreased everywhere between the two wars.

Czechoslovakia was the most highly educated country. The number of schools swiftly rose by more than one-fifth in Slovakia at the end of the First World War. Yet this little state had been more neglected during the Hungarian regime than either of the Czech lands of Bohemia or Moravia. The cultural development of the Slovak people was exemplary. Not only did illiteracy almost disappear within twenty years but also the numbers of the Slovak intelligentsia so increased that they fulfilled the main needs of the whole country.

Czechoslovakia became a 'land of readers'. Nowhere else was there such a demand for magazines and books. More than 10,000 books a year were published. They included translations of not only the world's leading authors but also the books of less known or more esoteric writers.

Technical culture was on a Western level. Typical Czechoslovakian democratic trends and the cultural aspirations of the Slovakian people meant that the mental development of the country was extraordinarily extensive. Possibly more energy was devoted to the organization of culture than to actual creation, yet in music, painting and poetry these people attained a very high standard.

Although the cultural needs of the masses in the other countries were neglected, the cultural level of the intellectual élite was high – particularly in Poland, Rumania and Hungary.

In a sense the aristocratic nature of these Society intellectuals showed itself even in the domain of culture. So it would be wrong to dismiss these countries generally as 'culturally backward', especially as a relatively high percentage of illiteracy is not necessarily a sure yardstick with which to measure the civilization of any country. The countries of East Central Europe – with the exception of Czechoslovakia and Austria – felt above all the lack of a technical intelligentsia. They suffered from a surplus of lawyers, and from students of the arts and the humanities, and teachers. Because there were not enough official posts to occupy these humanists, or adequate salaries to keep them from need, many of them, particularly in the Balkans, fell the victims of political radicalism – turning either to Fascism or Communism out of a feeling of social frustration.

Throughout East Central Europe Western influence (not only cultural but also political) predominated over the Russian. Czechs and Slovaks were 'Russophiles', but only in their foreign policy, seeking in Russia a counterbalance to the German policy of expansion. In this they looked to France as well as to Russia. But all their culture, social customs, national traditions, manner of thought and 'way of life' were very Western. The social style of their life was to a marked degree under German and Austrian influences, while politically and psychologically they were close to the English and the French. They loved Russian literature, which was known even among the ordinary people, but their rational and experimental (or pragmatic) outlook kept them from having any deeper understanding for the type of thinking so peculiar to the Russians in which there is much that is irrational and Messianic.

Despite their national aversion to Russia, the Poles are better able to understand 'the Russian soul' than the Czechs. The Russian influence was most notable among the Bulgarians. In the seventies they reacted sharply to Czarist emissaries who acted in the same way as their Bolshevik and Soviet successors in this century and tried to rule the country as though it were a Russian colony. Bulgarian Agrarian policy accepted much of the nineteenth-century Russian popular movement, which meant that the Bulgarian Agrarian movements differed greatly from those of other Central European countries.

The cultures of France and Germany had the strongest influence on Middle Europe. At the end of the First World War French civilization was the most attractive of all Western cultures even to Hungary, which was inclined politically to follow Germany and Italy. Excellent French Institutes and Lycées in Middle Europe spread French thought very effectively. At the end of the thirties English cultural influences, always strong in the Baltic states, began to spread more widely. During and after the last war the United States and Britain began to have the greatest influence on the East Central European states for reasons of international politics. These two Great Western Powers were expected to give the greatest help in thwarting the expansionist ambitions of Communist Russia.

The nations of East Central Europe took a lively interest in the Western world, but knowledge of Russia was generally incomplete and notably one-sided. The truth was not easily obtainable. Everything depended on whether people were antipathetic or sympathetic towards Communism, and, if knowledge of Russia was based on prejudiced hearsay, the peoples of Middle Europe knew perhaps even less about each other. In spite of various bilateral societies (the Czechoslovak-Polish or Czechoslovak-Yugoslav, or Polish-Hungarian and so on) detailed information about each other was confined to narrow circles of specialists or to those who were actively interested. The average Czechoslovak, Pole or Rumanian had a far greater knowledge about life in the Western countries than he had about his neighbours' activities, and in this way various mutual prejudices and diffidences were preserved.

The Serbs and Bulgarians shared with the Russians an unshakeable loyalty to the Greek church, but this played only a small part in their national development. Many people forget that Orthodox churches are nationally independent. This is precisely why they were able to play such an important role during the Turkish overlordship, preserving the consciousness of particular national traditions. The Orthodox Rumanians were always anti-Russian, resisting a Russian Protectorate. And the Hungarians never forgot that their national revolution, led by Kossuth in 1848, was crushed by Czar Nicholas I, and after that their nationalism could always provoke propaganda against Russian 'Pan-Slavism'.

It is not easy to estimate to what extent religious differences actually hindered mutual understanding. The Czechs and Poles are Roman Catholics; the Serbs and Bulgarians members of the Greek Orthodox Church. Yet not much harmony existed among them. Similarly there was constant tension between the Catholic Poles and Catholic Lithuanians because of the occupation of Vilno, but there was friendly co-operation between the Catholic Czechoslovaks and the Orthodox Serbs on the one hand and Rumanians on the other. The Calvinist Hungarian aristocrats found friends and allies among the Polish Catholic aristocrats, but between the Czech and the Slovak Catholics there was much misunderstanding. Agreements or disputes were far more influenced by nationalist than by religious views. Indeed, nationalism was such an influential force that it had an effect on religion itself.

Polish Catholicism became a sort of national religion. Under the influence of the counter-reformation it took on a militant character and, definitely separating the Catholic Poles from the Orthodox Russians and Ukrainians on the one hand and from Protestant Germans on the other, it became a nationally powerful, spiritual shield against Germany and Russia.

In contrast, Catholicism in the Czech lands suffered because the Czechs who, for two hundred years, had been Hussites after their defeat at the White Mountain in 1620 (close to, but not identical with Protestants), were forcibly returned to the Catholic fold and deprived of their national independence. In the national struggles of the nineteenth century against the Habsburgs, who were supported by the Vatican, the Czechs often came into conflict with the Catholic hierarchy. The cleavage was emphasized because the Czech struggle, which was not only a religious but also a national revolution, was consciously inspired by the Hussite tradition, and in the new era was, in the spirit of liberalism, interpreted as a movement for freedom. With the exception of a religiously inflamed minority, Czech Catholics, preserving the conventions of the church, were as a rule tolerant, often lukewarm and even indifferent to religion. Some foreigners found it was difficult to decide whether the Czechs were Protestant Catholics or Catholic Protestants. In such circumstances it was not surprising that after the fall of the Austrian Empire, where the Roman Catholic was the state church, about a million Czechs turned away – more for nationalist than for religious reasons – from Catholicism to join the new national, so-called Czechoslovak Church which was schismatic. Or they remained without denomination.

In Slovakia, where the Hussite influence was weaker than in the Czech lands, the spirit of the counter-reformation had a strong attraction for the Catholics and psychologically estranged them from the Czech Catholics. 'Slovak autonomy' was passionately advocated by the local Catholic priests as against 'Czech atheism'. And Catholicism became the welcome ally of Slovak national feeling against the Czechs, just as it did in Croatian national feeling against the Serbs.

It was only in some instances and only to a certain extent that religious differences strengthened national antagonisms. Religious beliefs were not the main or decisive reason for such antagonism. Many Slovak Protestants were supporters of autonomy, but a separatist policy which, aimed at an independent Slovak state, was opposed by the majority of the Slovak Catholics. While there was constant tension between Orthodox Serbs and Bulgarians, the Catholic Slovenes knew how to co-operate successfully with the Serbs, neglecting their Catholic neighbours, the Croatians, with whom they made common cause only when it appeared beneficial to Slovene national interests.

The dispute between the Serbs and Croats did not stem primarily from religious differences, but from their conflicting aspirations: Greater Serbia versus Greater Croatia.

The Hungarian Catholics and Protestants competed in ardent support of the national aspirations of their country. The relatively weak influence of religion on the policy of the Central European nations was most notable in the disputes between the Vatican on the one hand and Czechoslovakia or Lithuania on the other. The majority of Catholics in these countries supported the policy of their Governments against the Vatican.

Nationalism everywhere showed itself to be more powerful than religion. This does not mean that religion did not have a deep influence on the national development and character of the nations in East Central Europe, or that it was without importance in their mutual relations. But the instances we have examined support the opinion that as a general rule religion retreated before national interests – at least in the foreign policies of these nations. This seems to be a common phenomenon, occurring all over the world. In our time it is most strikingly apparent in Asia.[1]

DIFFERENCES IN POLITICAL REGIMES

All these economic, social and cultural differences explain also

[1] Here is a survey of religions in East Central Europe:

The Catholics predominate in: Poland 90 per cent – before the war, 65 per cent – while the rest were Orthodox, Uniate Ukrainians, Bielo-Russian Jews, German Protestants; Czechoslovakia 75 per cent; Hungary 86 per cent; Austria 98 per cent.

Catholic minorities are in: Latvia 24 per cent; Rumania 7 per cent; Albania 9 per cent; Bulgaria 3 per cent; in Estonia and Finland they do not even amount to 1 per cent. Yugoslavs, Croats and Slovenes are almost all Catholics, of which there are in the whole country 38 per cent.

The Protestants are in the majority in: Finland 98 per cent; Estonia 78 per cent; in the minority in: Hungary 27 per cent; Czechoslovakia over 20 per cent (before the war 13 per cent – the difference is caused by the decrease in population and partly through the transfer of the Sudeten Germans and the concession of Ruthenia); Lithuania 9 per cent; Rumania 7 per cent; elsewhere they are an insignificant fraction.

The Orthodox are in the majority in: Rumania 75 per cent; Bulgaria 90 per cent; in Yugoslavia – Serbs – almost 50 per cent.

Orthodox minorities are in: Albania 20 per cent; Estonia 19 per cent; Latvia 9 per cent; before the war they were also in Poland 11 per cent and in Czechoslovakia, particularly in Ruthenia, 5 per cent; the majority of whom were Uniates.

(*The Uniates*, the so-called Greek Catholics, must rather be classified with the Roman Catholics, since they recognize the Pope in Rome as their head. On the other hand in their liturgy they preserve the Orthodox rite: Rumanian Uniates are 8 per cent, and in Hungary 3 per cent.)

The Moslems have a majority in Albania of 71 per cent. They are in the minority in Yugoslavia with 11 per cent, and Bulgaria with 7 per cent. The tragic fate of the Jews is illustrated by these terrible figures: out of more than 3 million in Poland (about 10 per cent of the entire population of that land) over 2½ million were exterminated; in Czecho-slovakia, out of 360,000 (not quite 3 per cent) more than 300,000 died; in Rumania, out of 850,000 (5 per cent), half; in Hungary, out of 470,000 (6 per cent), half; in Austria, out of 350,000 (5 per cent), about 300,000 and so on. Of those who survived the Nazi terror or escaped it in time by going abroad, many emigrated after the war, thus also escaping the new Communist terror.

to a great extent the variety of political regimes in the individual countries of East Central Europe.

In the years immediately following the foundation of the nation-states, parliamentary democracies according to Western patterns (Franco-Belgian rather than Anglo-Saxon) were introduced everywhere. The new political parties represented, as a rule, definite social conditions or strata. A central European speciality was the Agrarian Party. The large number of political parties led to a clumsy system of coalition governments in which the inevitable compromises prevented a clearly defined policy. Sometimes it appeared that an adjustment of interests was made purely from a power point of view. This repulsed many of the intelligentsia, particularly the young people, who longed for more principled administration. In Czechoslovakia, in Austria and, to a certain extent, in Poland, political parties, particularly the Socialists and Agrarians, were well organized with fairly rigid discipline. The party system in these countries was in this respect nearer to the German than to the French. In contrast, in Hungary and in the Balkans the parties were usually only loosely grouped round certain personalities to help in the organization of elections or the formation of factions in Parliament.

The first deviation from a democratic regime, in the Western sense, came in Hungary when Bela Kun's Bolshevik dictatorship, which lasted for some months, produced a violent reactionary regime led by Admiral Horthy. A parliamentary façade was preserved, but such democratic freedom as electoral rights was considerably limited. The Horthy administration was not Fascist, as some people maintained, but was based on the social and political reactionary oligarchy of the Hungarian gentry and a section of the high aristocracy that had ruled Hungary for hundreds of years.

Count Bethlen, Prime Minister for ten years, was a typical representative of the ruling class: politically very gifted, socially very conservative, an opponent of land reform and socialism, a proud nationalist longing for the renewal of Greater Hungary, and convinced of the superiority of the Hungarian aristocracy and upper classes over their non-Hungarian neighbours. He despised the common people, yet Fascists were repellent to him and he stopped the anti-Jewish pogroms. The English aristocrat of the eighteenth century was his prototype, and his regime recalled to a remarkable degree the moderate absolutism of that time. Fascist elements in Hungary, supported by Germany and Italy, gained more influence towards the end of the thirties, but they came to power only towards the end of the war when, for a short time, under the leadership of Ferenc Szalasi, leader of the Arrow Cross Party, they introduced a reign of terror in which tens of thousands of people lost their lives.

More outstanding deviations from democracy occurred in other countries: in Poland, after Marshal Pilsudski's putsch in 1926, in Lithuania the same year, in Yugoslavia in 1929, in Estonia, Latvia, Austria and Bulgaria in 1934 and finally in Rumania in 1937. By the end of the thirties only Czechoslovakia in all Central Europe and the Balkans remained a democracy. She was struck down in 1938.

The reasons for the creation of dictatorships in these Middle European countries were not everywhere the same, even though in many ways they were similar. The inability of the numerous political parties to agree on a common policy within the framework of a coalition government, and the exaggerated rivalry of the political leaders made it easier for stronger or more astute individuals to establish a dictatorial or semi-dictatorial regime. In Poland and in the Baltic states financial and economic difficulties also contributed to the introduction of an authoritarian system. Events in Poland were confused to an even greater degree because the new united state contained cultural, social and political elements that had been inherited from Russian, Austrian and German occupations. They frequently came into collision with each other. There was much disagreement over policy towards the minorities, particularly the Ukrainian and Jewish. Anti-Semitism was still widespread

19

in Poland – just as it was in other Central European countries, in Russia, and in Nazi Germany.

The immediate motive for the declaration of a royal dictatorship in Yugoslavia was the danger of increased antagonism between the Serbs and Croats. Military circles, always fairly influential behind the scenes, played an important part in Yugoslavia, Bulgaria and Poland in plotting the revolutionary revolts that led to dictatorships.

The personal position and ambitions of a potential dictator were not without significance. Marshal Josef Pilsudski had a complex and contradictory personality. He possessed the character of an impatient and authoritative revolutionary. In his eyes, party politicians were demagogues worthy only of contempt. He was an ardent nationalist, carried away by the vision of The Greater Poland of the eighteenth century, and he longed for Poland to rank among the great European Powers. He made full use of his status as national hero, which he achieved in the battles for the independence of Poland before and during the First World War. Assured of the blind support of fanatically devoted followers – many of whom remained faithful to him even after his death in 1935 – Pilsudski did not hesitate to use brutal means when necessary. Taking refuge from criticism in his general popularity, in the thirties he imprisoned all the politicians who opposed him; among them the fine leader of the Agrarians, Witos, and the socialist veteran, Liebermann. Yet Pilsudski did not indiscriminately destroy freedom in every sphere. He preserved Parliament, although with only a limited jurisdiction, for which elections were conducted under the relentless pressure of the government.

The royal dictators of the Balkans were different altogether. Boris of Bulgaria knew how to play one politician against another. He dominated them through his thorough grasp of domestic affairs and his undeniable skill in conducting foreign politics. He was shrewd and cynical, sly and ruthless in his state-craft. Bulgaria never recovered from the disastrous results of the bloody putsch which in 1923 destroyed the great peasant leader, Stambolijsky, who dreamt of a federation of all the southern Slavs and strove for an agreement with Yugoslavia even at the cost of renouncing Bulgaria's claims to Macedonia. Hundreds of his supporters were murdered with him, and thousands more were brutally persecuted, and from that time on, except for a small break at the beginning of the thirties, Bulgaria became a police state, controlled by the harshest methods of armed, uniformed persecutors.

The ability of King Carol of Rumania bore no relation to his ambition. He dropped Titulescu, an outstanding administrator, who was also one of the most able diplomats in Europe; he exploited for his own ends the fact that the honest leader of the Agrarians, Maniu, one of the greatest Rumanian patriots, who nursed a vision of a Central Federation until he died in a Communist prison in 1955, remained in opposition while other politicians were either paralysed by mutual rivalries or competing for royal favours. Carol played a dubious game in which indulgence alternated with persecution of the Fascist, bitterly anti-Semitic Iron Guards. Yet not even his clever shadow-boxing with Hitler brought him any security. In the end, Carol was compelled by the Nazis to abdicate and to leave the country.

In contrast, the Yugoslav king, Alexander, a serious and brave man, was a patriot with good intentions. But he was more of a soldier than a politician. He spent his youth among the officers of the Czarist regime, and was prevented from completing his studies in the West by the outbreak of war in 1914. He had neither the wisdom nor the patience of a statesman and he was addicted to militarily dramatic but politically disastrous interventions in his country's affairs. After the death of the brilliant Serbian statesman, Nikola Pasic, the assassination of the fickle but able Croatian leader, Stjepan Radic, and the removal of Svetozar Pribicevic, a passionately impulsive but dependable Yugoslav patriot, there was no personality sufficiently astute and generally esteemed to cope with the unfortunate king's leanings towards military dictatorship. When he was murdered by Macedonian and Croatian conspirators in Marseilles in 1934 the way lay open for that insincere and cunning weakling, Prince Paul, and for the gifted but cynical Stojadinovic who led Yugoslavia into dependence upon Italy and Germany.

The dictatorships (and semi-dictatorships) of East Central Europe were not identical with those of Italy and Germany. The Fascists and the Nazis were dedicated to definite ideological doctrines and political systems. They pursued their barbaric course with ruthless fanaticism. The authoritarian regimes in East Central Europe lacked any sort of ideology. They merely leaned heavily on the power of the police and took advantage of the weakness of their democratic opponents. It was only towards the close of the thirties that ideas frankly borrowed from Nazism and Fascism gained any influence in these countries. And it was only during the war that the supporters of these movements were installed in power by the Nazis. Communist regimes are similarly established with the direct help of the Russians. The authoritarian regimes were rather primitive police regimes than Fascist dictatorships. But they were at one with them in the use of brutal methods of persecution and suppression and in their blatant exploitation of a false nationalism. In contrast to the German and Italian regimes they had no support from the people as a whole – with the possible exception of Poland, during the early days of Pilsudski's rule. The Middle European dictators, having at their disposal the army and the police, won over only the social 'déracinés' or the politically ambitious and the adventurers, while the majority of people remained partly indifferent and partly hostile. Government 'blocs' or similar organized bodies, 'won' the elections only with the help of police pressure.

They were not totalitarian regimes. With the exception of Yugoslavia and for a certain period Bulgaria also, where the dictatorships were harshest, political parties were allowed to exist even though their activities were constantly interrupted by the arbitrary actions of the Governments. Even newspapers were permitted to indulge in a limited amount of criticism of the Government. Certainly there was relatively more freedom in these countries than in contemporary Germany and Italy, and, of course, Soviet Russia.

They were regimes dominated by 'the strong hand' but at the same time a hand irresolute and groping. Their great weakness lay in superficiality and vacillation. Not knowing how to mobilize national energies for clearly defined goals, they merely assisted political and social demoralization. With the exception of Poland, which notably increased its economic potential under Pilsudski's administration, the other semi-dictatorships did not contribute anything towards the economic improvement of their countries. On the social side these regimes were reactionary. They failed to hide their indifference to the social needs of their people beneath a demagogic anti-Communism. Not one of these disastrous regimes withstood the test of war.

It has been said that these half-hearted dictatorships were a natural consequence of the social and cultural backwardness of the Central European countries. This is scarcely a satisfactory interpretation. How can it be explained that in Italy, which as a whole was certainly more advanced than Central Europe, and particularly in Germany, with a high social and cultural level, dictatorships took root far more firmly than anywhere in 'backward' East Central Europe?

How can it be explained that, with the exception of that part of Poland which was under Russian occupation, these 'primitive' countries, up to the time of the First World War, were more democratic than after it? It is certainly true that democracy can best function in a society with a high cultural level, a society where structure is most clearly defined but in which the social classes are not isolated one from another. In spite of this fact, Nazism was victorious in Germany. Obviously the economic crisis with its widespread unemployment facilitated Hitler's rise to dictatorship. Yet neither the devastating crisis which disorganized American society in the thirties, nor the mass unemployment in Britain led to the introduction of a Fascist dictatorship in these countries. Or why was democracy preserved in Czechoslovakia, badly hit by the economic crisis, when the overall social and cultural level of that country was not after all higher than in Germany?

Political and psychological factors are ultimately more important than economic and social development, and Czechoslovakia is in this way instructive. From the beginning of the nineteenth century Czechoslovakia evolved against a background of democratic liberalism; in a liberal sense the Czechs reinterpreted their tradition, and decided that their national character called for a constant striving for spiritual and social progress. A progress towards 'an even more perfect democracy' (in Masaryk's own words) seemed to them to be the meaning of their history. Being a nation of 'small people' they clung to democracy. They understood the social needs of the masses and ardently educated themselves, aiming at a policy 'of European and world orientation'. In this way they created, together with the Slovaks, the conditions necessary for building their national state, and for maintaining it on democratic foundations.

It was also important that at this time the leading figures in public life, from the Right to the Left, were inspired by democratic ideals. The majority of them were of humble origin. Very few were outstanding personalities, but the 'average' was remarkable. Certainly it was fortunate for the new Republic that it found such a great leader in its first President. T. G. Masaryk was an exceptional personality who, to a great extent, embodied Plato's ideal philosopher-statesman, and professed with profound conviction liberal democratic ideals, together with a deep understanding of the social needs of 'the fourth estate' of workers and peasants. His ideas became the national creed and in fact form part of the living faith of the Czechoslovak people to this day, even during the present period of subjugation.

Masaryk wished for federal co-operation among the Central

European nations and he was an ardent advocate of European unity. He never doubted that Communism would finally collapse. He considered it a morally perverted system, philosophically primitive and politically untenable. By the side of the old President (he became head of the state at 68 and carried out his duties for seventeen years) stood his young follower, Edward Beneš, who directed Czechoslovakia's foreign policy first as Foreign Minister and later as the second President. Beneš's knowledge of international politics was incomparable and he was without doubt one of the best diplomats of this century. The tragic disillusionment that he suffered through the lack of support from both East and West on both sides of the gap – which he hoped to bridge – showed with cruel clarity to what extent the fate of a small nation depends on the political games played by the Great Powers.

For internal policy Masaryk found some outstanding colleagues: Antonin Svehla, leader of the Agrarians, was a master of the art of political compromise and created a system of coalition government that protected the new state from severe internal crises; Antonin Hampl, a workers' leader with great political courage led the Socialists in a consistently democratic and sharply anti-Communist spirit; Alois Rasin, a progressive liberal, developed the cult of 'the Czechoslovak crown' as a stable currency and made thrift one of the principal civic virtues; Mgr Jan Sramek, a convinced Christian Socialist, deserved recognition for achieving not only religious peace but also the progressive social orientation of his Catholic Party; Vavro Srobar, an enthusiastic Slovak supporter of Masaryk, contributed fundamentally to the firm adherence of Slovakia to the United Republic; Milan Hodza, possibly the most gifted of Slovak politicians, strove for the economic betterment of Slovakia and acquired an international reputation through his interest in Central European federation.

In the democratic atmosphere that permeated the life of the whole nation, neither Fascist nor Communist tendencies flourished. Though the Communists polled about 10 per cent of votes in elections and in Parliament, the Party was, as long as Czechoslovakia remained independent, absolutely without influence on the policy of the state.

Czechoslovak democracy was not perfect. It suffered from the same weaknesses as the other democracies, and mistrusting a class of the élite it gave almost too much priority to the 'average person' with some special talent. Because of this it was unable adequately to overcome a certain provincialism, despite the great general interest in international politics and culture. But even with its many faults and shortcomings Czechoslovakian democracy was probably one of the most successful in Europe in the years between the wars. Its downfall did not harm that small Central European nation alone. 'The democratic tradition' was not so securely entrenched in the other countries of East Central Europe, and with the collapse of Czechoslovakia they could not stand out against anti-democratic tendencies, especially as the ruling classes, being mostly limited to the more commercial and financial rather than industrial members of the bourgeoisie, to the upper classes and to military and bureaucratic circles, did not have a broad enough sympathy for the needs and ideals of the masses. Also authoritarian tendencies made capital out of violent nationalism, which in these countries did not develop such a liberal spirit as it did in Czechoslovakia, although even there, narrow-minded, provincial nationalism sometimes resisted more liberal ideas.

Yet democratic elements were everywhere so strong in Central Europe that they prevented the introduction of totalitarian dictatorships. The Agrarian Parties, of democratic conviction, were always in sharp opposition to police-state semi-dictatorships. The Socialist Parties opposed them too, but – with the exception of Poland – they were too weak to be effective. Communist Parties were weaker still and were usually banned, while the intelligentsia were usually divided equally into the adherents and the militant opponents of dictatorships. Democratic forces were in a difficult position, because in the great neighbouring states (in Russia from the start, in Italy from the beginning of the twenties and in Germany from the thirties) there dwelt antagonistic anti-democratic, totalitarian governments. As for Austria, on the whole, political, economic and social conditions were similar to those in Czechoslovakia, even though the democratic tradition, except in Vienna, was weaker. Whereas Czechoslovakia was almost uninterruptedly governed by a 'national coalition' in which all the principal parties were represented, there developed in Austria a sharp dispute between the Catholic Party, led by the able, self-assured and diehard Conservative prelate, Mgr Seipel, and the Social Democrats at whose head stood several such outstanding politicians as Renner, Bauer, Seitz and Paul. They played a leading part in the European Socialist movement (and their party, by its radical Socialism, absolutely paralysed the Communist Party in Austria. In contrast to Germany and Czechoslovakia, Communism never gained many adherents among the Austrian workers). But Austria was too divided.

Hungary quickly overcame the catastrophe of 1918 by a firm nationalist policy supported by a general demand for the renewal of the old Greater Hungary; but Austria never recovered from the overthrow of the Habsburg empire in which she had held a privileged position, and failed to re-establish herself as a nation. Since there was no hope of a renewal of the Danube federation Austria quickly expressed her desire for an Anschluss with the German empire. Apart from the Great-German liberals, whose influence was not great, it was the Social Democrats who most ardently advocated the Anschluss. The Christian Socialists were not enthusiastic; they did not wish their country to become a Weimar Republic with, at least in the early years, Liberal Democrats predominating. Also Protestants were in a majority in Germany; and the Austrian Christian Socialists were under the influence of the Vatican and of Italy who did not wish to have a greater Germany extending to the North Italian frontier. The victorious Allies strenuously opposed defeated Germany's desire to extend her boundaries by acquiring Austria, and systematically resisted attempts at an Anschluss. Austria, unsure of her ability to survive, asked that those who were unwilling to agree to an Anschluss should give her assistance – and then treated this as an obligation on their part. In such circumstances it was difficult for any lively patriotism to arise.[1]

Nazis penetrated into Austria soon after Hitler established his dictatorship in Berlin. This was the time when the Christian Socialists ought to have joined the Social Democrats, who had turned away from the idea of an Anschluss as soon as Germany became a police state. Together they should have resisted Nazi pressure. But the possibilities of such united action were thwarted by Mussolini. He saw the opposition of the hated Social Democrats as a threat to his plan for making Austria, as well as Hungary, an Italian satellite. The ambitious Austrian Chancellor, Dollfuss, became the Duce's puppet, and founded the so-called Fatherland Front with Catholic, anti-Socialist, anti-Nazi but pro-Fascist tendencies; and in 1933 and a year later he dissolved all political parties. The Social Democrats rebelled, but after four days' fighting they had to capitulate.

And so a Catholic-Fascist regime was established in Austria, but proved too weak to withstand Nazism. The bloody extermination of democracy in Austria merely encouraged and helped Hitler's offensive, and at the decisive moment Mussolini did nothing to stop him.[2]

Authoritarian regimes were installed in other countries in East Central Europe without direct intervention from outside

[1] I remember that President Masaryk used to say that the Austrians would have to undergo the test of an Anschluss to understand and recognize that their place was not within the framework of Germany but by the side of their small neighbours, or within a Central European Union.

[2] Count Sforza, then living in exile, told me in Paris in the spring of 1934: 'It is not possible to fight 100 per cent Fascism with 50 per cent Fascism, only with 100 per cent democracy. The defeat of social democracy which completed the destruction of democracy in Austria benefits no one but Hitler.' Dollfuss was murdered during a Nazi putsch in July 1934 and Chancellor Schuschnigg, his successor, was thrown into a concentration camp by the Nazis after the Anschluss in 1938.

– even though Fascist tendencies were supported by Italy and Germany – but the Austrian dictatorship was installed under the direct auspices of Mussolini. Without his interference Austrian democracy might not have died: at least it could scarcely have been swept away so ruthlessly.

The Central European semi-dictatorships must always take the blame for frustrating the promising developments in their countries which began under the banner of democracy after the Kaiser's war. They failed to improve the social condition of their people, and through the excessive nationalism by which they sought to compensate for their deficiencies, they impeded closer co-operation among these nations. At the same time, lacking adequate support from the peoples of their own countries, they gradually came closer to both Fascist Powers, thus encouraging German and Italian penetration into East Central Europe. Yet it must be emphasized that, although the democratic elements in these countries were considerably weakened, they bravely opposed their dictatorial governments with every weapon left to them.

We should not blame these supporters of democracy because their nations succumbed to Communism after Hitler's war. There were no specific conditions to help Communism to flourish; only direct pressure of Soviet power made the establishment of Communist governments possible in these countries. In contradiction to the opinion fairly widely held in the West, there were much better conditions after the Second World War for the introduction and consolidation of democratic regimes in East Central Europe than after the First World War.

For the most part these nations had had enough experience of police states and semi-dictatorships. Wartime occupation and oppression by the Nazis increased in all these sorely tried nations the desire for a liberal administration. Twenty years of freedom contributed fundamentally in Czechoslovakia to the strengthening of the democratic tradition. Although the essential development of this people was also handicapped by authoritarian regimes, by the general economic crisis of the thirties and the disintegration of international security, the cultural level of the nations of East Central Europe in the period of their independence increased to a far greater extent than is frequently realized. Illiteracy decreased considerably. In some instances it was wiped out. The publication of periodicals and books greatly increased, and so did the number of schools of all grades. The hygienic services improved, while the level of social welfare in Czechoslovakia was among the highest in Europe. Almost everywhere literary, scientific and artistic output was intensified. Production – in agriculture and in industry – was expanding. Poland, Hungary and Rumania had started on a promising programme of industrial development. Czechoslovakia, almost self-sufficient in agriculture, had increased the output of its factories and was becoming one of the strongest states in Europe. Foreign trade in the Succession states was higher in relation to world trade than it was before the First World War. Altogether the formation of independent national states in East Central Europe had not meant – as it is sometimes argued in the West – any deterioration but had instead created an improvement in the cultural and living standards of the nations[1] in this area.

This development was stopped dead by the outbreak of the Second World War, and the forcible introduction of Communism into East Central Europe prevented those nations from being able to make the most of their creative capacities under more liberal regimes – for which they had all the necessary cultural, economic and political background.

This survey of the situation in East Central Europe in the era between the wars shows that the area was remarkably heterogeneous. Each nation had its own national traditions and particular interests, often conflicting with the interests of

[1] I gave data illustrating this in my study *Small and Great Nations*, London, 1944.

its neighbours. Differences in economic and social structure and differences in religion and culture increased national divergencies until co-operation became difficult or impossible. Strong, sometimes even over-exuberant, nationalism dominated the actions of the states, but not necessarily more than in the larger nations. The ancient Habsburg empire was swept away by a powerful tide of nationalism; the unbelievably speedy destruction of the 'Austrian' or 'Austro-Hungarian' tradition at least proved that this Empire had outlived itself historically. But, in spite of all their differences and antagonisms, the nations of East Central Europe felt the need for co-operation. That is why the Ententes and alliances were formed. More intensive and more all-round co-operation failed to develop among them. Each of them continued jealously to guard its new sovereignty and to follow its own interests, sometimes with short-sighted insularity. And attempts to help integration met with strong opposition from neighbouring Great Powers. The disastrous 'Balkanization' of East Central Europe cannot be blamed merely on excessive local nationalism; it was caused as well by the ambitions and rivalries of the Great Powers.

Only if we consider to what extent the Great Powers interfered in East Central Europe can we understand the complicated and dramatic history of this unquiet area of Europe.

CHAPTER II

Ambitions and Rivalries of the Great Powers

REVISIONISTS AND ANTI-REVISIONISTS

The formation of the national states in East Central Europe after 1918 produced an international situation that could not fail to influence the relationships (and the policies) of other European Powers. Germany had been weakened by the destruction of the Habsburg and Ottoman empires, for both of them had been her allies and were to a great extent dependent on her. Russia, having been removed from the 'concert of European nations' by revolution and civil war, was being ostracized by the rest of the world because of Bolshevik government, and with the loss of Finland, the Baltic states, Poland and Bessarabia, Russian frontiers were now too far to the east to be included in Europe. Italy had fulfilled her hopes of national unification by gaining southern Tyrol, Istria, Trieste and Fiume, and was strengthened by the disappearance of the Habsburg empire, her traditional enemy, from the European scene. Yet Italy still felt embittered because she had not managed to contrive the annexation of Dalmatia and Valona. France and Britain had the strongest international position after the war, and when, after playing a principal role at the Paris Peace Conference in 1919, the United States withdrew from Europe into traditional isolation, it was these two Western allies who accepted the leadership of the Europe created by the Treaty of Versailles.

Europe became divided into two camps: the revisionists and the anti-revisionists. Germany and Russia (soon to be joined by Italy) persisted in demanding the reversal of the 'Versailles *Diktat*', which was, in the eyes of Lenin, the work of capitalist, imperialistic bandits. The 'anti-revisionists', with Britain and

France at their head, defended the new constitution of the New Europe. But Britain soon began to show sympathy for some of the demands of the revisionists, particularly the demands of Germany, and gradually British policy moved towards a revision of the peace treaties 'by peaceful means'.

East Central Europe also became divided between the same two camps. While Hungary, Bulgaria, Turkey – and to a certain extent Austria – strove for a revision of the 'unjust' peace treaties, the rest approved them. Right from the start there was a marked difference in the approach of Britain and of France towards Central European problems. Britain preserved an air of reserve and detachment, but France, fearing the resurgence of Germany, sought friends in the East according to the centuries-old pattern of her foreign policy. Having lost Russia as an ally, she found new friends in Poland and the countries of the Little Entente, while these nations, failing to find an adequate guarantee of security in the League of Nations, tried to strengthen it by alliance with victorious France.

FRENCH FRIENDSHIP

In its general orientation the policy of France was correct. She was not mistaken in her belief that Germany, in spite of her defeat and territorial losses (Alsace-Lorraine had been given back to France, part of Upper Silesia and Pomerania fell to Poland, and Danzig became a free city), was still so potentially strong economically that she could soon regain her position as a Great Power able to threaten peace by renewing her traditional '*Drang nach Osten*' and '*nach Westen*'. That is why France was justified in her attempts to create a barrier against German expansion by a system of Franco-Central European alliances. The greatest weakness of her policy was that, concentrating on political security and military defence, she overlooked the economic weakness of her Eastern allies. The aid offered occasionally in the traditional form of loans or capital investments was not nearly sufficient for the improvement needed in the agricultural countries of Central Europe. At this time French commercial policy in particular lacked imagination and scope. Tardieu's plan of 1932, recommending in essence a system of preferences for the countries of East Central Europe, came too late. The crisis was then at its height, and Germany and Italy were already strong enough to frustrate the plan.

France always wished for close co-operation among the Central European nations – not only between Poland and the Little Entente but also between the Little Entente on the one hand and Austria and Hungary on the other. But she did not succeed in overcoming national rivalry and distrust among these nations. European 'revisionists' boldly asserted that the small Central European allies were nothing but satellites of 'French imperialism'; but if this had been true France would have compelled them to co-operate with Hungary, Austria or Bulgaria, especially as the union of these nations would have strengthened her influence on the Continent, and at the same time hindered German and Italian expansion. France limited herself to discreet advice without even attempting to impose her wishes. History contains only a few other examples of a great power exercising such tact and restraint towards small nations. The French alliance with the Central European nations was founded on the respect of equal partners without any intervention of the stronger in the affairs of the weaker.

The Central European allies did not all side with France in all circumstances. Czechoslovakia was very reserved about the French occupation of the Ruhr in 1923. And Poland continued to be unfriendly towards Russia even after the conclusion of the Franco-Soviet Pact. Altogether it must be recognized that France, who fought hardest for the liberation of the Central European nations during the First World War, had, of all the Great Powers, the most friendly relations with these nations, and, eager for reconciliation and co-operation in that area, she pursued a constructive policy in the interests not only of her own but also of European security. But France was frustrated not only by the jealousies of the Central European nations but also by the lust for power that governed German and Italian activities.

GERMAN 'MITTELEUROPA'

Berlin never relinquished the plan for '*Mitteleuropa*', conceived by the German publicist, Naumann, during the First World War. The entire Continent from Germany to Turkey was to be united under German leadership. Hitler had many predecessors who, using 'geopolitical', economic, strategic and other arguments, declared that this area, enlarged to include also the Ukraine, was the '*Lebensraum*' which the superior German race needed if the development of the particular talents that destined the Germans for the role of '*Herrenvolk*' was to be given full scope. The imperialist ambitions of the Germans were almost completely fulfilled in the spring of 1918, and when the efforts of the dilettante Emperor Charles for a separate peace with the Western Allies met with painful failure, Austro-Hungary became absolutely dependent on Germany. This produced a situation in which the Austrian and Sudeten Germans, in common with the Hungarians, saw their surest bulwark against the efforts of the other nations to liberate themselves. Bulgaria and Turkey were mere German satellites. The Peace of Brest-Litovsk in March 1918, which was up to that time the most outstanding expression of Pan-German '*Drang nach Osten*', subjected the Ukraine, the entire Baltic area, including Finland and Poland, to German domination. Finally, the Peace of Bucharest, in May 1918, dragged Rumania into subjection, and German hegemony spread not only over all East Central Europe but also over the whole of the Ukraine. But a few months later Germany capitulated and her new empire collapsed.

German nationalism, however, which eventually proved stronger than German democracy, kept alive the nation's imperialist ambitions. As long as defeated Germany remained weak, she limited herself to half-measures. She indulged persistently in propaganda against the 'Versailles *Diktat*', vehemently denouncing French hegemony over Europe – in this respect at least she gained sympathy for her claims in the Anglo-Saxon world, in the Scandinavian countries and in Holland. Relatively soon she was granted a revision of her reparations, and through the Treaty of Rapallo with Soviet Russia in 1922 she prepared the way for further manœuvring with the Allies. At the back of all these diplomatic moves lay the old Imperialist dreams.

While the leaders of the Weimar Republic in no way moderated their dislike of Poland, they preserved a cold but correct attitude towards the Little Entente. But they did not hide their sympathies for the movement striving for an Austrian Anschluss or for the revisionist claims of the Hungarians, and while they preserved official restraint they permitted nationalists to agitate in Austria and to incite the Hungarian and Bulgarian revisionists against their neighbours.

Nationalist disputes among the small Central European nations were tremendously helpful to Germany. Germans looked askance at the association of the three states in the Little Entente. Berlin publicists represented it as an instrument of French imperialism for the 'encirclement' of Germany, and Berlin advised Vienna not to go far in *rapprochement* and economic co-operation with Prague. German diplomats were determined to prevent full use being made of that article in the peace treaties according to which Czechoslovakia, Austria and Hungary could, five years after signing, negotiate a system of preferences among themselves. At the same time Germany encouraged Belgrade to establish a close friendship with Budapest merely to arouse distrust between Yugoslavia on the one hand and Czechoslovakia and Rumania on the other.

Germany's more active intervention in Central European affairs began only in 1931. Making capital out of the general economic crisis that hit Vienna particularly hard after the failure of the *Kredit Anstalt*, Germany arranged a customs union agreement with Austria. This was meant to prepare the way for Austro-German union, and as a first serious attempt at an Anschluss it failed only through the decisive opposition of the Little Entente and France. Germany took her revenge a year later when, with Italy, she ruined the Tardieu Plan aimed at uniting East Central Europe. The Germans did not want the Middle European nations to be united until an opportunity arose for bringing them together under her domination, and Hitler, once in power, lost little time in preparing to accomplish this objective. He abandoned the slow and moderate policy of the Weimar Republic in favour of bold aggressive expansion. First of all he set about breaking the French system of alliances. In this he achieved his first big success with a Non-Aggression Pact with Poland in 1934. This meant not only the alienation of Poland from France but also the first breach in the system of so-called collective security. And at the same time the Germans aggravated Polish hatred for Czechoslovakia. The French Foreign Minister, M. Barthou, tried to stop these threatening moves by proposing an Eastern Mutual Aid Pact (a sort of Eastern Locarno) that would bring into close association Germany, Russia, Poland, the Little Entente and the Baltic states. This suggestion was the last attempt made by French diplomacy before the Second World War to establish European co-operation. Russia and the Little Entente received M. Barthou's plan favourably but Hitler rejected it, not wishing to tie his hands with another Locarno in the East. With incredible lack of discernment, Colonel Beck, the Polish Foreign Minister, also rejected the French plan. He hated Russia above all else, and at the same time contemptuously under-estimated her strength, so he could never accept anything that appealed to Moscow. He even managed to persuade the Baltic states to refuse. Hitler found in Beck an active helper in the dissolution of any sort of collective defence against Nazi expansion.

The Western Powers began to retreat before the pressure of the dictators. They failed to stop Mussolini's aggression in Abyssinia; they confined themselves to empty protests against the occupation of the Rhineland by Hitler in 1936, and their alarming complacency had catastrophic results. Such passivity almost encouraged capitulation. The difficulty with which the French Parliament ratified the Franco-Soviet Pact showed that the Franco-Soviet alliance was hardly likely to prove effective. Belgium declared her neutrality. Prince Paul and Stojadinovic and King Carol began to make friends with both the Great Dictators, and Beck's example was widely followed. Germany at that time also successfully penetrated the agricultural states of Central Europe and the Balkans by taking over their agricultural surpluses in exchange for industrial goods and made them still more dependent on her by means of an ingenious credit policy. Germany was dominating the markets of Bulgaria, Rumania, Yugoslavia and Hungary by 1938. Economic penetration facilitated political penetration and paved the way for ultimate German hegemony.

Hitler made excellent use of the German minorities living in East Central Europe. The most numerous, and politically the most powerful, was the German minority of more than 3,000,000 in Czechoslovakia. The Germans themselves estimated their numbers in Poland at about 1,700,000. In Hungary there were about 500,000, in Rumania almost 800,000, in Yugoslavia about 500,000, in Lithuania 35,000, in Estonia 16,000, in Latvia 62,000. Thus there were in the East Central European countries nearly 6,500,000 Germans. Most of the members of these colonies willingly accepted the Pan-Germanic programme of the Nazis. Hitler's plans envisaged the annexation of the Austrian and Sudeten Germans, the Reich's neighbours, and a privileged position for German minorities in all the other states over which the protection of the Nazi hegemony was to be extended. Germans penetrated into East Central Europe during the Middle Ages as 'colonists'. They enjoyed a privileged status, and because they usually had a higher social and cultural standard than the people of the countries into which they moved they were inclined to consider themselves as members of a 'higher race', destined to rule over others. The Nazis had little difficulty in using them as a 'fifth column' in fulfilling their expansion programme in the same way that the Russians now use local Communist Parties for their imperialistic aims.

Altogether the Nazis fully exploited the national rivalries in East Central Europe. They incited the minorities against the states in which they lived, and they fomented the national aspirations of one nation against another. A treaty in 1919 aimed at the international protection of minorities through the medium of the League of Nations did not fulfil its object in the right way. Most of the states concerned did not normally respect the rights of the minorities and these minorities themselves were inclined to make use of international protection against their governments for strengthening their separatist, irredentist aims. Masaryk, systematically restraining the nationalist idiosyncrasies of the Czechs and Germans, the Slovaks and Hungarians, sought a symbiosis of all the nationalities in Czechoslovakia in a spirit of liberal tolerance, hoping that if peace were preserved in Europe for two generations, Czechoslovakia would develop into a second Switzerland. But this liberal Czechoslovakian policy, which manifested itself in the participation of representatives of the German minority in the governments of the Republic, was swept away by the rising tide of Nazi propaganda. The majority of Sudeten Germans were carried away and longed not only to be united to the Reich but also for the inclusion of the Czech lands and even Slovakia in Hitler's empire. At the same time, Nazis incited Slovak nationalists against the Czechs and raised the hopes of the Hungarians for the annexation of the frontier districts of Slovakia where a Hungarian minority lived. Because most of these German minorities willingly served Pan-German imperialism and prepared the way for the Nazi reign of terror over East Central Europe there was a mass transportation of such Germans from these countries back to the Reich after the war.

The Nazis incited not only the local Germans but also the

Ukrainian minority against Poland. Proposals for the future of the Ukraine always played an important part in Hitler's expansionism programme and they supplemented the '*Lebensraum*' policy, already expressed in the Brest-Litovsk *Diktat*. This was based on his racial conception of the right of Germans to rule over the inferior Slav races.

Following the classic method of 'divide and conquer', the Nazis, with malicious pleasure, aided Colonel Beck in his anti-Czech policy, enlivened the dispute between the Hungarians and Rumanians over Transylvania, and dexterously provoked quarrels among the Balkan nations with the help of Mussolini.

Gradually the Nazis prepared for the domination of East Central Europe by destroying the collective security system, by alienating France and all her Central European allies except Czechoslovakia (who remained faithful to her to the end), by using the German minorities as fifth columns, by the incitement of one nation against another, and by economic penetration. The last barriers were removed in 1938. The annexation of Austria took place in March. Czechoslovakia was compelled to capitulate in September and she was so crippled by having her frontier districts torn away that six months later (in March 1939) Hitler marched in to take possession of the whole country. The Czech lands became a German 'Protectorate', and Slovakia was declared 'an independent state', but at the same time immediately became subject to German 'protection' and control.

The consequences of the appeasement of Munich were catastrophic. Poland was isolated. One state after another in Central Europe and the Balkans fell into German dependence. Russia sought reconciliation with a tremendously strengthened Germany, and through the notorious pact of August 1939 hoped to direct Hitler's expansion towards the West. France became so demoralized that she lost faith in herself and eventually, when put to the test, she capitulated. Britain, in a state of bewilderment, was thrust into a war with Germany in which, for a time, she had to stand alone.

Through the determination of the British, led in their hour of need by that historic personality, Sir Winston Churchill, time was gained. Gradually a Grand Alliance was built up to overpower and finally smash Hitler's military colossus. But victory was achieved only at the cost of incredible energy and sacrifice. For years Germany had been the master of Europe from the Atlantic to the Caucasus; by seizing the Danube Basin and the Balkans, she gained a strategical advantage over the Western allies and over Russia. Had Hitler not underestimated the military power of Russia, had he not been wild enough to embark on a war on two fronts, Europe would obviously have remained in his power for a considerable time – all the more so because he would eventually have acquired the use of atomic weapons.

Bismarck's theory that 'whoever is master of Bohemia is master of Europe' is often quoted. Hitler knew that if he destroyed the Czechoslovakian bastion, he could conquer the whole of East Central Europe and that in this way he could dominate Europe.

The last war confirmed that East Central Europe occupies a key position on the European continent. But at the end of the war this was once again forgotten. The Central European key was placed in Stalin's hands.

For a better understanding of the present position in East Central Europe it is necessary to recall that the psychological consequences of Munich have not yet been completely overcome. Communist propaganda never fails to remind the Czechs and the Slovaks that they were deserted by the West at the time of Munich. This is a warning for all the other Central European countries, says Moscow. Even though the subjugated nations understandably expect help eventually from the Western democracies, distrust still persists and suspicion of Western motives was certainly not dispelled by the passivity of the Allies during the recent revolts in Hungary and Poland against the Soviet-dominated governments.

ITALY'S DILETTANTE IMPERIALISM

Germany systematically ruined all attempts at unification, and the game of playing one country against another proved rewarding when Hitler began his programme of expansion at the end of the thirties. Mussolini pursued a similar policy. But even before his time, democratic Italy did not favour plans for Middle European unity, fearing a revival of the Austrian Empire in another form. For the same reason she strongly opposed all attempts at restoring the Habsburgs, and supported Czechoslovakia, Yugoslavia and Rumania on this issue. It was a great misfortune that the dispute over Fiume and Dalmatia prevented any further agreement between Italy and Yugoslavia. This destroyed all hope of Italy playing a consolidating role in the Balkans and the Danube Basin similar to that played by France through her pacts with Poland and Czechoslovakia. Had France and Italy agreed to co-ordinate their policy in East Central Europe much of the confusion and many of the complications that led to conflict could have been avoided. Much of the responsibility for the more unfortunate developments after the First World War lies with Benito Mussolini, the Fascist dictator who was possessed by a wild ambition to restore the Roman Empire. Not having any personal creative ability, he conceived his Fascism merely as the negation of democracy. His corporatism as a sociological theory was over-simple and superficial. The theatrical pose of 'Duce' failed to hide a ridiculous imitation of the Roman Emperors or the Renaissance condottieri. In essence, despite his demagogic success, he was a poor dilettante, even to his cynicism. He was most obviously dilettante in his foreign policy, gaining temporary successes primarily because the policy with the democracies was weak and superficial. Hitler played skilfully with him and almost unnoticed led the unwitting, arrogant 'Duce' into dependence on Germany.

Being consumed by envy and possessed of an inferiority complex, Mussolini did his best to undermine France, especially in East Central Europe. France supported the Versailles order so Mussolini supported revisionism. Since the Little Entente had an alliance with France, Mussolini formed an opposing block with Austria and Hungary on the basis of the so-called Roman Pacts of the thirties. As soon as Poland split with France, Mussolini made friends with Colonel Beck.

Yugoslavia, annoyed by the Duce's plan for '*mare nostrum*', stood in the way of the hegemony of Italy spreading over the Balkans. That is why Mussolini made little Albania his protectorate; that is why he supported the Macedonian revolutionaries and Croatian Ustashi (who murdered King Alexander); that is why he sought to bind the Bulgarian King Boris to Italy by marriage with an Italian princess. The Balkan policy of the Italian dictator was nothing but a collection of intrigues and disruptive manœuvres.

Although during the First World War Mussolini was an ardent supporter of the Czechoslovak volunteers fighting on the Italian front (previously he had written an enthusiastic pamphlet about Jan Hus, a Czech religious reformer of the fifteenth century) he, as Fascist 'Duce', developed an equally passionate hatred for Czechoslovakian democracy and its leaders, Masaryk and Beneš. And he eagerly helped Hitler in the destruction of Czechoslovakia in 1938.

The poverty of Mussolini's foreign policy was notably emphasized in his attitude towards Austria. First he contributed to the collapse of Austrian democracy, and then he ostentatiously protected Austria's independence, sending his troops to the Brenner Pass after an unsuccessful Nazi putsch in Vienna in 1934. At that time Hitler had only started to create the army that was later to terrorize the Continent. And when the power of the Nazis grew to dangerous proportions Mussolini's interest in Austria gradually faded, until in 1938 he merely recognized the Anschluss. By then he was already dependent on Hitler. And it was only through Hitler's munificence that he gained anything further at all during the war. When Mussolini was hard-pressed in Greece, Hitler decided to send in his own troops, but the Belgrade Government refused to allow the German army to cross Yugoslavia. Then a putsch in Belgrade to remove the pro-Nazi ruler, Prince Paul, provided an excuse for Hitler to attack Yugoslavia in April 1941. Hitler allowed Mussolini to 'take' at that time some Slovenian coastal areas of Yugoslavia and to form the puppet kingdom of Croatia-Slavonia whose Prime Minister, Ante Pavelic, leader of the Ustashi (Croatian Fascists and terrorists) became his protégé. Two years later Mussolini capitulated, and with his death ended the disastrous game of Fascist expansion which only in fact aided German imperialism to the detriment of Italy's interests.

CONTRADICTORY SOVIET MANŒUVRES

The policy of the third neighbouring Great Power was no more helpful to East Central Europe in the twenty years of cursory peace than were the machinations of the German and Italian dictators. In the beginning the foreign policy of Bolshevik Russia was dominated by revolutionary dynamism. It is impossible to decide whether it would have taken a different course if Lenin's Government had been invited to the Paris Peace Conference. The Western Allies were still intervening against the revolutionary regime in 1919, hoping for its overthrow. But this policy of intervention was superficial and vacillating.

The Russian revolutionaries, profiting considerably from the weakness and disorder of the Czarist generals and their supporters, were victorious because of their decisiveness, their recklessness and their demagogy. They did not hesitate to use every weapon, political and military, that they could find, or to make fraudulent promises. They parcelled out land to the peasant farmers, postponing agricultural collectivization to a later date. They gave extensive autonomy to the non-Russian nations within the Russian empire, fettering them soon afterwards by a central 'dictatorship of the proletariat' within the Soviet Union. Lenin then thought that the capitalist world, weakened by war, was also ready for revolution and he hoped that the German proletariat at least would follow the Bolshevik example. His attention was centred on provoking Communist revolutions. But he was disappointed. All the Communist revolutions in Hungary, Germany and Bulgaria failed miserably. The Bolsheviks were forced to admit after 1924 that the capitalist world had achieved a 'temporary relative stabilization'. Despite the proclamations of Trotsky, Stalin, a realist who never shared his revolutionary colleague's enthusiasm for a 'permanent world revolution', began to pursue a policy of 'socialism in one country', concentrating on the consolidation of the Soviet system in Russia. Rapid industrialization and forcible collectivization of the land were part of his programme. Everything and everybody was sacrificed to the creation of a strong Soviet state.

That is why the 'Third International' and the 'Comintern' were gradually subordinated to the interests and needs of Soviet foreign policy. Communist Parties were consigned to a minor role, serving either the defence or the expansion of the Soviet Union. During this period revolutionary agitation among Europe's masses virtually ceased. Because the Soviet Communists were at the same time weak in power, Communist Parties in Europe had little influence in local politics. Communists became merely an unpleasant nuisance. Their attempts to upset the workers only weakened the Socialists to the benefit of the Conservatives, who adroitly made use of the Communist bogy for their own ends.

Bela Kun's Communist regime in 1919 contributed substantially to the restoration of a politically and socially reactionary regime in Hungary. A Bulgarian Communist putsch in 1923 strengthened Cankov's government, encouraging its persecutions and brutalities. A Communist attack on the Yugoslav Minister of the Interior, Draskovic, provided an excuse for the disbanding of the Communist Party in Yugoslavia in 1920. In all these countries (and in Poland and Rumania, too) the Communist Parties were outlawed. They were forced to vegetate underground. The keen, vigorous radicalism of the Austrian Social Democrats in opposition to the Government prevented Communism from gaining any ground in Austria.

Communists were strongest in Czechoslovakia, but even though they made full use of their democratic rights they remained far weaker than the Socialists. Czechoslovakia had proportional representation and Communists numbered 10 per cent in Parliament. All the other local parties were organized according to nationalities but the Communists were a united 'international' party – Czech-Slovak-German-Hungarian-Ruthenian. They gained more votes among Sudeten Germans than among the Czechs, and by their demagogic approach attained their greatest success among the politically less mature Slovaks and Ruthenians.

Moscow is the Mecca of Communists, and local Communists met with greater or lesser obstacles according to the attitude of this or that nation to Russia. Poland and Hungary (and to a great extent Rumania) were traditionally anti-Russian; Bulgaria and Czechoslovakia were more friendly towards Russia. But the influence of such national policies was definitely smaller than a first glance would suggest. This is corroborated by Yugoslavia and Germany. Russophilism was widespread not only among the Serbs but also among the Slovenes and Croats in Yugoslavia. Yet the attitude of Yugoslavia towards Soviet Russia was unfriendly or at least non-committal until the beginning of the Second World War. The persecution of Yugo-Slav Communists did not meet with any apparent opposition from the rest of the people. And although German nationalism thrived on anti-Slav propaganda, the Communist Party nevertheless gained about 6 million votes.

Czechoslovakia had definite Russophile tendencies, and many Sudeten Germans and Hungarians voted for Communism, yet the Party remained to the end of the Republic without any influence on the internal and foreign policy of the state. Communists were not allowed to join the coalition Government even after the signing of a pact with Soviet Russia in 1935 and, in contrast to France, the Czechoslovakian Socialists consistently rejected all Communist efforts to form a 'people's front'.

Judged as a whole, Communism in East Central Europe did not constitute any influential political force between the two World Wars. Even if we admit that police regimes in other countries hindered Communist development by constant persecution, Czechoslovakia, where it was able to flourish quite freely, proves that the communization of East Central Europe in 1945 was not the work of native Communist forces but the product of external pressure by the victorious Soviet Union. But after the failure of the Communist putsch instigated by Moscow in East Central Europe in the twenties, the Soviet leaders did not pay much more attention to the countries involved. Their relations with the Baltic countries remained aloofly correct. Only Lithuania, angry with Poland because of the occupation of Vilno, had anything akin to friendship with Moscow.

Relations between Poland and Russia were always very tense. During the war unleashed by Pilsudski in 1920 – after conquering Kiev, he dreamed of forming a Polish-Ukrainian union – Poland was endangered when a Red army, having repulsed a Polish attack, halted before the gates of Warsaw. The Poles were saved at that time not only by the intervention of the French General Weygand but also through the strategical and psychological mistakes of the Bolsheviks (among them Stalin in particular) who scattered their forces and underestimated the dynamic spirit of Polish patriotism. The Russians paid for their defeat by heavy territorial concessions in the Peace of Riga in 1921. There was never any doubt that they could ever become reconciled to this frontier which removed them so far from Europe and gave to Poland extensive Ukrainian and White Russian areas. But victorious Warsaw ignored the danger of Russian revenge, relaxing in the belief that Russia had been too weakened to be able to create another army worthy of respect in the next twenty years. (The aspirations of power-seeking Pilsudski, bordering on megalomania, become more comprehensible when we recall that in the twenties both Germany and Russia were militarily feeble and few people in Europe at that time foresaw the possibility of this unusually swift development in the next ten years.)

Moscow's attitude to the three states in the Little Entente was not affable. She considered them satellites of French imperialism, which she denounced as vehemently as she criticized British imperialism. She supported Germany's opposition to the Versailles Treaty after the Rapallo Agreement. Only the unconcealed enmity between the Soviet leaders and the Horthy regime prevented Moscow, in spite of her basic attitude towards the 'imperialist' Paris peace treaties, from actively supporting Hungarian revisionism. But Russia had no interest in the existing position advocated by the Little Entente, especially as she had never recognized the annexation of Bessarabia by Rumania, who, on her side, sought to consolidate this gain by an alliance with Poland. The other countries of the Little Entente did not follow even when France, Italy and Britain entered into diplomatic relations with the Soviet Union in 1924, and normal diplomatic relations between Czechoslovakia and Rumania and Russia were not established until after Hitler's ascent to power in 1934, when Soviet policy began to turn in the direction of a *rapprochement* with the West. Even then Yugoslavia did not join her partners. She did not establish diplomatic relations with the Soviet Union until the beginning of the Second World War – even later than Bulgaria, whose relations with the Soviet Union were always strained.

Hitler clearly declared in *Mein Kampf* his hatred not only of Bolshevism but also of Russia and all the other 'inferior' Slav races. Obviously the Soviet leaders had to strengthen their defences and alter the orientation of their foreign policy after the victory of Nazism in Germany. The Soviet Foreign Minister, Litvinov, negotiated non-aggression pacts with the states of

East Central Europe from Finland to Turkey, with the exception of Bulgaria, Hungary and Austria, in 1933, a year later the Soviet Union entered the League of Nations, and, after the failure of Barthou's plan for an Eastern 'Locarno', representatives of the Soviet Union signed treaties of alliance with France and Czechoslovakia in 1935. Stalin's henchmen also became more friendly with Britain at this time. The Russians now decided that 'revisionism' (which they had previously supported) was an instrument of Fascist reaction. They defended, in the name of 'anti-Fascism', the position established by the Versailles Treaty rejecting, among other points, the Austrian Anschluss, and arguing in favour of a system of collective security partly within the framework of the League of Nations, partly on the basis of special alliances. It seemed that Russia was eager to revive the Franco-Russo-British Entente. At the same time relations between Russia and the Little Entente improved, and Moscow became particularly friendly with Czechoslovakia. During this period Soviet Russia also took care to create the impression that, having abandoned the imperialist dreams of Czarist Russia, the Communists were resolved to respect the independence of the small Central European nations.

But relations between East and West began once more to deteriorate in the middle thirties when the Western Powers unwillingly accepted the Nazi occupation of the Rhineland and Mussolini's attack on Abyssinia. While the Western Powers decided not to interfere in the Spanish Civil War, the Fascist Powers helped Franco, and the Russians, in their own strange way, sided with the Republicans. These episodes helped to widen the new gap between East and West, and Russian suspicions were aroused by passionate ideological 'anti-Communist' and 'anti-Fascist' campaigns. France was dangerously divided during the days when the people's front provided a government. The minds of the people were so confused by the fashionable militant passions that to many it seemed as though they must choose either Hitler or Stalin. This confusion, purposely cultivated by Fascist propaganda, described Czechoslovakia as a 'bastion of Bolshevism' and contributed to the French desertion of their faithful ally. The Fascist Powers united in the 'Rome-Berlin Axis' in 1931 to pursue an increasingly offensive policy, but Britain and France inclined more and more towards 'appeasement'. Finally came the disastrous agreement of the Four Powers at Munich in September 1938. Russia was ostentatiously left out of this meeting of the leaders of the Great Powers, and the Munich Agreement was obviously directed against her. Many influential statesmen in the West hoped that Hitler, leaving the West in peace, would try to fulfil his programme of expansion at the expense of Russia.

It is difficult to avoid wondering whether the world would have been spared six years of war had the Franco-British-Soviet alliance placed itself in decisive opposition to the Fascist Powers in 1938. German generals testified at the Nuremburg trials that Hitler would have been removed if the other Great Powers had declared their opposition openly to his military adventures. Even if this had not happened immediately, the Nazis would probably have yielded fairly soon to a war on two fronts. This would have been forced on the Nazis right from the start of the war if the Franco-British-Soviet alliance had lasted, and it must be remembered that the Germans were militarily and politically far weaker in 1938 than a year later when war actually broke out. Some people think that Stalin would have avoided taking part in a war on the side of the Western Powers in 1938 despite all his public promises, but documents published so far do not confirm this opinion. Yet the Communist assertion that Russia was willing to help Czechoslovakia even without the support of France is untrue and is repeated only because it serves the needs of Moscow's propaganda machine. It seems though that the Russians were convinced in 1938 that Hitler could not withstand the united forces of an alliance of the Western Powers and Russia, to which the armies of Czechoslovakia and other Central European nations would inevitably have been added. And it is likely that after careful thought Poland would also have joined the Allies. All this confirms the belief that the Russians would have joined France and Britain in 1938 – especially as such a course would have been so much in the interests of Soviet Russia.

But developments took another turn. Stalin answered the shortsightedness of the West with his own shortsightedness. He negotiated a pact with Hitler in August 1939 in the desperate belief that the war could be limited to Western Europe and that he would intervene only when all the 'imperialist' powers were exhausted. Moscow counted on a long 'war of attrition' in the West. The speedy collapse of France in 1940 ruined these cynical calculations. Molotov sent Hitler a telegram congratulating him on his victory over France, but in reality the Kremlin was consumed by anxiety at that time. The Russian hierarchy could not ignore the possibility that the victorious Nazis would hurl themselves on Russia once their task in the West was completed.

The failure of the co-operation between East and West was catastrophic for Eastern Europe. We have seen how the fall of Austria and Czechoslovakia made the nations of the Danube Basin and the Balkans dependent on Nazi Germany. The frenzied policy pursued by Colonel Beck merely brought catastrophe to his country all the sooner. Hitler and Stalin agreed on a new division of Poland. Czechoslovakia had already gone and now Poland, too, was wiped off the map of Europe. The Baltic states, Bessarabia and Bukovina, were swallowed by Soviet Russia, and Finland was threatened.

The German-Soviet Non-Aggression Pact, relieving Hitler at an opportune moment of the danger of war on two fronts, enormously helped the Nazi dictator not only in his fight against Poland but also in his struggle with the Western Powers. But the secret agreement on the partition of Poland was no less significant. Hitler offered Stalin an opportunity such as he had never had before to revive the ambitious dreams of Russian imperialism for Central and Balkan Europe. From that time onwards Stalin never lost sight of his objective, even though he concealed it for tactical reasons when the Western democracies became his allies in 1941. From the partition of Poland the path leads, even if in a roundabout way, to the agreements with the Western democracies that culminated at Yalta and actually placed East Central Europe within Russia's sphere of interest.

The Soviet-Nazi pacts of 1939 represented an association of 'revisionist forces' against the order established by the Treaty. Co-operation between the 'revisionist' Great Powers was brief but it lasted long enough for the decisive destruction of the European pattern based on the leadership of Britain and France. The collaboration of the German and Russian dictatorships also put an end to the independence of the nations of East Central Europe – an independence that was the child of democratic conceptions and could only be preserved in an international democratic order.

Hitler and Stalin did not last long as a team; Nazi and Soviet ideas of imperialism soon clashed. Attempts to reach agreement on 'spheres of influence' failed, and irreconcilable rivalries concerning East Europe were soon reawakened. Conflict was almost inevitable as soon as Germany and Russia again became next-door neighbours, and became all the more so because the pact negotiated in 1939 was only an expedient for both dictators. The partition of Poland, which at one time served to strengthen Russo-German friendship, also gave Hitler an opportunity for a direct attack on Russia in 1941. In the Balkans, German imperialism had adopted old ambitions of the former Austro-Hungarian Empire, and when Soviet policy clashed with their imperialistic traditions, friction developed between Moscow and Berlin. Conflict was hastened by Hitler's impatience. Feeling himself sufficiently secure in the West after the defeat of France, he wished speedily to carry out his expansionist plans in the East, hoping that within a few months he would be issuing orders from the Kremlin.

Previous experience shows that it is possible to reconcile the imperialist rivalries of Germany and Russia only if they do not clash against each other or at least as long as they are separated by the independent states of East Central Europe. Their brief period of co-operation between 1939 and 1941 should now be a warning not only to the small nations lying between them but also to Western Europe. An alliance between Russia and Germany, today as yesterday, threatens all other European nations, including the British, with the danger of becoming dependent on those two Great Powers; or, because such an alliance gives them a dangerous preponderance of power over the others, it can lead to world conflict.

In the first part of the Second World War the 'revisionist' Great Powers attained many of their objectives. The Europe created by the Versailles Treaty disappeared. France, Belgium, Holland, Denmark and Norway fell into Germany's hands; Britain was isolated; Hitler was master of the greater part of Poland, of the Czech lands and of Slovakia. His voice was decisive throughout the Danube Basin and the Balkans, even in Greece. Mussolini took possession of Slovenia, Dalmatia, Croatia-Slavonia and Albania. Stalin absorbed the Baltic states, eastern Poland, Bessarabia and Bukovina. The Central European and Balkan nations became the satellites of the neighbouring Great Powers. Poland and Czechoslovakia had been erased completely from the map. Yugoslavia was torn to pieces.

This was a triumph for imperialist power politics. The small nations were helpless in the cynical game played by the three totalitarian powers. The strongest of them was Nazi Germany. Fascist Italy achieved its Balkan gains only by virtue of Germany's generosity. Hitler realized a Pan-German *Mitteleuropa* stretching from the North and Baltic Seas to the Black Sea and the Mediterranean. In a way he attained even more. He extended German power to the Pyrenees and, after the successful invasion of Russia, to the Caucasus. The 'new European order' was a hegemony of the German *Herrenvolk* over all others. For the people of these countries there was slave labour, the concentration camp or the gas chamber.

Soviet Russia was shaken to her foundations by the terrible initial defeats she suffered in conflict with Hitler's army. Without the substantial aid given by the Anglo-Saxon countries she could not have resisted the overwhelming German blows. But as soon as the Germans were forced to retreat after their defeat at Stalingrad, Stalin began to make plans not only for the recovery of his territorial winnings in the early days of the war, but also for increasing them. Moscow started planning Soviet domination of East Central Europe in 1943.

CHAPTER III

Soviet Rule over East Central Europe

SPHERES OF INFLUENCE

Hitler wanted to drive the Russian Bolsheviks far back into the steppes of Asia, but he merely helped them to settle in Central Europe. Nazism was a remarkable return to the paganism and expansionism of the primitive Germans, and it ended as miserably as the German Empire of the seventh century. From the Crimea, which they had penetrated in the fourth century, the Germans were driven back to the Elbe and the Saale. 'L'hitlerisme, en ramenant le germanisme à ses origines, . . . ne réussira finalement qu'a provoquer le retour des Slaves jusqu'au bassin de l'Elbe.'[1]

The United States and Britain could have prevented the expansion of Russian power had they recognized in time that he who holds East Central Europe has the predominant position in Europe. Western statesmen failed to realize the danger of allowing Russian Communists to dominate East Central Europe.

Winston Churchill tried to lessen the dangers he foresaw by suggesting to Stalin a division of spheres of interest in the individual countries of Central and Balkan Europe. Washington diplomatists, shocked by such 'imperialist' bargaining, had to agree at Yalta to Soviet Russia's having the decisive influence in East Central Europe.

It would not appear from available documents that either Roosevelt or Churchill expressly relinquished this area to the Communists. The Yalta Declaration on Liberated Europe promised on February 11, 1945, 'the earliest possible establishment through free elections of governments responsive to the

[1] René Grousset, *Bilan de l'Histoire*, Paris, 1946.

will of the people'. But the Russians interpreted the terms 'freedom' and 'democracy' in their own undemocratic way. To Western statesmen it seemed legitimate that 'governments friendly towards the Soviet Union' should be formed in the liberated countries. But Moscow considered as 'friendly' only a government that blindly fulfilled her wishes and orders. Stalin himself observed at the Potsdam Conference that governments freely elected in Eastern Europe would be anti-Soviet. This he could not allow.

Western statesmen were justified later in reproaching the Russians that they – in the words of the American Secretary of State, Stettinius – 'failed to live up to the terms of the Yalta Agreement'. There were so many ambiguities in the Yalta Agreements that the policy of 'spheres of influence' could not be avoided. No matter what the intentions of the Western statesmen may have been, the fact remains that in Europe and the Far East a division of power between the Western Powers and Communist Russia was reached according to whether the countries were occupied by Allied troops or the Red Army. When East Central Europe was 'liberated' by the Russian soldiers she came at the same time under the domination of the Kremlin.

The Potsdam Conference was the last opportunity that the Western Powers were given to change the situation. By then they had gained enough experience to realize that Russia intended to dominate the countries of East Central Europe by means of puppet governments controlled by the Communists. Two weeks after the signing of the Yalta Agreements the Communists, protected by the Red Army, provoked a rebellion against the legal government in Rumania. Vyshinsky travelled to Bucharest and, ordering Soviet artillery to be posted in front of the royal palace, he compelled King Michael to name a new government headed by Groza, a hireling of the Communists. British and American protests were useless. It became ever more obvious from March 1945 that Moscow, ignoring the Yalta Agreements, intended also to install a Polish government that would be dominated by Communists. Under strong pressure from the Americans and the British, Stalin yielded so far as to allow Stanislaw Mikolajczyk, former Prime Minister of the Polish Government in exile in London, and a few other Polish democrats to join the new administration. In spite of this, the Polish Government formed in June 1945 was in the hands of local Communists on whom the Kremlin could depend. Rumania and Poland were ominous signs of Stalin's determination to keep East Central Europe under his will.

A few hours before his death on April 12, 1945, Roosevelt, in a telegram to Churchill on Poland, said, 'We must be firm . . .' And Churchill at the end of the war was unhappy with gloomy foreboding at the threat of Soviet domination and the spread of Communism in Europe. He even considered the possibility of not dispersing the defeated German Army and of using it, if necessary, against Soviet expansion.

But military operations against Russia were out of the question at that time, and for the same reason that extensive intervention against the Bolsheviks was impossible after the First World War. The Allied nations were exhausted by a long and terrible war and, apart from this, the victorious Red Army then enjoyed considerable popularity in America, Britain and the other West European countries, as in the same way the Bolshevik 'workers' revolution enjoyed the sympathy in 1918 of Western workers and of many Socialists. Yet the Western statesmen could have forced Stalin at Potsdam to guarantee the democratic and independent development of the countries of East Central Europe. Russia was so weakened and devastated by war that Stalin, who learnt at Potsdam that the Americans had the atom bomb, could not then have afforded an open break with the Anglo-Saxon Powers.

There is no doubt that the Russians were better prepared than the Western Allies for the 'battle for peace'. This is proved by their plans for East Central Europe, for Japan and China. But Stalin moved cautiously, not wishing to provoke a too violent protest, particularly from the Americans. With the continued advance of the Red Army into Europe he became more reckless and demanding because the Western Allies became more compliant. It was to his advantage that the Americans and the British were not always united in their reaction to his activities. It is probable that Stalin would not have acquired such a strong position in Europe if the war policy of the Western Allies had followed Churchill's line. His plans for a Balkan invasion showed great political foresight, and it can not be doubted that had the Western and not the Soviet armies occupied Berlin, Prague and Vienna, Soviet influence in Central Europe would have been considerably limited, to the advantage not only of the Western Powers but also of democracy in East Central Europe.

But the decisions of the Allies on the future structure of the world were based on a division of 'spheres of influence' – to the lasting profit of the Russians. Italy and Greece found themselves in the Western sphere, but East Central Europe in the Eastern. Manchuria fell under Soviet influence; Japan under American. Korea was divided into a northern Soviet area and an American southern area. For future developments it was regrettable that Germany – with the exception of Berlin – was not subject to a joint occupation, but was divided into four occupation administrations, and the same thing happened to Austria, again with the exception of Vienna which, like Berlin, came under joint Allied administration. Thus the way was prepared for the later division of Germany into Western and Eastern zones, and the Russians consolidated their positions on the Elbe and in Saxony with its uranium mines. But such a division of Germany into Western and Soviet spheres meant a division of all Europe.

Stalin also arranged at Potsdam in the summer of 1945 that the new Polish frontier should be on the Oder-Neisse rivers. Poland was in this way to be compensated for the loss of her eastern provinces, which had been handed to Russia. The eastern frontier of Poland was roughly located according to the Curzon Line proposed at the Paris Conference in 1919. Poland also gained Danzig and the southern portion of East Prussia. Russia annexed the northern portion with Königsberg. It is true that the German provinces given to Poland at Potsdam were only formally placed under Polish administration until a final peace settlement with Germany. And the Western Allies still do not recognize the Oder-Neisse frontier as final. This legal reservation in no way alters the existing state of affairs, and it is necessary only to arouse the suspicions of the Poles about Western intentions for the Oder-Neisse to make them qualify their dislike for Russia, without whose help they could scarcely hope to keep this frontier.

During the war even the Western Allies acknowledged that Polish claims, particularly to Silesia, were justified and that it was only just that the Poles should receive compensation for their big territorial losses in the East at the expense of Germany, who was guilty of starting a war in which Poland was the first victim.

The Russian leaders have always realized that Poland would be under an obligation to them as long as they insisted that the Oder-Neisse line should become a permanent feature of the map of Europe. In this attempt to tie Poland to Russia as firmly as possible they have ardently supported the new frontier and derived smug satisfaction from the reserved and irresolute attitude adopted by the Western Allies on this issue. Moscow tried by unofficial hints to persuade Czechoslovakia to make demands on Germany for Lusatian territory. Some Slavonic Serbs or Wends remain in Lusatia and I provoked Czech Communists into making violent protest when, in July 1945, in agreement with President Beneš, I categorically opposed these designs. It was obvious that the Russians wished in this way to strengthen Czechoslovakia's dependence on Moscow.

Yet it is wrong to believe that the Russians instigated the transfer of the German minorities from Central Europe. At least as far as Czechoslovakia is concerned, the Russian Government delayed a long time before making any decision on this question. The Czechoslovak Communist Party included at that time many Sudeten Germans, and Moscow was apparently considering if it would not be possible to make the Sudeten Germans put pressure on the Czechs, whose liberal tendencies were as suspect to the Bolsheviks as they were in the past to Czarist officials. The Soviets agreed to the transfer of the Sudeten Germans only after the British and Americans approved the move in principle in 1943. The Potsdam Conference then decided that all German minorities in the Central European countries should be sent 'home'. This was an attempt to strengthen European security by removing those minorities in Central Europe that had always been so willing to intrigue to help plans for German expansion. When the Soviet Government suddenly stopped the transfer of those Sudeten Germans who were to be admitted to the Soviet Zone of Germany, they were obviously toying again with the idea of playing the Germans off against the Czechs, as they did the Slovaks against the Czechs.

Russia fulfilled her promise to send the Sudeten Germans 'home' only when, observing that the Americans were punctiliously meeting their obligations, her leaders began to fear that the Americans might become too popular with the Czechs to the detriment of Moscow.

The Potsdam Conference, conducted on the basis of decisions previously reached by the Allied leaders at Yalta, was meant to decide how temporarily to meet the situation that would be created by the defeat of Germany. The new European order, it was thought, would be created at the inevitable peace conference. But peace treaties were negotiated only with Italy, Finland, Hungary, Rumania and Bulgaria in 1946, and to this day there has been no peace treaty with Germany. Potsdam established the basis for a settlement in Europe for a far longer period than was imagined at that time. We are still suffering from the consequences of Potsdam and it is unlikely that those who took part in the conference ever dreamt what the results would be. Western statesmen hoped that from 'definitive' peace treaties there would eventually emerge a new order that would generally be in accordance with the principles of the Atlantic Charter and the United Nations Organization founded in San Francisco in June 1945. Their hopes were not fulfilled. The Russians, paying only lip service to democratic principles, were determined to secure full domination over all East Central Europe, to gain points of vantage in the Far East and to extend their power and influence wherever opportunity offered. The end of the war was also the end of the Grand Alliance between the Western Allies and the Soviet Government. The war was followed not by peace but by the cold war. Winston Churchill was already prophesying at the beginning of 1946 that an 'Iron Curtain' would soon fall to hide the eastern part of Europe that had slipped into Communist hands. Tension between the West and the Soviet empire rapidly increased. It soon became obvious that the main contenders in the international arena were the U.S.S.R. and the U.S.A. Few other politicians immediately after the war saw with such penetrating vision as Winston Churchill that even though the world had been saved from the dangers of Nazism it was still threatened by the even greater imperialist ambition of Soviet Russia, whose self-confidence had grown alarmingly through her great wartime victories. It is unlikely, on the other hand, that Stalin ever expected that the United States, emerging from the war as the strongest world power, would continue to be interested in Europe. After the First World War the Americans soon lost interest in Europe, but this time they showed their willingness to defend Europe against aggressive Soviet moves. True enough they quickly disbanded their wartime armies, but within a few years American troops were back in Europe.

In spite of the United Nations the world remained split. The policy of 'spheres of influence' begun during the war could scarcely have led to anything else. Measures adopted at the end of the war by the Allies either for military purposes or for temporary occupation tasks (Germany, for example), later influenced political decisions. Power politics and 'expediency' outweighed political and moral principles. Whereas the Versailles decisions were based on the elements of political power and on democratic principles, Potsdam's decisions rested, if not exclusively, certainly to a great extent on nothing but power politics.

THE SOVIET EMPIRE

Russia would only profit from such a policy. In the first place she greatly expanded her empire, starting with the territory she gained after the conclusion of the pact with Hitler in 1939–40. From Finland she acquired the Karelian Isthmus, the Salo sector, and Petsamo with its lead mines. She further incorporated three Baltic states – Estonia, Latvia and Lithuania – into the Soviet Union. From Poland she took the eastern provinces just beyond the Curzon Line; from Czechoslovakia she took Ruthenia; from Rumania she took Bukovina and Bessarabia which connected her to the mouth of the Danube; and finally from Germany she took the northern part of eastern Prussia. In the Far East she gained the ports of Dairen and Port Arthur, Sakhalin and the Kuril Islands. For a time she occupied Manchuria, establishing an advantageous position that helped her economy and communications. Finally she acquired a decisive influence in northern Korea, even though she returned to Communist China in 1954 some of the positions they had 'won' after the war.

Thus Stalin made good all the losses incurred by Russia through her defeat by Japan in 1904 and through the First World War. He not only realized, but he also surpassed the imperialist dreams of Peter I and Catherine the Great, except that he did not become master of Constantinople, the Dardanelles and the Bosphorus. Russia expanded into territory she had never controlled before: Königsberg, eastern Galicia, Bukovina and Ruthenia. On the Baltic, Stalin reigned over the east coast from the Gulf of Finland to Königsberg and, because of the dependence of Poland, virtually all the way to Stettin, too. Russian predominance in this area and the fundamental reduction of German influence made a renewal of German expansion in the Baltic very difficult. Having reached the mouth of the Danube and – for the first time in history – having penetrated to the south of the Carpathians into the lower reaches of the Danube, Russia won a position from which she could exert a decisive influence in Central and Balkan Europe.

And the might of the Soviets extended far to the west of her own frontiers. She dominated not only East Central Europe and East Germany, but she also controlled the whole area from the Bay of Lübeck on the Baltic to Trieste and Valona on the Adriatic and Varna and Burgas on the Black Sea. After the quarrel with Tito in 1948 Russia's power in the Balkans was notably lessened. She ceased to be a direct threat to Italy. Yet the Kremlin's leaders still hold Albania, where they built air and submarine bases and from where they still threaten Yugoslavia and Greece. In both these countries, and particularly in Yugoslavia, there is an Albanian minority numbering more than half a million, and they are dangerously near Albania's frontiers.

Neutralization of Austria brought great relief to the people of that country in 1955. It meant they need no longer endure the presence of Soviet and Western occupation forces. But the power of Soviet Russia in Central Europe was not seriously weakened. To a certain extent she benefited by this arrangement. Austrian neutrality cuts communications between Western Germany and Italy.

To emphasize the strength of the Russian position in Central and Balkan Europe it is only necessary to point out that from Thuringia, now occupied by the Red Army, Bonn, the capital city of West Germany, is only a little over 120 miles and the Franco-Belgian-Luxemburg frontier about 200 miles. From the Western frontiers of Bohemia to Strasbourg the distance is not much more than 250 miles. Trieste is not more than 160 miles distant from Hungary. The distance from Bulgaria to Istanbul is not more than 100 miles, to Salonika not quite

70 miles. The air route from the Elbe, occupied by the Red
Army, to London covers about 470 miles. In an age of tanks,
planes and guided missiles such distances are negligible. By
dominating East Central Europe and East Germany the
Russians have secured for themselves an exceptionally advantageous position for the defence of Russia and for a possible
offensive against Western Europe and the Eastern Mediterranean. The improbability of a general war does not exclude
the possibility of one, and Russian power, having the heart of
Europe at its disposal, represents a dangerous threat that
should be oppressive to Western Europe—and to Britain.

From the time of Catherine the Great in the second half of
the eighteenth century Russia has been trying to acquire a firm
anchorage on the Baltic and Black Seas, seize Constantinople
and the Straits and have under her protectorate at least the
eastern half of the Balkans. That is why she protected the
Orthodox Rumanians, Bulgarians and Serbs, and temporarily
the Greeks, and waged war with the Sublime Porte for their
'liberation'.

Czarist Pan-Slavism was limited to Orthodox Slavs. It was
not interested in the Catholic Croats and Slovenes or Slovaks,
still less in the liberal Czechs. The Catholic Poles were merely
suppressed. The Czarist Government suffered or supported
Pan-Slavism only in so far as it served its imperialist ambitions.
Liberal Russian 'Slavophiles' remained in disfavour or were
actually persecuted. In this the Soviet Government followed
Czarist tradition. During the last war she made use of the 'Slav
idea' only in so far as it made good propaganda for Soviet
penetration into Slav countries. Russia's interest in the 'Slav
idea' was soon forgotten after the war, and once more gave
way to purely Communist propaganda.

Czarist Russia held a great part of Poland in domination, but
the Communists expanded the Czarist conception of a Russian
empire by adding Czechoslovakia.

When it seemed that Marshal Brussilov would penetrate into
Slovakia and the Czech lands in the autumn of 1916, the

Czarist Foreign Ministry, in a secret memorandum, proposed the creation of a Czech Kingdom which was to be under direct Russian influence. It suggested supporting those Czecho-slovak émigrés living in Russia who were willing to accept a Czarist Protectorate, and sharply rejected Masaryk, 'the English agent', who was in favour of Western orientation for the new Czechoslovak state. It was necessary – according to the memorandum – to place at the head of the Czechoslovak exiles 'a man who is sincerely convinced that it is to the immediate interest of Bohemia to join forces with Russia'. The Soviets followed this policy, using the Czechoslovak Communist exiles living in Moscow during the last war for the same ends as Czarist diplomacy.[1]

Wishing to consolidate Russian domination Stalin even toyed with the idea during the war of deporting the majority of the Hungarians from their own country to Siberia or Turkestan and settling Russians or other Slavs in Hungary.

By holding Poland, Czechoslovakia and all the Balkans, Soviet imperialism surpassed the most audacious Czarist ambitions – if we forget Constantinople, Greece and Yugo-slavia. Stalin outstripped Ivan the Terrible, Peter, Catherine the Great and Nicholas I. He was more akin to such Mongolian conquerors as Jenghiz Khan and Tamerlane than to his Czarist predecessor. His empire stretched from the Elbe to Vladivostock and North Korea, and his influence was felt over the whole of China down to North Indo-China. The extent of his dominion and power put Napoleon and Hitler in the shade. He was one of the most successful and most terrible con-querors the world has ever known.

Soviet expansion followed the same pattern of Czarist Imperialism but there was a fundamental difference between them. Czarist Russia tried to achieve her aims in the same way as any other great power; Soviet Russia in addition must seek to spread her own ideology over all the other nations – 'being

[1] E. Pezet, *'Panslavisme d'hier et d'aujourd'hui'* – *Revue Politique et Parlementaire*, June 1949.

ready at all times to spread Communism with all the force at her command'.[1]

The real objectives of Soviet conquest go far beyond the aims of the old-fashioned Russian imperialism without neglecting them. The totalitarian character of the Soviet regime drives the Soviet leaders inexorably to expansion. They feel themselves threatened as long as all other nations are not subject to their domination. That is also the main reason for their being afraid to relax their authority. Allowing even limited freedom seems at once to threaten the foundations of the regime. The preservation of international tension and internal 'vigilance' against foreign and internal 'counter-revolutionaries' is for Soviet dictators an inevitable condition in the preservation of their power. 'If they do not pursue global rule as their ultimate goal, they are only likely to lose whatever power they have already seized.'[2]

Soviet expansion in East Central Europe is an example of this. The Russians were not satisfied with the extension of their territory. They were not satisfied (as Czarist Russia would have been) with exercising a predominant influence in the neighbouring small countries on their western border. They subject these nations to direct rule, forcing puppet Communist administrations on them. Not even the Communist tendencies of these countries, as Yugoslavia, Poland and Hungary have shown, was enough to satisfy the Russians. They demand total obedience from their satellites. The Czars subjugated Poland and for a time had Rumania and Bulgaria under their protectorate, and to a certain extent even little Serbia was their vassal state; but because their autocracy was not absolute, they failed to absorb Poland as part of Russia and they quickly lost even their influence over the Balkan countries. Soviet imperialism is far more successful because it purposely and systematically

---

[1] J. Salwyn Schapiro, *The World In Crisis*, p. 297, New York, 1950. Schapiro, in a modification of Lenin's well-known definition of Bolshevism, says: 'Soviet Russia is historic Russia plus Marxism.'

[2] Hannah Arendt, *The Origins of Totalitarianism*, p. 378, New York, 1951.

combines the powerful strength of Soviet Russia with Communism when imposing Soviet authority on the lands that come within its sphere of influence.

GENERAL PLAN OF COMMUNIZATION

By a cunning combination of power and ideological force the Russians achieved complete domination over all East Central Europe soon after the war. They abused shamefully the trust that the leaders of the Western Powers had shown in them at the wartime conferences at Teheran, Yalta and Potsdam. They simply ignored the obligations they had accepted in the treaties and agreements concluded with their allies, contemptuously forgetting promises about free elections in the countries of East Central Europe, calmly violating the United Nations Charter and the later Declaration of Human Rights.

They took advantage of the fact that, after the speedy demobilization of the Western armies after the war, the balance of power in Europe disappeared. Winston Churchill was right in saying that only the atomic bomb, not then possessed by the Soviets, prevented the Red Army from marching into western Europe. The Western Allies frequently protested at the way in which the Russians violated their promises in the countries behind the Iron Curtain, but their protests, without force behind them, had no effect on the Soviet leaders. They merely became offended because the Western Powers were 'interfering' in their sphere of influence. But above all else it was the occupying Red Army which enabled Moscow to shape East Central Europe to her will. If these countries had been liberated by the Western armies (or simultaneously by them and the Red Army), they would never have succumbed to Soviet rule. Austria is the best example of this. It is beyond all doubt that – except possibly for Yugoslavia, where Tito's partisans represented a strong force – the Communists would have been unable to enforce their leadership of the East European people without the backing of Soviet troops. The presence of Russian troops, even though they did not directly intervene, was sufficient to prevent anti-Communists from preparing or undertaking open revolt against Moscow's puppets. Whenever Communists met with serious difficulties they did not hesitate to terrorize their adversaries by threatening the imminent intervention of the Red Army. This happened in Czechoslovakia during the 1946 elections and the February crisis of 1948.

An official document exists to prove the decisive part played by the Red Army in making Communists of the people of the East European countries. During the dispute between Stalin and Tito, the Central Committee of the Soviet Communist Party in a letter of May 4, 1948, to the Central Committee of the Yugoslavian Communist Party declared that 'the services of the French and Italian Communist Parties to the revolution were not less but greater than those of Yugoslavia', and added:

> 'Even though the French and Italian Communist Parties have so far achieved less success than the Communist Party of Yugoslavia this is not due to any special qualities of the Communist Party of Yugoslavia, but mainly because . . . the Soviet Army came to the aid of the Yugoslav people, crushed the German invader, liberated Belgrade and in this way created the conditions which were necessary for the Communist Party of Yugoslavia to achieve power. Unfortunately the Soviet Army did not and could not render such assistance to the French and Italian Communist Parties.'[1]

Similar assistance had been given by the Red Army in Poland, Czechoslovakia, Rumania, Bulgaria and Hungary, and in this way the Russians created the conditions needed by local Communist parties when they were achieving power.

It is very important to remember that no country in Europe which had not been within the direct grasp of the Red Army eventually succumbed to Communism and Soviet domination. The bayonets of the Red Army were a decisive

[1] *The Soviet-Yugoslav Dispute*, Royal Institute of International Affairs, p. 51, 1948.

and very efficient method of bringing foreign people under the total sway of Moscow.

Backed by the Red Army the Russian Communists converted East Central Europe to their way of thinking with tenacious thoroughness. During the war the Communist leaders of these countries, living in exile in Moscow, had already been given the task of arranging, under the guidance of Soviet experts, a general plan for progressively turning the whole area from the Baltic to the Mediterranean into a Communist empire. The three Baltic states were simply to be incorporated into the Soviet Union; so the plan mainly concerned the other countries. Briefly, these aims were laid down in this way: the establishment of 'National' or 'People's Fronts' under Communist leadership; the seizure of key positions in the Government, especially the Police and the Army; the unification of the trade unions, agricultural institutions, cultural, youth and other organizations under Communist control; replacement of the old administration by the local 'National Committees' created by the Communists; the confiscation by the State of economic enterprises ruled by the Germans or Nazis; the severe punishment of those who had collaborated with the Nazis by the so-called 'people's courts', which helped as well to persecute and 'liquidate' many anti-Nazis who were also unfriendly to the Communists; the banning of political parties suspected of collaboration with the Nazis; the gradual nationalization of industry, of the banks and insurance companies, radical land reforms and so on. At the same time, the foreign policy of the states 'liberated' by the Red Army, emphasized the need for friendship with Russia and gradually reduced to a minimum relations with the West. Even before victory was achieved – victory which was possible only through the united efforts of the West and Russia – Moscow was already intentionally preparing for rivalry and struggle with her wartime allies. The Moscow plan, briefly outlined, for gradually introducing Communism was then put into practice in all the countries of East Central Europe, and even in Yugoslavia, although there the Communists under Tito's leadership (in contrast to the Communists of all the other countries) were not only fighting the Nazis but also gaining a position of political superiority. Communists everywhere proceeded according to a general plan worked out in Moscow, and the Comintern, ostentatiously disbanded for tactical reasons in 1943, in actual fact continued its activities.

When I was in Moscow in June 1945 as a member of the Czechoslovak Government delegation, I went one day through the city by car with Clementis, a pre-war Communist and at that time Under-Secretary of State in the Foreign Ministry. Clementis ordered the driver to stop at a certain building, and when I asked him where he was going, he calmly replied: 'To the Comintern.' Seeing that I was absolutely dumbfounded he smilingly added: 'Of course, the Comintern no longer exists, but the building remained and there "we" (i.e. the Communists) gather. . . .'

The Communist plan was carried out systematically but with varying intensity and not always simultaneously. The Russians began to intervene directly and ruthlessly, immediately after the signature of the Yalta Agreements. Vyshinsky forced King Michael to accept a new puppet Government. This brutal intervention in Rumania's affairs was inspired by complete mistrust of the Russo-phobe Rumanians. Rumania was strategically vital to the success of Moscow's plan. Only through total subjugation could the Russians secure their position on the Danube and their road to the Balkans and Constantinople. Their brutal treatment of Rumania and Bulgaria reveals their determination to enforce Soviet domination on the Balkans and the Mediterranean.

In Hungary the Russians early secured a firm hold on the big industries and on the local oil wells. They did the same in Rumania. Without insisting on their nationalization, they formed joint controlling companies with Russian and local directors, but politically they did not urge these countries to become Communist. They hoped that radical distribution of land – to smallholders – would destroy the old regime, the 'gentry', the bureaucracy and the army, and convert the people to Russia's ideology.

At the same time, the Communist Vice-Premier, Matyas Rakosi, the strongest personality apart from Marshal Tito among the Central European Communists,[1] began in 1946 to use with mounting success the so-called 'salami tactics'. This meant that his opponents were cut into thin slices by his cutting machine and discarded slice by slice until nothing was left of them.[2]

The opposition of the democrats was broken by the Soviets exacting reparation payments, according to need, or otherwise increasing economic pressure on Hungary. The same tactics were used in other countries.

Poland was a particularly hard nut. The ancient antagonism of the Poles towards the Russians (and vice versa) was initially a tremendous stumbling-block, and Polish patriotism was only increased by the ardent local Catholicism that naturally rebelled against atheistic Communism. The Russians had no reason to trust the Poles. They were not people who could easily be subdued. The Russians realized that Polish farmers would cling passionately to their private ownership of the land. Yet Poland was the largest state in East Central Europe, and it became impossible for the Russians to ignore the large number of Poles who, having remained in exile, began to make the free

[1] It is interesting that they included so few significant personalities. Stalin obviously favoured the blindly obedient '*aparatchik*' (the Party man) rather than strong individualists. Other more outstanding personalities were possibly the Bulgarian Dimitrov and the Rumanian Anna Pauker. Among the Polish Communists there were a few intelligent individuals such as Berman or Minc, but none with the abilities of a true leader. Gomulka is, it would seem, a man of tough character, but he was brought to the front far more by circumstances than by force of personality. The Czechoslovakian Communists are notable for their mediocrity. Some of them are clever and cunning. The most able of them were Gottwald and Slansky, and of those still alive, Široký, Dolansky, Novotný and Barak.

[2] George Mikes, *The Hungarian Revolution*, p. 33, London, 1957.

world conscious of what the Russian Communists were doing to their homeland. The Polish soldiers in the famous army led by General Anders remained faithful to their commander. Political émigrés formed the Council of National Unity in London. The American Poles supported a vigorous propaganda campaign against the Moscow and Warsaw Communists. Facing serious opposition, the Red Army posted units at various places in Poland and maintained military control on the main Polish railway linking Russia with eastern Germany. The Russians insisted on the immediate communization of the police, army and industry. For them this was urgently necessary because the Polish Communists were not as strong as they should be if they were to control the country. At the same time every effort was made to crush the powerful peasant party, led by Mikolajczyk, which had such a strong appeal for the individualistic democratic and religious-minded peasantry. (Similar tactics were adopted in Bulgaria where Nikola Petkov and Dr Georgi Dimitrov were very strong.) Dr Dimitrov should not be confused with Georgi Dimitrov, the leader of the Bulgarian Communists who gained world-wide repute during the trial in Leipzig (after the burning of the Reichstag) by defying Goering with stubborn provocation. Georgi Dimitrov was for long Secretary-General of the Comintern. After the last war he became Bulgarian Prime Minister. Dr Dimitrov, a very gifted man, was one of the younger leaders of the Bulgarian Agrarians. He is now in exile in the United States.

For the first two years after the war the Russians proceeded cautiously in Czechoslovakia, taking a much milder attitude than in other neighbouring countries. They relied mainly on 'infiltration' practised by the Czechoslovakian Communists, and on the nationalization of the bigger industrial and banking enterprises. Czechoslovakia enjoyed the special friendship of the Western democracies, and as she occupied such a vital position in the very heart of Europe it was not to the advantage of the Russians to alarm the Western world by openly and rapidly turning her into another Communist slave state. For a time they even benefited by Prague's policy of maintaining friendship with the Soviet Union as well as with the Western Powers. Czechoslovak economy, dependent in large measure on foreign trade, soon recovered from the war, and developed successfully from the middle of 1946. Extensive trade with the West, which far exceeded trade with Russia and Central Europe, was mainly responsible for this. Czechoslovakia's trade with the West represented roughly three-quarters of her entire foreign trade at the close of 1947. It now amounts to not quite a quarter. Czechoslovak democracy deteriorated when the tension between the West and Russia began to increase. Stalin prevented Czechoslovakia (and Poland) from taking part in the Marshall Plan in June 1947, yet even the Czechoslovak Communists had originally agreed to it (so had the Polish Communists). Moscow's distrust and dislike of the Czechoslovak democrats increased when they urged a renewal of the previous alliance with France, and simultaneously rejected Communist proposals, inspired by Soviet diplomacy, that the new treaties of alliance with the other Central European states should be directed not only against Germany but also against any aggressive policy. This was meant particularly as a criticism of the Western Powers' desire to form economic and military pacts to act as bulwarks against Communism. The Russians began to realize that they would never persuade Czech democrats to agree to an anti-Western policy. Yet Moscow was alarmed because of the increasing strength of the Czechoslovak democratic parties. It was clear that the Communists would suffer heavy losses at the elections to be held in the spring of 1948. By the end of 1947 Stalin and Tito were beginning to quarrel, and Moscow rightly feared that an open break with Belgrade might encourage the Czechoslovak anti-Communist parties to take full advantage of the situation. How could Stalin allow the Communist empire to be damaged in the south by a split with Yugoslavia, and in the north by a break with Czechoslovakia – and at the same time? It was as intolerable to the Bolsheviks as it was to the Nazis before them that democracy should flourish in the centre of Europe. So democratic Czechoslovakia had to be sacrificed for the sake of power politics as well as for ideological reasons. The Russians told the Czechoslovak Communists to overthrow democracy and create a Communist regime dedicated to Moscow. At this time the Russians were in open disagreement with the United States, and they gave no sign of being troubled by Western reactions. They seemed convinced that the Western Powers would limit themselves to diplomatic protests. In this they were justified. The Communist *coup d'état* in Prague in February 1948 was directed by a Moscow Vice-Minister, Zorin, previously Soviet Ambassador in Czechoslovakia, and sent by Moscow to make sure that the putsch was a success. The destruction of a democratic and independent Czechoslovakia meant the end of all hopes for the West of reasonable co-operation with Soviet Russia. The sick President Beneš, who had long nursed such hopes but had, also, counted on the preservation of a certain balance of power between West and East, soon afterwards resigned. Some months later he died, bitterly disenchanted, sad and lonely. Those democratic Czechoslovak politicians who did not succeed in escaping to the West suffered cruel persecution.[1] The Russians incorporated Czechoslovakia in the Soviet bloc, thus completing their dominion over all East Central Europe. For the Czechs and Slovaks it was no comfort that their subjugation, emphasized to the Free World by the tragic death of Jan Masaryk, son of the first Czechoslovak President, accelerated the consolidation

[1] A particularly brutal example of the Communist terror was the execution of Milada Horakova, a member of Parliament and President of the Council of Czechoslovak Women, in 1950. She had been imprisoned by the Nazis for five years during the war.

Democratic politicians who escaped to the free world founded the Council of Free Czechoslovakia in Washington in 1949 under the chairmanship of Dr Petr Zenkl, former Mayor of Prague and a Deputy Premier. Zenkl spent the whole war in Buchenwald. Dr Jozef Lettrich, leader of the Slovak Democrats, became Deputy Chairman of the Council. In a similar fashion the exiles of the other East Central European countries founded National Councils in the U.S.A.

of Western defence plans in the North Atlantic Treaty Organization.

THE SOVIETIZATION OF THE SATELLITES

The Prague putsch completed the first phase of Soviet subjugation of East Central Europe. At that time the Russians and their Communist puppets concentrated – according to the plan conceived in Moscow during the war – on destroying political, economic and social systems and on strengthening the power of the Communist parties in all fields of public life. They strengthened the bonds tying their countries to Moscow and made sure that they had little contact with the Western Powers.

From the second half of 1947 it had been obvious to the Russians that such methods would not suffice alone. The United States reacted against the more alarming Soviet moves by introducing the Truman doctrine and the Marshall Plan, and the opposition of the anti-Communist elements in eastern Europe began to increase. It was with alarm that the Kremlin recognized that not only the non-Communist parties but also the Communists in Warsaw, Prague and even in Bucharest were willing to accept the benefits offered by the Marshall Plan. For the first time Moscow realized that foreign Communists had a tendency towards independence and saw that their satellites were still willing to strengthen the economy of their countries by co-operation with the West, despite Moscow's disapproval. Hilary Minc, Polish Minister of Industry and Commerce, told me (I was at that time Minister of Foreign Trade) in June 1947 in Prague: 'Our countries are not at all in the same situation as a Great Power such as the U.S.S.R. We need American help. I am convinced that the Soviet Government will take that into account.' Minc was mistaken. Stalin took not the slightest interest in the needs of our countries and brutally compelled us to refuse the offer of the Marshall Plan.[1]

[1] See my book, *Czechoslovakia Enslaved*, pp. 52–53, London, Gollancz, 1950.

So Russia decided to tighten the screw on the Central European countries. The Comintern was re-established in the form of the Cominform by September 1947. Its manifesto demonstrated a revival of a militant policy for Communist parties throughout the world under the leadership of Soviet Russia, whose power – after victory in 1945 – was far stronger than ever before.

This reawakening of belligerent Communism opened the second stage in the subjugation of Central and South-Eastern Europe to Moscow. Anti-Communist parties were to be liquidated. The Communists intended holding all the power in their own hands. Ferenc Nagy was ousted from the Hungarian premiership in June 1947. Nikola Petkov, leader of the Bulgarian Agrarians, was executed three months later. In the following weeks Juliu Maniu, one of the foremost democratic statesmen in Rumania, and Dragoljub Jovanovic, the leader of the Serbian Agrarians, were arrested. Maniu was sentenced to solitary confinement for life, and died in 1955. Jovanovic was sentenced to nine years' imprisonment and was released in 1955. Stanislav Mikolajczyk, Vice-President of the Polish Government, saved his life by escaping from Warsaw. Then the Communist *coup d'état* in Prague destroyed Czechoslovak democracy in the beginning of 1948.

All these countries then saw the opening of a vigorous campaign of religious persecution. The Roman Catholic Church was attacked with significant intent. Cardinal Mindszenty in Hungary, Archbishop Beran in Czechoslovakia and Cardinal Wyszynski in Poland, with many other dignitaries and thousands of priests were arrested or sent to 'concentration monasteries'. Side by side with political and cultural persecution new economic and social measures were introduced to strengthen exclusively the power of Communism. Industry and trade, including small businesses, were nationalized. Only about 3 per cent of commerce remained in private hands. Collectivization of the land began in the formation of state farms or agricultural co-operatives. Compulsory labour was introduced and convicted persons were sent to 'labour camps'. Economic links with the Soviet Union were tightened. Moscow created, in January 1948, the 'Council for Mutual Economic Assistance' for 'the organization of broader economic co-operation between the countries of the people's democracies and the U.S.S.R.' A 'Molotov Plan' was to save the East as the Marshall Plan saved the West.

The political integration of the East European countries in the Soviet bloc was being achieved by a series of treaties of friendship and alliance not only between Russia and individual Iron Curtain countries but also among those countries themselves. While maintaining the international status of sovereign states they became mere satellites. Thus a new Soviet empire was created.

In all the Central and South European countries the Communists made considerable headway in the late forties. But it was at that time that Tito's heresy began to embarrass Soviet domination in Central Europe. Tito's defection from Moscow opened another phase in Soviet policy – or at least accelerated this move. Until about the end of 1948 political persecution was directed only towards the liquidation of the anti-Communist opposition, but in the following years 'Titoists' or 'national deviationists' among the Communist Party members themselves were purged in vast numbers. At the same time the political, economic and cultural 'communization' of all the Central European countries was accelerated and accomplished strictly according to the Soviet pattern. The appointment of the Soviet Marshal, Konstantin Rokossovski, to the post of Defence Minister of Poland and Supreme Commander-in-Chief of the Polish Army in November 1949 was a spectacular demonstration of an important development in Soviet policy in the Central European countries. The Kremlin rulers had begun their 'Sovietization', which meant total communization, slave-like imitation of the Russian example in everything and complete submission to Soviet will and might. This process was to lower the satellites to the status of Communist colonies. And it brought a reign of terror – arrests, imprisonments, executions. The despotism of the secret police was complete – and merciless. Anyone considered even a potential opponent of the regime was liquidated in one fashion or another. Denunciation was declared a civic duty. About ten thousand non-Communists were thrown into prison, many were executed or beaten to death, and hundreds of thousands suffered in concentration camps. Those who campaigned against the churches recognized no limits. Persecution of the Jews, under the pretext of fighting against 'Zionism', started all over again. It is doubtful whether we will ever be able to account for all the victims of this terror.

Communists were persecuted with non-Communists. Hunting 'Titoists' became a fashionable sport. Any Communist who appeared to Moscow to be even slightly confused about his ideology was removed without further consideration. Rajk in Hungary, Kostov in Bulgaria, Slansky and Clementis in Czechoslovakia and Koci Xoxe in Albania were executed with dozens of others. Gomulka and many others were thrown into prison in Poland; Anna Pauker in Rumania was interned, others were imprisoned. Today, Hungarians are still giving evidence of the brutality with which 'confessions' were extracted from the accused and of the barbarous conditions in which prisoners, Communist and non-Communist, were expected to live. The same inhuman methods were also employed in the other countries.

The middle classes were systematically liquidated in this political terror and the nationalization of the economy included even quite small enterprises, businesses and shops. Workers were submitted to relentless discipline. They soon realized that from mercenaries of 'private capitalism' they had been turned into slaves of 'state capitalism'. They were deprived of the right to strike. Trade unions, instead of protecting the interests of the workers, served only as an instrument for increasing productivity and for enforcing labour discipline. Officials became the helpless, reluctant slaves of the Communist Party which controlled the Government, the police, the army, the administration, the schools, the economy, public life and even private life. Peasants were driven, sometimes by the most brutal means, into the collectives. 'Private' farmers were so cruelly oppressed that they sometimes sought escape from the sufferings inflicted on them by volunteering for the collective farms. But not even the Communists could pretend that the introduction or maintenance of the collectives was possible without brutal pressure being exerted. Resistance to them was general. Tito himself publicly admitted that it was impossible to destroy a thousand-year-old tradition of private ownership of the soil.[1]

All spiritual and cultural life in the satellites was made to fit the Soviet pattern. Marxism-Leninism-Stalinism (or rather, Stalin's conception of Marx and Lenin) was the only admissible doctrine. Any deviation was mercilessly punished. Children, students, adult workers, officials, officers, teachers, priests and farmers had this doctrine crammed into their heads. Deafening propaganda prevented thought. All life – public and private – was regulated according to orders and 'plans' from above. Stalin's ideal Russia was the example in everything. Western civilization was treated with contempt and derision. Russian was a compulsory language in schools. Everything was done to prevent the nations of East Central Europe having any contact with the West. Radio broadcasts from the free world were jammed. Astounding efforts were made to fill people with hatred

[1] The 'socialist sector', that is, the *sovchozy* (farms actually owned by the state) and *kolchozy* (farms maintained by agricultural collectives under the direct control of the Communist Party) comprised the following percentages of arable land in 1954–55:

Poland 20 per cent, Czechoslovakia over 40 per cent, Rumania 25 per cent, Hungary 35 per cent, Bulgaria over 60 per cent, Albania 13 per cent; Yugoslavia in the year 1951 about 25 per cent, later she disbanded a large number of collectives.

After the revolution the Hungarian peasants at once took back their own land which had been gathered into collective farms; the present agricultural situation in Hungary is chaotic. After the Polish revolt of October 1956, 90 per cent of collective farms were disbanded.

for Western 'warmongers' and disdain for 'decadent' Western culture. Even local culture was frequently disparaged in favour of the Russian version. Every national tradition that might cause people to feel proud and possibly inspire a spirit of revolt against foreign domination was suppressed or falsified. Communism, one hundred per cent pure, was injected into these subject peoples by order of the Kremlin. Soviet Russia was the one friend, Soviet experience the one example, Red Moscow was the Mecca, Stalin the only true prophet.

In economy one-sided emphasis was laid (again according to the Soviet pattern) on heavy industry, on coal and oil production; increased output in these branches was intended primarily to serve the military and economic needs of the Soviet Union. And the Russians achieved remarkable results.[1]

The output of crude steel, pig iron, coal, lignite and crude petroleum increased remarkably in all six Communist countries, surpassing France and representing roughly 60–65 per cent of the production of Britain or Germany. This has meant a vast

[1] Here is a brief survey of the statistical data concerning increased output in basic products and raw materials. The year 1937 was the last year before the territorial changes in Europe began to occur.

TABLE OF STATISTICS
In metric tons

		Crude steel	Pig iron	Coal	Lignite	Crude petroleum
Poland	1937	1,500,000	720,000	36,000,000	18,000,000	501,000
	1954	4,000,000	2,500,000	91,000,000	7,000,000	250,000
Czechoslovakia	1937	2,300,000	1,500,000	16,500,000	18,000,000	19,000
	1954	4,430,000	3,000,000	21,500,000	36,000,000	196,000
Hungary	1937	665,000	360,000	1,000,000	8,000,000	2,000
	1954	1,500,000	843,000	2,000,000	20,000,000	1,194,000
Rumania	1937	240,000	130,000	300,000	2,000,000	7,000,000
	1954	630,000	432,000	400,000	4,000,000	10,000,000
Yugoslavia	1937	169,000	44,000	400,000	4,500,000	
	1954	616,000	370,000	1,000,000	12,500,000	216,000
Bulgaria	1937				2,000,000	
	1954				8,500,000	
Together	1937	4,500,000	2,700,000	54,000,000	52,500,000	7,500,000
	1954	11,000,000	7,150,000	116,000,000	88,000,000	12,000,000
U.S.S.R.	1937	18,000,000	14,500,000	112,000,000	16,000,000	28,500,000
	1954	41,500,000	30,000,000	267,000,000	80,000,000	59,000,000
U.S.A.	1937	51,000,000	38,000,000	448,000,000	3,000,000	173,000,000
	1954	80,000,000	54,000,000	378,000,000	2,500,000	313,000,000
Great Britain	1937	13,000,000	8,500,000	244,000,000		
	1954	19,000,000	12,000,000	227,000,000		
Germany with Saar	1937	20,000,000	18,000,000	184,000,000	183,000,000	451,000
	1954	20,000,000	15,000,000	149,000,000	272,000,000	2,500,000
France	1937	8,000,000	8,000,000	44,000,000	1,000,000	79,000
	1954	10,500,000	9,000,000	54,000,000	2,000,000	526,000

development of Russia's economic potential. This would be still more obvious if it were possible to give the facts about the production of machinery and arms. But it is possible only to say that the productive capacity of Czechoslovakia is now greater than it was before the war. This is proved by the export of these products not only to Russia and the satellite countries but also to the Middle East and to the Asian countries. The Polish economist, Jan Wszelaki, in his excellent study, 'The Rise of Industrial Middle Europe',[1] estimated that 'The 90 million satellite population produces as many goods per capita as the 200 million or more inhabitants of Soviet Russia. Roughly speaking, the captive European countries produce one-half as much hard fuel and electric power, about one-third as much steel and more than one-fifth as much oil as Russia.' And it is worth mentioning that Germany needed about 16 million tons of steel in her preparations for World War II. Yet five of the satellite countries alone (we are leaving out Yugoslavia) produced 10 million tons, Soviet Russia over 41 million in 1954.

Again and again the one-sided increase in production or output of materials must be emphasized; it primarily serves to increase the power of the state and develop the military strength of the Communist world without benefiting the individual countries of East Central Europe. The industrialization of these agricultural countries was necessary. There was no other way of overcoming their poverty. But their social needs could best have been served by the development of those light industries that would produce consumer goods and of the engineering industry which could contribute to the modernization of agriculture and light industry. Special care should have been devoted to technical improvements in mining coal, metals and other industrial raw materials. The Communists neglected such development. Everything was concentrated on heavy industry in which enormous capital was invested. They drew remorselessly on national incomes. Great industrial combines were

[1] *Foreign Affairs*, October 1950, New York.

feverishly constructed without any thought for remuneration or for the finances of the country concerned. Many undertakings of this kind had to be left uncompleted when it was proved that they could not be maintained – physically or financially. An astounding amount of capital was wasted in this way. The local standard of living inevitably fell, all the more so because the budget of every one of the Communist countries was incredibly burdened by the high costs of the army, the police and the over-staffed bureaucracy.

Czechoslovakian Communist newspapers complained in March 1957 that for every thirty-eight workers in Czechoslovakia there were eleven unproductive employees: planners, controllers, officials, factory militiamen, Party and 'cultural' (propaganda) workers.[1]

The nations of East Central Europe suffered heavily when, under pressure from Moscow, they were compelled to refuse the Western invitation to join the Marshall Plan, to limit their trade relations with the West to a minimum and trade only with Russia on Russian terms – high prices for her exports, too, and low prices for her imports from these countries. The price Russia paid for Polish coal was so low that it amounted almost to robbery. The condition of the satellites deteriorated still more when, during the Cold War, the West replied to Soviet threats by putting an embargo on strategic materials.

Even among non-Communists in the West it was agreed that though the violent methods used by the Communists must be regretted, the industrialization of East Central Europe could only lead eventually to an improvement in the standard of living. But the Polish and Hungarian revolts revealed for the first time the truth about the state of affairs behind the Iron Curtain. There could be no further doubt about it. Communism did not improve but lowered the standard of living of the people under its domination. Everywhere there is a shortage of industrial, agricultural and consumer goods. Where they are

[1] '*Cechoslovak v zahranici*' – *The Czechoslovak Abroad*, London, IX, 14, April 6, 1957.

available, as in Czechoslovakia, extortionate prices mean that only the minority can buy them. Agricultural production, compared with the pre-war period when, with the exception of Czechoslovakia, farming was neglected, has, on the average, remained the same or actually declined. Yet the demands for the products of the farms and the factories have increased, especially now that so many agricultural workers have gone into the new industries. And, of course, the population has increased. Countries that suffered before the war because they could not find markets for their agricultural goods are not even self-supporting any more. They must import grain from Russia (Yugoslavia buys from America). Even in Czechoslovakia, where the economic situation is better than in the other slave states, the population has become poor. Everywhere there is more tiring, often exhausting work, but fewer goods and less food. Everywhere there is industrial conscription, but nowhere has anybody any social rights. Russia has brought the countries it dominates to the verge of bankruptcy, keeping itself in power even though the subjugated people suffer through shortages, under-nourishment and the misery of living under a totalitarian regime. These countries, brutally converted into Communist states without the slightest consideration for their social needs and economic capacities, have been mercilessly exploited as colonies of Soviet Russia – the country that so frequently criticizes the more benign Western powers for imperialism.

COMMUNISM – A 'NATURAL PHASE' OF
DEVELOPMENT?

The conversion to Communism of the countries of East Central Europe has to some extent been considered by some Western experts as a sort of natural stage in their development. To the point of weariness it has been argued that these nations with their primitive social and cultural structures and without democratic traditions were more suited to a dictatorial, Communist regime than to a democratic form of government. To decide that what happened *had* to happen is comforting, all the more so because it does away with any question of responsibility. Sometimes it is true; usually it is not. As far as East Central Europe is concerned, it is in obvious contradiction to the facts. In these countries conditions for democracy were better after the Second World War than after the First. The pre-war police states or semi-dictatorships were irreparably compromised. Each was responsible for weakening its people's ability to resist the Nazis or, with the exception of Poland, guilty of collaborating with Hitler. The yearning for a free democratic regime was thus all the greater. Immediately after the war there was a powerful agrarian movement in East Central Europe which demanded radical land reforms. There is not the slightest doubt that the Agrarian parties supported by the others would definitely have strengthened the independent farmers tilling their own soil. There was a great wave of social reform in East Central Europe just as there was in Western Europe. The welfare state became the general aim for the liberal-minded *bourgeoisie*. It would have been achieved in East Central Europe too – probably on the British pattern – if it had not been for the Communists. Extensive development of industry would also have been achieved without the Communists, all the more so because in many ways it had received fresh impetus from the war, and industrial development had already begun in Poland, Hungary and Rumania in the thirties. But the democrats would have industrialized their countries according to their particular economic possibilities and the social needs of their peoples. The democratic parties in East Central Europe were all dedicated to fulfilling political, economic and social ambitions. Their programmes, the declarations and efforts of their leaders between 1945 and 1948 all give convincing proof of this. Without the intervention of Soviet Russia the countries of East Central Europe would probably have developed into liberal, socialist democracies, supported by the Socialists, Agrarians, Christian-Socialists and Liberals. At least the principal conditions necessary for such a development existed.

Of course the Communist parties would also have played an important part. They would have exploited the strong feeling of admiration aroused by the victories of the Red Army and the greatly increased strength of Soviet Russia in world politics. They would, also, have used to their advantage any crisis in the ranks of democratic Socialists – as in Italy when Togliatti gained the co-operation of Nenni. In some countries they would obviously have occupied, at least for a time, a leading place in the government coalitions. But they would never have been able to introduce a Communist regime by themselves and by democratic means. Everywhere they were in the minority. In some countries, such as Rumania, Poland and Hungary, they were in an absolutely insignificant minority. The Communists had their biggest electoral success in Czechoslovakia in 1946 in circumstances which were extraordinarily favourable to them. But they were in retreat from 1947 and they were pre-pared to suffer heavy losses in the elections planned for the spring of 1948. They were saved only by the Soviet putsch in February. Perhaps only in Yugoslavia, where they had ac-quired decisive strength even before the end of the war, did the Communists have sufficiently favourable conditions to enable them to establish their pattern of government. But even for Tito, Soviet help was important, and only the most brutal terrorism was able to suppress the democratic forces of Yugo-slavia.

All these facts can only prove the stupidity of the supposition that the political and social 'immaturity' or 'backwardness' of the countries of East Central Europe made it necessary for them to go through a Communist experience. The British historian, Hugh Seton-Watson, one of the greatest experts on Eastern Europe, discussing this question, wrote in his book, *The East-European Revolution*,[1] 'It is true that nations of the Eastern Europe have lived for generations in poverty. . . . It is also true that except in Czechoslovakia there was little political liberty before the war for any but the upper class, and that even they

[1] p. 379, Methuen, London, 1959.

lost most of their liberties in the thirties. But it is not true that these peoples do not understand what liberty means and do not passionately desire it. Their crude but vivid notions of their national history and their simple but powerful religious convictions are the best proof of the contrary. Nor does it follow that economic improvement can be obtained only by political oppression. Economic reforms have long figured in the plans of democratic parties, especially peasant parties and social democrats. The combination of economic change and terror is not inevitable. It is a result of Communist policy.'

The suggestion that the political and social backwardness of the peoples of East Central Europe made them easy victims for the Communists is equally misleading. Neither East Germany nor Czechoslovakia was backward, yet each succumbed to Communism. Despite her highly developed economy and in spite of her deep-rooted democratic tradition, Czechoslovakia became as completely Communist as any other country in East Central Europe. This proves that neither the 'communization' nor the 'sovietization' of Central Europe was part of an organic historical evolution. Instead, it was the result of the circumstances in which the Russians were able to impose their rule on the weak and isolated small nations.

DISPUTE WITH TITO

Before his death Stalin completed with brutal thoroughness the total enslavement of the nations of East Central Europe. Yet he could not have been utterly content or satisfied. Tito's Yugoslavia which, after the war, was even more wholeheartedly Communist than the rest, managed to escape from his iron domination.

The Yugoslavs were the only Communists in East Central Europe who conducted partisan warfare on a large scale and formed their own administration in the districts they occupied. They also acted according to the general plan worked out in Moscow: they founded an 'Anti-Fascist Council of the National Liberation of Yugoslavia', in which non-Communists were represented, but which was completely under the Communists' control, and they formed local 'National Committees'.

By the end of the war the Yugoslav partisans represented the only organized force in the country. The other remaining political parties were completely disorganized. The bands of *'chetniks'*, led by the brave but politically inexperienced General Draga Mihailovic, were dispersed, and Mihailovic himself was finally captured in the spring of 1946 and executed soon afterwards. It was to the advantage of the Communists that the young King, Peter II, did not take part in the fighting in his country. His father, Alexander, was almost constantly at the front during the First World War. Also the democratic leaders, in exile in London, could not agree in time on a constructive programme for the future of Yugoslavia. But the Communists had agreed on a clearly defined objective – to maintain a united Yugoslavia on a federal basis. Later they applied a nationalist policy of the Soviet pattern, allowing local national autonomy but at the same time limiting it by the centralized dictatorship of the only political party, the Communist Party. The Federal People's Republic of Yugoslavia, consisting of six federal republics – Serbia, Croatia, Slovenia, Macedonia, Montenegro and Bosnia – was established in November 1945. Right from the end of the war the Yugoslav Communists set to work on systematic reorganization of their country. Communists in the other countries, aware of their own weaknesses and realizing they must depend to a great extent on help from Moscow, were compelled to go warily. Extensive purges carried out with unheard-of brutality and without any consideration for even the most primitive principles of justice and simple humanity, helped the Yugoslav Communists to take over the police, the army and the entire administrative apparatus and to carry out radical nationalization of the economy. They soon started, also, on forcible collectivization of the land. They persecuted the church, particularly the Roman Catholic Church. The Croatian Archbishop Stepinac was sentenced to sixteen years' imprisonment, but was conditionally released in 1951, elected Cardinal in 1952, but not allowed to go to Rome for his Cardinal's hat, nor to carry out his duties.

Yugoslavia became Communist far sooner than the other countries of East Central Europe and it was entirely the work of Tito's supporters, without substantial or direct help from Russia. Even before the beginning of the Cold War between Russia and the West, the Yugoslav Communists engaged in a campaign against Western 'imperialism' and 'capitalism' – in fact, against Western civilization. The Western Powers were also condemned because of their attitude to Yugoslavia regarding Italian claims to Trieste. The Yugoslavs shot down an American plane in the summer of 1946. To the Yugoslavs, Moscow was the centre of the new Communist world. Tito was considered – and rightly – the most decisive advocate, the most resolute protagonist and the most dependable ally of the Russians among foreign Communists. He was presented to them as an example to be followed – frequently to their great displeasure. I know from my own experience that several Czechoslovak Communists such as Gottwald, Clementis and Nosek (the Minister of the Interior) did not like Tito, being extremely jealous of the favours shown him by Moscow at that time. Dimitrov and Rakosi were equally jealous of him.

It was only natural that Belgrade should be chosen as the seat of the Cominform, in the founding of which, in September 1947, the Yugoslav Communists, next to the Soviet representatives, played a leading role.

For this reason the astonishment of the world was all the greater when the Kremlin confirmed, on June 28, 1948, that the Yugoslav Communist Party with Tito at its head had been expelled from the Cominform. The accusation brought against them was serious in the eyes of the orthodox Soviet Communists. It was charged that 'the leaders of the Yugoslav Communist Party . . . have taken the path of seceding from the unified Socialist front against imperialism, have taken the path of betraying the cause of the international solidarity of the working people and have taken up a position of nationalism'.

They maintained an anti-Socialist order 'where much land is concentrated in the hands of the *kulaks*, and where hired labour is employed'. Their nationalism can 'only lead to Yugoslavia's degeneration into an ordinary bourgeois republic, to the loss of its independence and to its transformation into a colony of the imperialist countries'.

Andrei Zhdanov, the principal Soviet delegate at the Cominform conference in Bucharest, overcame the embarrassment of some of the other delegates present, by the categorical declaration: 'We possess information that Tito is an imperialist spy.'[1] As soon as the Cominform had pronounced its judgment the Communists throughout the world unleashed a furious, unending tirade against Tito and his followers, representing them as Fascists, Nazis, lackeys and agents of Western imperialism, counter-revolutionaries, Trotskyites, *kulaks* and treacherous vipers. They used every insult and fantastic accusation that had been invented by the Communists to use against their enemies from the time of the great trials of the thirties, that were used by Stalin to have all his real and imaginary opponents (and hundreds of thousands of innocent persons) condemned to death. The 'dictionary' of abuse was used recently against the Hungarian rebels.

Not one of the charges made against Tito had any foundation. Tito had converted his country to Communism in every way possible. He even went further with his radical collectivization of the land than the majority of the other leaders of 'people's democracies', and he abandoned this policy only after 1951. Even the accusation of 'nationalism' was not justified. Tito's nationalism in no way deviated from the official doctrine of nationalism; certainly Stalin never ceased at any time to advocate great Russian chauvinism or the nationalist passion of one nation against the other.

Tito was condemned simply because, refusing to be a mere puppet in the hands of Stalin, he rebelled against having to fulfil, without a word of protest, the Kremlin's wishes and

[1] Vladimir Dedijer, *Tito Speaks*, p. 370, Weidenfeld, London, 1953.

orders. He was expelled because he did not wish the Yugoslav Communist Party, the administration, the police, the army and the economy to come under direct Soviet control. Communists in the other countries could not prevent this happening because it was only with the help of the Russians that they were able to acquire power and keep it. Tito, speaking about the conflict with Moscow, recalled that during the war the Kremlin 'wanted a resistance movement in Yugoslavia which would serve the interests, not of the people of Yugoslavia but of Russia's Great Power policy – its policy of gaining the power needed to bargain with the other great nations'. And he continued: 'Stalin coolly and systematically prepared to subjugate Yugoslavia as the central point in South-Eastern Europe. Not satisfied with having attached six European states with over eighty million inhabitants to the Soviet Union after the war, he reached out for Yugoslavia.'[1]

Stalin inspired the conflict with Yugoslavia, and, according to Khrushchev's testimony, was convinced that he could settle Tito without much difficulty. Khrushchev claimed that Stalin said, 'I will shake my little finger – and there will be no more Tito. He will fall.' And Khrushchev adds: 'No matter how much or how little Stalin shook not only his little finger but everything else he could shake, Tito did not fall. Why? The reason was that . . . Tito had behind him a state and a people who had gone through a severe school of fighting for liberty and independence, a people which gave support to its leaders.'[2]

Tito was able to withstand Stalin's attack because he had the Party, the police and the army completely under his control. Those who were even suspected of sympathizing with the Cominform judgment were remorselessly hunted down and executed. Unlike all the other subjugated countries, Yugoslavia did not have a common frontier with Russia and this was of great advantage to Tito. The unfriendly actions of the

[1] Dedijer, *op. cit.*, pp. 265 and 266.
[2] 'The dethronement of Stalin.' Full text of the Khrushchev speech of February 25, 1956, p. 25. Published by the *Manchester Guardian*, June 1956.

neighbouring satellites, instigated by Stalin, were less dangerous. The Bulgarians, Rumanians, Hungarians and Albanians knew that if they were to attack they would en-counter the passionate resistance of all Yugoslavs, who have often proved themselves resolute fighters. Finally, Tito was able to defy and withstand the long boycott imposed by the Russians and their satellites because he received effective help from the United States and other Western Powers.

At the beginning Stalin clearly hoped that the malediction which he had pronounced against the Yugoslav leaders would lead to their being overthrown in a local revolt. When this did not happen, he was not sure, once America had offered help to Tito, that he dare use armed force against Yugoslavia without starting a general conflict. He had to limit himself to an econo-mic boycott of Yugoslavia and to provoking frontier incidents. With the help of the West, Tito was able to overcome his economic difficulties and had little difficulty warding off the frontier forays. For his army far surpassed those of his neigh-bours. Even so, he would have succumbed had it not been for his great courage and the resolution displayed by his supporters.

The quarrel with Belgrade was a debilitating embarrassment to the Russians. Their power in the Balkans was considerably weakened. The loss of Yugoslavia could not be counter-balanced entirely by their domination over Bulgaria and Albania. They were cut off from the Adriatic Sea – except from Albania, which is an important strategic base for them. They could no longer maintain pressure on Italy and Greece, and had to limit their activities from that time to those internal political actions that could be undertaken by the local Communists. As well as losing political power, the Russians were seriously alarmed by the effects of their conflict with Tito on the Com-munist world. The mists of international Communist solidarity were dispersed. And Soviet imperialism had appeared for what it was. It was now obvious that Moscow demanded blind obedience to her will from foreign Communists. They were not permitted the slightest independence, particularly in affairs of international policy. Trotsky, in agreement with Lenin, believed in a world federation of autonomous, Communist republics, possessing equal rights, but Stalin's conception was strictly realistic. Communist countries must be Soviet slave states. Tito's revolt, in essence a nationalist revolt against foreign imperialist domination, showed that nationalism could in certain circumstances defy Moscow without committing suicide. This meant that the conflict between Moscow and Belgrade endangered the solidarity of the Communist empire. 'Titoism' or 'national Communism' developed into a new political force that seriously threatened Soviet supremacy. Belgrade gradually became the centre of attraction for many Communists yearning for a greater measure of independence – or at least for less dependence on Moscow. It is not surprising that Stalin devoted himself to preventing this Tito infection from becoming endemic in the satellite countries or in other Communist parties. About a thousand Communists died in the persecution of 'Titoists' in East Central Europe in three years.

Tito stayed in power despite all the attacks and manœuvres instituted against him by Moscow. And the brutality and terror with which Stalin enforced his will on the other slave states increased to such an extent that they not only emphasized the hatred of the oppressed nations for Soviet domination but also evoked a 'crisis of conscience' among Communists.

Hopes of the satellite countries following Tito's example were not fulfilled. It must be realized that Tito did not tear himself away from Moscow. He was expelled by Stalin from the Communist community. It took a long time for Tito to realize that it was Stalin himself who caused the rupture. Khrushchev was clearly not mistaken when, in his attack on Stalin, he said: 'There was no significant basis for the development of this "affair", it was completely possible to have prevented the rupture of relations with that country [Yugoslavia].' But other satellite countries inspired by Titoism were not in a position to break with Stalin. Undoubtedly many a Communist was attracted by Titoism. But the rank and file

Communists had no nationalist leaders who were the equal of Tito. Potential 'Titoists' had been swiftly executed or imprisoned. Outstanding personalities, such as Rakosi, were more Stalinist than Stalin. Most of the other Communist leaders were mediocre and less than mediocre *aparatchiki*.

They recognized that without the constant and effective help of Moscow they could not hope to stay in authority. Also the Russians had the Communist Party and the entire state apparatus of each satellite under their direct control through the medium of special agents. 'Titoism' could not spread or become powerful. The events in Poland and Hungary in October 1956 were not inspired by Titoism, even though some Communists clearly had his example in mind. These revolts were made possible mainly because Stalin's death brought a slight relaxation of the cruel tyranny that he had so relentlessly enforced throughout his dominions.

There were hopes, too, that Tito's national Communism would gradually form into Western democratic Socialism. In this there was only wishful thinking. Tito did not fundamentally deviate from Communist doctrine, still less from Communist policy founded on the Dictatorship of the Party. His only significant retreat from this policy was the abandoning of forcible collectivization of the land. This was forced on him by the opposition of the peasants and fear of a catastrophic drop in agricultural production. But even land collectivization remains among the aims of the Yugoslav Communists. The introduction of economic decentralization (now being tried in Russia) and the formation of workers' committees to help in the administration of state enterprises could only benefit Yugoslavia's economy – neither is likely to lead to a more democratic regime. Tito's Yugoslavia remains a Communist dictatorship which, despite minor changes and a softening of police brutality, does not hesitate to treat harshly any real or imagined opponent. Milovan Djilas, formerly one of Tito's principal advisers, paid for his efforts to introduce more democracy into Yugoslavia by expulsion from the Party and conditional punishment and finally, at the end of 1956, by imprisonment.

The Hungarian revolution caused Tito great anxiety. In a moment of disquiet he betrayed his fears about the possibility of the waves of democracy inundating his country and washing away his national Communism. Though his quarrel with the Kremlin was patched up temporarily by Stalin's successors in 1955, Tito remained in conflict with Soviet Russia. He is determined to follow 'his own path to Socialism', and his example alone is not responsible for the difficulties now facing 'Muscovite Communism' or 'national Communism'. The contradictions that are inherent in the Communist system itself are helping to embarrass the Russian overlords.

CHAPTER IV

Crisis in the Soviet Empire

A CRISIS OF AUTHORITY

Stalin seemed to stand at the height of his power at the end of 1952. His extensive empire appeared to be secure for a long time. Tito's defection had been an unpleasant experience, but it seemed an isolated incident which could not seriously endanger Soviet domination of the satellites of East Central Europe, including East Germany. So powerful was the word of Moscow that these countries had sunk to the level of powerless colonies. Mao Tse-Tung was asking for help from his great Communist neighbour. It was no longer possible to hope for the conquest of all Korea, but the northern half was secure for the Communists. They were already sure, too, of achieving fresh successes in Indo-China. The XIXth Congress of the Soviet Communist Party in Moscow in October 1952 gave a stupendous ovation to Stalin. The delegates competed with such vigour to pour superlative praises on their leader that they revealed their bad taste, their fear and their insincerity.

Fear was more than justified. Within two months the conspiracy of the Jewish doctors was 'discovered'. They were supposed to have intrigued against the Soviet leaders. Another extensive purge was obviously being prepared. According to Khrushchev's statement (in February 1956), Stalin was ready to rid himself of a number, possibly of the majority, of his closest advisers. Their liquidation was prevented by the liquidation of Stalin himself, whether by a natural or an unnatural death we do not know. It was merely announced on March 6, 1956, that he had died after a short illness.

The Western world soon realized the insincerity of the ovations with which Stalin had been overwhelmed in Moscow during his lifetime. The funeral orations were freezingly correct – only Molotov showed any sign of emotion. Stalin's name gradually disappeared from speeches and newspaper articles. His mystique was replaced by the cult of Lenin. 'Collective leadership' took the place of personal autocracy. Everything indicated that Stalin's successors felt the *necessity* to change not perhaps the objective, but at least the strategy of Soviet policy. This was all the more necessary because the oppressed masses both inside and outside Russia felt on the day of Stalin's death, the *possibility* of change. The leaders themselves betrayed their fears when, in the official communiqué announcing his death, they promised an immediate reorganization of the Party and the Government 'to avoid panic and disorder'.

With Stalin's removal there ended an era of Soviet development. The beginning of the next era was marked by frequent drastic changes not only in the Kremlin's hierarchy but also in the policies pursued by the new rulers. The autocracy was replaced by a 'collective leadership'. This was an expedient, since no personality of sufficient authority was left to take Stalin's place. But the 'collective leadership' did not prevent fierce struggles among Stalin's many second-rate heirs. Beria was shot; Malenkov, Molotov, Kaganovic, Marshal Zhukov and Bulganin were gradually robbed of power and then of their jobs.

Khrushchev seemed to be strong enough by the end of 1957 to dismiss the mockery of 'collective leadership' and put himself in Stalin's place as dictator. Khrushchev showed a genius for self-preservation that was rare even among Communist leaders. He realized the likelihood of Party dictatorship being replaced by a military dictatorship, and having made a bargain with the military leaders who saw him through his more precarious days, he finally got rid of Zhukov and Bulganin in a way that not only left him in sole control but also prevented any serious reaction from the Red Army.

He proved that the Soviet leaders are merely conservative-minded guardians of the Soviet pattern. Only a few of the present Communist leaders have the ardent passion and the humble dedication that distinguished the early Bolsheviks. They adhere to Communism not only from deep-rooted tradition but also because without it they would no longer have an easy method of retaining power over the world's largest and most powerful group of states. Khrushchev spoke frankly when he said after the Geneva Conference (September 17, 1955): 'If anyone believes that our smiles involve abandonment of the teachings of Marx, Engels and Lenin, he is badly deceived. Those who wait for that must wait until a shrimp learns to whistle.'

Though Communist leaders do not quarrel about the fundamentals of their belief, their jealousy and rivalry become all the more intense as their addiction to the traditional doctrine and to the power cult is strengthened by the passing years. Their conservatism makes them ideologically sterile. They can only repeat the old slogans. In answer to the dynamic ideas that were revealed during the Polish and Hungarian upheavals, the Kremlin rulers could only declaim about the evils of the Fascists and the reactionaries. They had no spiritual weapons – only the Red Army. They resist national Communism only by strengthening the 'unity' of the Communist alliance under the domination of Moscow. The more sterile and conservative their political outlook, the more they depend on power as a method of maintaining their rule. That is why the struggle among them is so violent and permanent.

It explains also to a large extent the vacillations and contradictions of their policy. They are aware of growing dissatisfactions among all classes of Soviet society. They tried to avert discontent by the 'gentler course' (introduced by Malenkov in 1953) that led to the first famous Cold War 'thaw'. But the new liberty that allowed criticism of the Government became embarrassing, and soon surpassed the limits that the Kremlin wished to preserve. It became necessary to revert again to threats and prohibitions.

Malenkov had tried to win popularity for a Government that

is lacking in true legitimacy. That is why in addition to 'Socialist legality' he promised the people more consumer goods to raise their standard of living and began to talk about giving concessions to the farmers. But within two years, in February 1955, he was removed from office as Prime Minister because of his 'non-Leninist' policy. He was succeeded by a new leadership of Khrushchev and Bulganin, and once again priority was given to heavy industry and to collective farming, the two central pillars of the Communist economic system. Malenkov's policy satisfied the most urgent needs of the poverty-stricken people, but threatened the output of heavy industry, especially the output of the arms factories. Neither of these must suffer if Russia is to maintain its Big Power policy. The priority given to heavy industry and the army makes it difficult for the Russian leaders to improve the general standard of living. This means, too, there can be no relaxation of the severe discipline of their police state. Only the harsh regime of a dictatorship could continue to exact such great sacrifices from ordinary people. A more extensive liberalization of the dictatorship will affect the entire economic system of Russia. Yet if the totalitarian harshness is not eased in some way, internal discontent can only grow.

The new Soviet rulers were compelled to adopt a 'gentler course' because of the social discontent that was created during Stalin's reign of terror. But is it possible for the Russian leaders to relieve this dangerous accumulation of hate? The peasants remain in defiant opposition to the *kolchozes*, but collective farming is an essential part of the Communist system. The agrarian problem is no less explosive in Soviet Russia than it was in Czarist Russia. It may yet prove as dangerous to the present rulers as it did to their Czarist predecessors. The urban workers and artisans have a better standard of living than the peasants, but it is still very low. Khrushchev admitted to a delegation of French Socialists in the spring of 1956 that Soviet workers are far from attaining the standard of living of French workers. But how is it possible to improve their social conditions when there is a permanent shortage of consumer goods and homes? And how is it possible to give them social freedom when severe labour discipline must be maintained if Communist Russia itself is to be maintained?

Perhaps it might help if more advantageous material conditions were offered to the less numerous class of bureaucrats of all kinds, the officer class and the so-called intelligentsia. But the demands of this new Soviet middle class are growing all the time, and it is these people who have increasing difficulty in tolerating the Communist dictatorship. They yearn for greater personal security and a certain amount of freedom. The Khrushchev plan, announced at the beginning of 1957, for the decentralization of the economic administration is mainly concerned with finding a means of achieving greater efficiency, which cannot be achieved by bureaucratic centralism. But it also has a political aim. Khrushchev hopes to restore rigid Party control over the powerful economic bureaucracy which, being lukewarm and indifferent at present to Communist doctrine, could become, in some circumstances, dangerous to the regime itself. This is the insoluble dilemma with which the Soviet leadership is now faced: relaxation of the iron grip of dictatorship appears to be necessary if internal tensions are also to be lessened; but the maintenance of a strict dictatorship is implicit in the maintenance of such a totalitarian regime.

This constant dilemma is inherent to every totalitarian system. Khrushchev could not overcome it, when later on he tried to throw all responsibility for the sufferings of the Russian people on Stalin.

Contradictory tendencies were also apparent in the foreign policy of Stalin's successors. It is possible that, feeling their home ground unsure beneath their feet after the death of the autocrat, they wished to ease tension abroad to prevent further embarrassment and insecurity and to prevent the present heavy cost of arms, particularly of nuclear weapons, becoming even more oppressive. The old campaign for peaceful co-existence was renewed with the intention of weakening the vigilance of the Western Powers and of introducing disharmony among the members of the Atlantic Alliance. Khrushchev's 'policy of smiles' was a great success at the Geneva Conference in July 1955. It definitely improved the international position of the Russians without bringing equivalent advantages to the Western Powers. But at the second Geneva Conference of the four Foreign Ministers in October 1955, the Russians began to confirm the belief that they were not willing to make any genuine concessions. Molotov, the old Bolshevik who was still the powerful Stalinist Foreign Secretary, assumed the same intractable attitude for which he had become renowned. And Khrushchev and Bulganin, on their ostentatious journey through India, Burma and Afghanistan at the end of 1955, began their great campaign against 'colonialism', flattering Asian nationalism in every way possible and promising economic aid to all and sundry. The beginning of this Soviet policy in Asia coincided with the opening of a new offensive in the Middle East. Even during the Geneva Conference, as though to stress their insincerity, the Russians began to supply arms to Egypt and Syria. Even though the Cold War was not reopened in its most acute form, tension between Russia and the West again increased. No other development was possible. The 'gentler course' adopted since Stalin's death had its limits both at home and abroad. The new Russian leaders could not do otherwise than continue to pursue a policy of imperialist expansion. This was imposed on them by Communist tradition and Russian Messianism which, even though different in aim and motive, have now gained strength through their collaboration.

Up to the Second World War, Communists were too weak to pursue successfully a policy of expansion, but they have always cherished imperialist or expansionist aims. When they became the second strongest Power in the world after their victories in 1945, they frankly adopted a policy of aggressive imperialism. Internal difficulties might even force them into temporary 'peaceful co-operation' with other countries, but they can never relinquish their expansionist ambitions. They would not abandon them even if the superior power of the United States and her allies compelled them to withdraw from the positions they now hold. Also international tension gives Russians an excuse for justifying to their people the sacrifices and hardships extracted from them for maintaining a dictatorship.

Yet the international tension purposely created by the Russians can only increase the internal tensions that threaten them. Soviet citizens pay dearly for the imperialistic ambitions of their rulers. There is the crushing burden of arms production. Russians must also suffer privation because their rulers offer help to Communist China, because they supply arms to the Middle East and because they want to compete with the United States in giving economic aid to the under-developed Asiatic countries. Until recently Russians benefited from the exploitation of their colonies in East Central Europe. Since the Polish and Hungarian revolts they have been compelled to give economic help to the majority of these countries.

This only increases the already high demands that a policy of expansion makes on the Soviet economy, and it suggests that the Soviet leaders have overstrained their own forces and capacities, thus sustaining (and even increasing) the crisis in which they found themselves after Stalin's death.

DISTURBANCES IN EAST CENTRAL EUROPE

The oppressed nations in East Central Europe felt that the departure of the dreaded autocrat offered an opportunity for liberation. They quickly recognized and assessed the uncertainty that existed in Moscow. And they felt encouraged because President Eisenhower's administration, considering Truman's defensive containment policy inadequate, proclaimed a policy of active liberation.

Workers started demonstrating in Plzeň, a well-known industrial centre with the great 'Škoda' armament works in June 1953, and there were also disturbances in other Czech and Slovak towns. The main reason for the demonstration was to protest against a currency reform that hit all classes equally hard. But as soon as the demonstrations started spreading, political demands were made. The workers asked for free elections. They hung American flags out of their windows (Plzeň was liberated by the Americans in 1945), and ostentatiously displayed pictures of Masaryk and Edward Beneš, the first two Presidents of the independent Czechoslovak Republic. These riots were swiftly quelled, with the help of reliable militia brought from Prague. They were isolated incidents, yet their political importance was tremendous. The workers themselves were the first to revolt against the 'Government of the workers'; the demonstrators demanded freedom in the spirit of Masaryk, who was condemned by the Communists as a servant of capitalism. And they displayed their sympathy for the Western democracies, especially the United States, a country that for years has been described by the Communists as the sworn enemy of the workers and of Socialism. The Plzeň demonstrations proved that the Czechoslovaks, headed by the workers, rejected Communism and desired a free democracy.

Two weeks later (on June 17, 1953), a workers' revolt in East Germany quickly spread throughout the entire Soviet-occupied zone. The local Communist Government was powerless. The outbreak was crushed only through the direct intervention of the Red Army – a foretaste of what was to happen in Hungary three years later. The East German revolt, which, because of its bloody character, aroused much greater attention throughout the world than the brief demonstrations in Czechoslovakia, confirmed beyond all doubt that the Communist regime is generally loathed by the workers as well as by other social classes. Obviously Russian Communism is kept in power only by the Red Army. It was equally clear that the people of East Germany ardently desired to be united with democratic West Germany. Soviet force alone frustrated the fulfilment of this desire. The East German revolutionaries were truly fighters for freedom.

The Western Powers did not offer to help those who took part in these demonstrations against Communist dictatorship.

The Allies, taken by surprise, were quite unprepared. It is a pity that the Czechoslovak demonstrations and the East German revolt were not afterwards studied in the West with the greatest attention. A thorough assessment would have suggested practical action to be taken during similar revolts in the future in the other slave states. But at that time it was thought that both in Czechoslovakia and in East Germany it was only a question of isolated incidents lacking far-reaching importance.

Yet these two episodes were the first serious symptoms indicating that the subjugated countries in East Central Europe were no longer willing to continue to accept Soviet domination without protest. Even the oppressed Russians themselves were at last being stirred by obscure unease. This was proved by strikes in the forced labour camps and a bloody rising in Vorkuta. Obviously inner tensions in the entire Soviet empire were increasing.

Russian leaders were aware of this. They suppressed the East German revolt, but they did not afterwards impose mass persecution of the rebels. There was not the customary brutality in the punishments inflicted on the East German and Czechoslovak demonstrators. It was still believed in Moscow that, after the shock of Stalin's death, the 'gentler course' introduced by Malenkov would in the circumstances be the best way to overcome general discontent.

THE NEW COURSE

The 'gentler course' became Soviet policy not only in Russia but also in the satellite countries of East Central Europe. Rakosi, leader of the brutal regime in Hungary, was compelled by Malenkov himself to withdraw. Imre Nagy became Prime Minister and administrator of the 'new course' in 1953. But Rakosi remained Secretary of the Party. Nagy sharply criticized on July 4, 1953, 'the grave mistakes' of the previous police and bureaucratic regime. He condemned the unjust purges. He defended the intelligentsia and promised them support. He rejected the excessive concentration on heavy industry. He pronounced himself in favour of the production of consumer goods. He announced the cessation of forcible collectivization of the land and promised that legal procedure would replace police despotism.

During Nagy's regime the situation in Hungary improved. But, encouraged by this gentler regime and the diminution of violence and the improvement in living conditions, the growing desire for freedom overcame all fear of the totalitarian masters. The peasants deserted the *kolkhozes* and started their own small commercial and industrial undertakings. Nagy soon faced again the dilemma that confronts all Communist leaders once they begin to soften in their strict dictatorship. After the fall of Malenkov, Rakosi was restored to power in February 1955 and Nagy was not long afterwards expelled from the Party. When, during negotiations for a reconciliation between Moscow and Belgrade, Tito expressed his dissatisfaction at the restoration of Rakosi, a wildly outspoken anti-Titoist, Khrushchev said: 'I have to keep Rakosi in Hungary, because in Hungary the whole structure will collapse if he goes.'[1] Khrushchev was not mistaken in believing that a Communist dictatorship could be maintained only by Rakosi's methods, but it was precisely these methods that precipitated the outbreak of the Hungarian revolution.

Communists in the other subjugated countries submitted to the 'new course' ordered by Moscow, more in word than in deed. No other satellite leader went so far as Nagy. Concessions were made to the peasants (without stopping collectivization), and the slave state rulers promised their people more consumer goods. They lessened the severity of the police terror, but continued to persecute 'opponents of the People's Democracy'. Heavy industry remained their chief preoccupation but the exhausting demands of production, previously the main cause of the social misery of the people, were reduced. Changes in Party leadership were not of great political significance.

[1] George Mikes, *The Hungarian Revolution*, p. 61.

'Collective leadership' was praised and the tasks of the First Party Secretary and Prime Minister, until then normally performed by one person, were divided. Czechoslovakia's President, Gottwald, died soon after his return from Stalin's funeral (on March 14, 1953). Antonín Zápotocký then became President of the Republic, and Viliám Široký, a Slovak, succeeded him as Prime Minister. Antonín Novotný was appointed First Party Secretary. Since that time Novotný's influence has greatly increased.

The satellite regimes were made even more dependent on Moscow. The so-called Warsaw Treaty of Mutual Assistance was signed by representatives of the Soviet Government and the seven satellite Governments on May 14, 1955. An East German delegate was present but East Germany was not admitted to the bloc for some time, and a Chinese general attended as 'an observer'. Marshal Koniev was placed in command of the united military bloc. The Warsaw Pact only confirmed publicly the long-established Soviet military control of the Communist states in East Central Europe. It also contributed to the co-ordination of the military forces and to the strengthening of Soviet rule over the countries in this area. It was not by chance that the Warsaw Pact was signed virtually on the eve of the Geneva Conference. The Russian Government wanted to strengthen Communism's bargaining power by creating an Eastern military bloc similar to the North Atlantic Treaty Organization. Russia was to say that she would be 'willing' to relinquish her alliance on condition that the Western Powers would disband the Atlantic alliance. If the West had agreed to this, Europe would have been at the mercy of the Russians. Once American and British forces left the Continent, Moscow's military power would dominate Europe, while keeping the slave states of East Central Europe in her power. Soviet propaganda is always calling for the dissolution of these military 'blocs', yet NATO is kept in existence only because of the Russians' own aggressive policy. In addition to its declared aims the Warsaw Pact offered Russia a legal justification for maintaining troops in Hungary and Rumania. According to earlier treaties the Red Army should have left Rumania after the evacuation of Austria. The Hungarian revolution showed that the Warsaw Pact secured for Moscow a 'legal reason' for military intervention in the internal affairs of subjugated countries. This treaty became a serviceable instrument in Moscow's hands both for exerting pressure on the Western Powers and for strengthening her domination over East Central Europe.

Russia's economic policy was also directed to this end. From 1956 the economic programme of all the subjugated countries had to fit the pattern of Russian planning. The Russians had been preparing for that since 1954. *The Cominform Journal*, in its issue of September 9, 1955, said: 'We now have every possibility of developing the economy of all the (Communist) countries . . . on the basis of a new international socialist division of labour.' At the same time it was clearly indicated that the proposed co-ordination of economic planning was intended primarily to increase the military potential of Russia. The Communist economist, Dudinsky, in the same issue of the *Journal*, wrote that the eight-nation Warsaw Treaty of Mutual Assistance 'was an important landmark on the road to the further development and expansion of economic ties between the signatory nations'. But the troubles in Poland and Hungary in 1956 spoiled these plans – at least for a while – and seriously upset economic relations of the U.S.S.R. and its satellites.

AGREEMENT WITH TITO

Stalin's successors seemed until then to be holding firmly to their inheritance in East Central Europe. The Czechoslovak and East German demonstrations were forgotten. Rakosi reigned again in Hungary. The other satellite Communists were blindly and devotedly obedient to Moscow. To the Kremlin rulers, then beginning a 'peace offensive' on the basis of 'peaceful co-existence', it seemed the time had come to strengthen their position by ending their feud with Tito. A new Soviet ambassador was sent to Belgrade in June 1953, and each of the satellite governments made a similar gesture. The Russian hierarchy showed that they wished for an improvement in their relations with Tito.

Finally, Khrushchev and Bulganin, accompanied by Mikoyan, visited Belgrade at the end of May 1955. Molotov did not go. He had been too outspoken about Tito's behaviour. This was one of the first signs of Molotov's eventual disgrace. Khrushchev then laid all the blame for the discord between Russia and Yugoslavia on 'the provocative role' played by those 'enemies of the people', Beria, Abakumov and others. They had now been unmasked as 'despicable agents of imperialism'. It was a year later that Khrushchev explained that it was Stalin who was guilty of the quarrel with Tito. After many overt gestures of renewed friendship (and a series of long secret talks) the Russians and Yugoslavs published a communiqué on June 3, 1955, announcing that they were once again in agreement. The most important paragraph in the communiqué emphasized 'mutual respect and non-interference in internal affairs for any reason whatsoever . . . since questions of internal order, different social systems and different forms of the development of socialism are the exclusive business of the peoples of the respective countries'.

Tito had achieved another great victory. The Soviet visitors to Belgrade not only condemned the campaign that was to have destroyed him but also explicitly recognized the primary principle that he upheld about the 'different forms of the development of Socialism (meaning Communism).' Tito's prestige increased enormously. The Soviets took a calculated risk. They hoped that their recognition of Tito would not inspire the satellite countries to emulate Yugoslavia's deviationism. The risk was considerable, for Tito naturally demanded the removal of those Communist leaders who had agitated most violently against him. And he asked for the rehabilitation of those who had been victims of anti-Titoist persecution. To some extent his wishes were granted. The Communist satellites had to accept – even if with considerable reluctance – the new Kremlin policy on Yugoslavia. The Moscow dictators obviously believed they could control without difficulty Tito's increased influence in their slave states. They clearly hoped to thwart any new moves towards 'national Communism', and until the Polish and Hungarian revolts they seemed justified in this appraisal of the situation.

The powerful Soviet leaders did not visit Belgrade in vain. They returned to Moscow with considerable political advantages. Tito, because of his independence, became a useful ally in the Soviet policy of 'peaceful co-existence'. He could effectively influence the neutrals in the Western world, especially since he had acquired great international prestige from his official visits to India and Burma at the end of 1954. His friendship with Egypt's dynamic President, Colonel Nasser, could also be used to the advantage of the Russians. Because Tito had affirmed that he was dedicated to 'an uncommitted policy', 'active co-existence' or 'active neutrality' in common with Nehru and other Asian politicians, he was a valuable social asset for the Russian leaders. They had announced with martial fanfares the establishment of the Warsaw bloc as an Eastern NATO in May 1955, but that did not stop them declaring in the Belgrade communiqué a few weeks later that 'the policy of military blocs increases world tension, undermines trust among nations and increases the danger of war': a declaration which confirmed the belief that their campaign against military blocs was insincere. They were merely trying to undermine Western alliances. Tito's support for Russia's 'peaceful co-existence' propaganda had its effect in the Western countries, to the undoubted benefit of Moscow.

The Soviet leaders also hoped that by ending the dispute with Tito they might weaken or even dissolve the Balkan alliance on which Yugoslavia, Turkey and Greece had agreed at Bled, in Yugoslavia, on August 4, 1954. This had guaranteed military aid to any partner who might be attacked. By this alliance these three states strengthened their defences against attack which, in the circumstances, could only come from either Russia or her satellites. At the same time the defensive power of the Atlantic Alliance was reinforced by this treaty, because both Greece and Turkey (though not Yugoslavia) were members of it. Tito preferred to stay outside the Western military system even when, after prolonged and acrimonious negotiations, an agreement was signed in London by representatives of Italy, Yugoslavia, the United States and Britain, settling the violent dispute over Trieste. The western zone of the Trieste free territory, with the town and the port, went to Italy; the eastern zone with a small area in which there were several thousand Slovenes, was given to Yugoslavia.

The Russians were determined to weaken the newly created defence system in the Balkans and in the eastern Mediterranean area. To a certain extent they succeeded. The agreement with Tito caused distrust among Yugoslavia's Balkan allies and also in the West. The disastrous dispute over the future of Cyprus, causing tension between Greece, Britain and Turkey, was all to Russia's advantage.

The *rapprochement* between Russia and Yugoslavia developed successfully. The Russians offered Yugoslavia advantageous loans and credits from the autumn of 1955. Khrushchev's attack on Stalin in February 1956 was welcome to the Yugoslav Communists because 'it removed obstacles that have kept the fighters for Socialism apart'. Tito sent a message of greeting to the XXth Congress of the Soviet Communist Party in February 1956 in which he declared Russia to be 'a great Socialist country' and intimated that after *rapprochement* between governments would come *rapprochement* (and eventually cooperation) between Russian and Yugoslav Communist Parties. The Cominform, which eight years previously had so sharply condemned Tito, was disbanded in April 1956, and soon afterwards Molotov was removed from his post as Foreign Minister. Favourable conditions were thus prepared for the continuation of friendly relations between Moscow and Belgrade.

Tito was welcomed in Moscow in June 1956 as though he

were a hero returning in triumph. No prodigal son had ever been given such a reception. The people of Russia seemed genuinely delighted to see him. During the Russian leaders' visit to Belgrade, Tito was still suspicious of Soviet intentions, and negotiations were limited to talks between the two Governments. On Tito's arrival in Moscow co-operation between the Soviet and Yugoslavian Communist Parties was renewed. In a special declaration on June 20, 1956, both parties agreed on mutual co-operation on the basis of certain principles, of which the most important were expressed thus:

'Abiding by the view that the ways and conditions of Socialist development are different in different countries, that the wealth of the forms of Socialist development contributes to their strengthening, and starting with the fact that any tendency to impose one's own views in determining the ways and forms of Socialist development are alien to both sides, the two Parties have agreed that the foregoing co-operation should be based on complete freedom of will and equality, on friendly criticism and on the comradely character of the exchange of views on disputes between our Parties.'

The Soviet Communists recognized the main principles on which Tito had defied them. They agreed to equality of status of the Communist Parties and accepted that there should be different forms of Communist development. The Soviet Communists promised not to try to force their will on other Communist Parties. This was a remarkable success, even though, as the Hungarian revolution showed, it was only a temporary and problematical achievement. Khrushchev secured Tito's adherence in the more important international issues dividing the Western world and the Communist bloc. It was agreed that the question of Formosa and other islands should be solved 'according to the legal rights of China to those territories'. It was announced that Russia and Yugoslavia considered 'that at the present moment, when two sovereign states have been formed on the territory of post-war Germany, negotiations are essential for the unification of the Federal Republic of (West) Germany and the (East) German Democratic Republic'.

Similar joint attitudes were adopted over disarmament and European security. In all these the Russians secured what they wanted from their new Yugoslav partner. Tito, persisting in his formal independence and on equality of rights, did not agree to direct Soviet control over his state and party, but in other matters he gave way, supporting agreed principles and tactics on the major questions of world policy. The triumph of the Yugoslav dissident was more than counterbalanced by the gains derived from the agreements by the Russians.

It was at this time that Moscow, pursuing the campaign for 'peaceful co-existence', renewed the call for 'people's fronts'. In the declaration on the co-operation of the Soviet and Yugoslav Communist Parties emphasis was given to co-operation according to agreed principles 'with other Communist and workers' parties as well as with Socialist and other progressive movements in the world'. Also, it was necessary, according to the declaration, to have 'the wide co-operation of all progressive and peaceful forces' in the world 'in the interests of the struggle for lasting peace . . . as well as of social progress'. It was not only a question of former 'people's fronts' or only of co-operation between Communists and Socialists but of co-operation among all leftist and 'progressive' forces in the world. By this the Russians meant Nehru and other Asian neutrals – such as Nasser. Moscow hoped that in all this Tito would be an incomparable mediator, especially as he enjoyed the understanding and sympathy of Western Socialists and Asian neutrals. Indeed, only a few weeks after his return from Moscow, Tito talked at Brioni with Nehru and Nasser. The Moscow agreements between the Soviet and Yugoslavian Communists were aimed at the Western Powers. Marshal Georgi Zhukov even went so far as to declare at a reception in the Kremlin on June 20, 1956, that: 'Should war be imposed upon us, we (the Soviet and Yugoslav military forces) will

struggle shoulder to shoulder for the benefit of mankind.'
Tito nodded agreement and shook Zhukov warmly by the
hand, thus creating considerable suspicion among the Western
Powers, particularly the United States, who questioned the
advisability of sending further aid to Yugoslavia. Such an
estrangement between Tito and the West was naturally not
displeasing to Moscow. As usual, it was the Russians who
gained the principal advantages from renewed co-operation
with Belgrade.

Tito obviously tried to persuade the Soviet leaders to allow
greater internal freedom in the Communist countries of East
Central Europe. This was in harmony with the belated Russian
recognition of the principle of 'various ways and forms of
Socialism'. Khrushchev and his colleagues were obviously
tempted by the possibility of allowing the satellites enough
internal autonomy to produce the appearance of independence.
They believed they would in this way improve their position
inside these countries and win the favourable opinion of the
West and of Asia. Tito's visit to Moscow took place during the
era of 'deStalinization'. There were great hopes of 'peaceful
co-existence' between East and West. To allow a certain
amount of 'Titoism', carefully controlled by Moscow, in the
subjugated countries did not seem to some of the Soviet
leaders to be a great risk, especially as Tito himself had at that
time fallen into line with Soviet policy in general.

At a rally in Moscow's Dynamo Stadium on June 19, 1955,
Khrushchev acknowledged that 'there are still many differences
of principle between us'. It would appear that, during the
exchange of opinions, there was general agreement, but many
ambiguities remained. Khrushchev thought that by maintaining a certain moderate liberalization within the limits set down
by the Soviet leadership, he could gradually bring the Yugoslav Communists into line with their Soviet comrades. And
Tito, his self-confidence greatly restored by the ovations
arranged for him throughout Russia, hoped that he could use
his increased prestige in the Communist world to spread his

influence over Central and Balkan Europe. The mental reservations and divergent ambitions of the partners who could not rid themselves, in the special atmosphere of totalitarianism, of suspicion and rivalry, soon led to fresh misunderstandings. The problem of 'national Communism' was not settled during Tito's visit to Moscow.

Outwardly, Tito was triumphant. He could scarcely have realized at that moment that precisely by renewing co-operation with Moscow he would considerably limit his chances of attaining his objective. But the October revolts in Poland and Hungary soon brought this home to him. It is even possible that the beginning of Tito's inevitable downfall will one day be linked with his triumphal journey through the Soviet Union.

When he took leave of his Soviet hosts, they all beamed with contentment. They all thought that by overcoming their disagreements and renewing friendly co-operation they would greatly strengthen the Communist Party throughout the world. But the self-satisfied Yugoslav dictator had scarcely left Russia when all the Communists, including the Yugoslavs, had their dreams destroyed by a workers' revolt in Poznan.

'DESTALINIZATION UNDER CONTROL'

At the beginning of 1956 the Soviet leaders must have looked to the future with optimism, even though coolness between East and West was noticeable because the Foreign Ministers' Conference in Geneva had failed to achieve anything, and Khrushchev and Bulganin had sharply attacked Western 'colonialism' on their Asian tour. But the Russians, having been reassured at Geneva that the United States had no aggressive intentions, felt that they could safely develop, on the basis of 'competitive co-existence', a political campaign against the West, especially in Asia and the Near East. They even entered into competition with America, promising economic aid to Asian nations, and they began to plan a Middle East defence organization with Egypt in opposition to the West's

Baghdad Pact. Politically the West was forced on to the defensive. At home the Kremlin's leaders had the impression that they had successfully overcome the uncertainties and difficulties that appeared after Stalin's death. Much was expected of this new Five Year Plan into which, with the exception of Bulgaria, the economic programmes of the satellites had been fitted to form a general Communist pattern. The satellites boasted about the increase in industrial output in 1955.[1]

The Russians leaders felt that the slight relaxation in the Communist world was producing general satisfaction. They were confident of being able to control their more outspoken critics or the deviations from official orthodoxy that had occurred, especially in Poland.

In this atmosphere of self-confident optimism Khrushchev made his crushing attack on Stalin in February 1956. He thought that by blaming the dead dictator for every error and brutality, he had not only found a convenient outlet for all the accumulated discontent but had also found a way of winning trust and hope in his 'collective leadership'. But his revelations stunned the orthodox Communist following. His attack on Stalin was the biggest shock that the Communist world had ever known. Obviously he had not realized that by criticizing the criminal actions of an 'absolute ruler' he would inevitably provoke criticism of the whole system from which such a regime evolved.

By opening the Pandora's box of Communism Khrushchev allowed the 'demons of scepticism and criticism' to escape. The so-called policy of 'deStalinization' inspired the liberation movements in Poland and Hungary which at one time threatened the Soviet domination of the whole of East Central Europe. Yet 'deStalinization' appeared to Khrushchev to be

[1] By comparison with the previous year there was in Poland a rise of 11 per cent, in Hungary of 8·2 per cent, in Czechoslovakia of 10·6 per cent, in Rumania of 14 per cent and in Bulgaria of 9·6 per cent. Agricultural production, it was vaguely stated, was 'generally satisfactory'; only in Czechoslovakia had it risen by 11·5 per cent and in Poland by 3 per cent.

the best way to re-establish his undisputed dictatorship not only inside Russia but also over the satellite countries.

Even the little that is known about the repercussions in Russia to Khrushchev's condemnation of Stalin shows unmistakably that Communists there were thrown into dangerous confusion, tortured by uncertainty and torn asunder by doubt. The Government had adequate power to suppress the criticism and discontent that Khrushchev aroused by his onslaught on the most outstanding and most powerful exponent of the Soviet system. But not even the totalitarian Russian Government could do anything about the 'crisis of conscience' and restore a faith that had been brought to the verge of disintegration. 'DeStalinization' speedily led to sharp criticism of the regime in Russia. This was disquieting to authoritarian rulers. Official newspapers soon began to admonish menacingly audacious criticism. The Government was prepared to curb impassioned opinion.

Great discontent spread also through the oppressed countries of East Central Europe. The satellite Communist Governments were, in common with the Communist leaders in the free countries, surprised by 'deStalinization'. They adapted themselves to it only out of necessity, limiting themselves to oral condemnation of 'the cult of personality'. When the State Department published at the beginning of June 1956 the text of Khrushchev's speech, the people behind the Iron Curtain found out about it only from foreign broadcasts. Local Communist newspapers had reprinted nothing more than articles and speeches against 'the cult of personality' from Soviet sources. It seemed that satellite Communists had estimated better than Khrushchev the dangerous consequences of 'deStalinization'. They knew it could lead only to 'deCommunization'.

Czechoslovakian writers and students began in April 1955 to reveal their desire for freedom of thought and criticism, and for the liberty to express themselves as creative artists and not merely as Communists. Other demands were made for the restitution of writers wrongfully imprisoned or silenced because they refused to conform to the Communist doctrinaire pattern. The poet, Frantisek Hrubin, speaking at the Second Congress of the Czechoslovak Writers' Union, said: 'The poet hollows out within himself the biggest possible space for freedom. The larger the area for freedom he excavates within himself, the larger the area he wins for it outside also, for his nation, for humanity. By freedom I mean that state in which a man finds himself rid of superstition. Superstitions are not only inborn and acquired through upbringing, they are also proclaimed and imposed.' The poet Jaroslav Seifert quoted those words of John Stuart Mill: 'She or he who permits the world or the respective part of the world to choose for him his life's goal does not need any other ability than the ability to copy like a monkey.' Seifert, recalling the glorious tradition of the Czech poets who led the struggles for freedom and justice, exclaimed: 'It is with some trepidation that I turn to our dead writers to ask them if they would be willing to be seen standing by our side.' And Hrubin, reproaching contemporary writers for their cowardice, declared: 'If we are not ashamed today then our children will have to be ashamed for us. . . .'

The students were politically more outspoken and audacious. They wanted the compulsory Marxism-Leninism courses to be restricted and voluntary. They asked for the renewal of academic freedom and the independence of universities and colleges. They demanded objective information about life in the capitalist countries of the West. They said they needed to know more about the triumphs of the West, particularly in technology. They suggested that they should be told about the mistakes made by the people's democracies and the Soviet Union. They insisted that the jamming of foreign broadcasts should stop; that the trials of persons unjustly accused should be reviewed; that those who violated 'Socialist legality' should be punished; and that foreign books and films should be imported. They argued that they should have freedom to travel abroad. The students also sought information about the ownership and management of the Jachymov mines, about their country's uranium resources and also about 'the privileged position of Soviet citizens in the Jachymov mines and elsewhere' (the Soviet School in Prague). They charged that 'the function of the other "non-Communist" parties of the National Front is purely formal' and demanded permission to create an opposition party and indulge in free elections. The young Czech intellectuals criticized the slogan 'the Soviet Union – our model' ('we arbitrarily and uncritically accept everything they have in the Soviet Union'). The majority of these demands were contained in a draft resolution issued by the students at the Institute of Pedagogics in Prague in May 1956.[1]

This critical mood, revealing the obvious longing of the students for freedom and for friendship with the West, disturbed the Communist leaders far more than the 'unprincipled liberalism' of the writers. These words were used by Novotný, First Secretary of the Czechoslovak Communist Party at the National Party Conference in June 1956. Referring to the writers and students, he declared: 'Independence of the Press from the Party and its ideas we have always rejected and will continue to do so.' Vice-Premier Kopecký, referring to the writers at the same conference, said: 'We were astounded at the transports of liberalism which it fell to our lot to witness at the Congress.'

Before being admitted to Czech universities and colleges, students had to be carefully screened. Children from working-class homes or peasant families were given priority over those of 'boorgeois origin'. Similarly, zeal in Party activities was more highly valued than talent, the ability of learning, knowledge, or technical qualifications. And it is all the more significant that these students, so carefully selected for the universities because the Government thought them dependable young Communists, should turn against the regime, and exhibit dangerous 'liberal tendencies'.

Even among the workers and the rank and file of the

---

[1] Its text was published in *News From Behind The Iron Curtain* (now *East Europe*), July 1956, pp. 42–44.

Communist Party there were articulate critics of the Government. Novotný bitterly reproached these opposition elements in his speech at the National Party Conference, saying: 'Many party workers have an indifferent, indeed, a frivolous attitude . . . to Leninist principles.' He said: 'Some demand relaxation and agreement in the ideological field with regard to the capitalists', and he explained: 'the former dogmatic "certainty" (of some ideological workers) has been replaced by absolute uncertainty so that they have almost begun to have doubts about the very principles of our world opinion. Wrong liberalistic tendencies, testifying to under-estimation of the role and meaning of security . . . reflect petty bourgeois criticism of Party policy, and in some cases turn into malicious attacks on the Party and its principles. . . .'

The Czech Communist leaders were very troubled by this movement against the regime towards independence. They feared (as one of them privately admitted) that if they relaxed their grip on the country even slightly, everything would collapse. That is why, immediately after the students' demonstrations, the Government took determined steps to suppress even the mildest critics. Vaclav Kopecký, a Deputy Prime Minister, told the National Party Conference: 'The condemnation of the cult of personality does not mean that the Party line has changed. . . . Various criticisms which were aimed against Leninist principles must be rejected . . . the Party can now move in the direction of overcoming wavering, and breaking various ideological and political conceptions spread by petty bourgeois elements and often inspired by enemies.'[1]

While in the other subjugated countries the 'victims of Stalinism' – dead and alive – were ostentatiously forgiven for their sins, their names cleared and their families brought out of disgrace, the Czechoslovak Government released only a few less important persons. In Hungary and Bulgaria, Rajk and Kostov were rehabilitated, but in Czechoslovakia Slansky was further blamed, as an 'agent of Beria', for violation of 'socialist

[1] *News From Behind The Iron Curtain*, July 1956, p. 44.

legality', for the brutality of the police and other sins. It was reluctantly admitted that the accusation of supposed intrigues with Tito might be unjust (the Czechoslovak Communists had to make some concession to Moscow's desire to appease Tito). Not even Clementis was rehabilitated – obviously to prevent any encouragement of 'bourgeois nationalism' in Slovakia. Some Slovak Communists were released from prison for 'good behaviour', but the accusations of 'bourgeois national-ism' were not withdrawn.[1]

The Minister of the Interior, Rudolf Barak, said that more than 25,000 had been released from prison since 1953. It is not known how many of these were political prisoners. Un-doubtedly only a few. No important non-Communists were released. The Hungarian Archbishop Groesz was 'forgiven' in May 1956, but the Czechs showed no eagerness to allow Archbishop Beran to return to his diocese. Only two Slovak bishops were released from prison in October 1956: the 79-year-old Mgr Jan Vojtassak and the 71-year-old Mgr Michal Buzalka.

Elsewhere, leading exponents of 'Stalinism' were forced to resign, but in Czechoslovakia only one was found guilty of the 'cult of personality': Alexej Čepička, a First Deputy Prime Minister of National Defence and member of the Politburo, was relieved on April 25, 1956, of all his functions in the Party and Government 'for fostering the cult of personality in the Army' and for 'shortcomings and mistakes committed in the execution of state and party functions'. Čepička was probably chosen as a scapegoat because he was equally hated by members of the Party and by Non-Communists. He surpassed all the other leaders in arrogance and brutality, and he was suspected by non-Communists of having taken part in the plot to kill

[1] It is not yet clear why the Czech Communist leaders so obdurately refused to rehabilitate either Slansky or Clementis. Indeed, it has never been satisfactorily explained why Slansky was removed in the first place. But it was easy to accuse Clementis of Slovak nationalism, and to recall his former 'deviation' when he was guilty of condemning the Ribbentrop-Molotov Pact in 1939.

Jan Masaryk, Petr Zenkl and Prokop Drtina in September 1947. It is possible that some Communist leaders feared that this cynical egomaniac might discover during the era of 'deStalinization' that he had 'Titoist leanings' and use the Army to further his ambitions. Yet they behaved considerately towards him. He did not vanish through the usual trap-door but was put in charge of the Office for Inventions. This means he can still be invited to Government meetings.

The Czech leaders went no further with 'deStalinization' than the Soviet leaders themselves. Oppression became a little less brutal, and the Czech rulers retreated for a while before the pressure of a discontented public, but no weakening of the authority or dictatorship of the Party was allowed. When they saw the growing opposition to Soviet Communism in neighbouring Poland they were all the more convinced of the need for keeping the masses and irresponsible intellectuals under control.

At this time the liberalization movement in Poland and Hungary was gathering strength, but in the other 'people's democracies' 'deStalinization' did not even go so far as in Czechoslovakia. There was a certain amount of discontent among Rumanian and Bulgarian writers and students, just as there was everywhere else. But scarcely had the writer, Alexander Jar, raised a critical voice when he was expelled from the Party. Bulgarian intellectuals who were – according to the Sofia paper, *Rabotnichesko Delo* of June 10, 1956 – so 'foolish' as to advocate 'freedom of criticism and freedom of the Press' and to oppose 'the guidance of the Central Party Committee' were also sharply silenced. Zwetan Kristanov was expelled from the Party because at a meeting of Communists in the Academy of Sciences he hinted that the entire Party policy in the villages was vicious, and made proposals which in practice would lead to the dissolution of the 'collectives'.[1] Official newspapers in both countries indignantly refuted the 'vile slanders' against the Party, and spoke of 'cosmopolitan, idealist

[1] *News From Behind The Iron Curtain,* July 1956, p. 53.

and mystical tendencies', 'anarchistic, bourgeois, individualistic eruptions' and 'bourgeois nationalism'. The Bulgarian Party Central Committee categorically declared in September 1956: 'There can be no place for liberalism and reconciliation when the Party must be defended against the machinations and slanders of its outward enemies'. In a similar fashion the Congress of Rumanian Communists declared: 'There is no question of a "pause" in the ideological struggle.'[1] It was typical of the unyielding severity of the Rumanian and Bulgarian regimes that at this time they should attempt to extend collectivization of the land.[2]

Only in Bulgaria was there a more serious change in the Communist leadership. The Prime Minister, Vulko Chervenkov, having been rebuked by the Party Central Committee for encouraging the 'cult of the individual', handed in his resignation on April 16, 1956. His place was taken by Anton Yugov who, in 1950, was reprimanded by Chervenkov for tolerating 'Kostov's conspiratorial activities'. But this exchange did not mean any relaxation in the severity of the Government's domestic policy. Yugov, as Minister of the Interior after the fall of Boris's regime, was renowned for his brutal persecution of non-Communists. The change was made primarily to placate Tito. At the same time the name of Traicho Kostov, executed in December 1949, was officially cleared. It was declared on April 14, 1956, that 'The accusations in the Kostov trial, based on ties with Yugoslav agencies and leaders, are cancelled. All defendants in this trial are rehabilitated.' Those still alive were then released from gaol.

But Anna Pauker in Rumania was not rehabilitated. On the

[1] *News From Behind The Iron Curtain*, November 1956, p. 53, and July 1956, p. 54.

[2] Households in collective farms and peasant associations rose from 390,000 to 577,000 in Rumania in the first half of 1956. The Socialist sector of agriculture represented 29·3 per cent of the arable land of Rumania. During the same period, the number of collectives rose in Bulgaria from 2,735 to 3,100, from 63 per cent to 78 per cent of the arable land.

contrary, 'the Pauker clique' was once more accused of advocating 'the cult of personality' and attacked for 'violating Socialist legality and Communist principles'. Presumably no changes in the Government were necessary! 'DeStalinization' in Rumania was limited to curbing slightly the brutality of the police and to releasing some political prisoners, among them a few Social Democrats. Under pressure from the Government they then declared themselves in favour of active participation in the 'construction of Socialism'.

Even in Albania no attempt was made to lessen the cruelty of the existing dictatorship. Koci Xoxe, executed in 1949, was cleared of the accusation of conspiracy with Tito, but he was not rehabilitated because he and his associates 'were hostile to the Party and State'. Enver Hoxha, the First Party Secretary, declared himself – merely in order to placate Moscow – in favour of friendship with Yugoslavia. But another misunderstanding between Moscow and Belgrade in the autumn of 1956 caused Hoxha to start attacking Tito again.

CHAPTER V

The Polish Rebellion

POZNAN RIOTS

DeStalinization in Poland and Hungary created such a wave of 'liberalization' that open revolt became inevitable. In these countries the voices of opposition and criticism made themselves heard far more clearly than they had for a long time in many of the other oppressed nations. Even before Khrushchev's attack on Stalin, Rakosi had been trying to damp down discontent. In Poland, at the same time, critics grew ever louder. At the beginning of November 1955, one supporter of the Government complained: 'The sense of the "thaw" does not lie in more intense criticism of evil symptoms (such criticism is wholesome and creative), but in ideological chaos and defeatism . . . in withdrawal . . . from the proletarian dictatorship and the leading role of the Party in the life of our society.'[1]

Khrushchev only added to the 'ideological chaos' and encouraged severe criticism of the regime, and indeed of the Communist doctrine itself. After he had told the truth about Stalin at the XXth Congress of the Soviet Communists in Moscow, Warsaw announced that the decisions of the Congress must be translated into the Polish language: 'Certainly there will not be more meat, fats or milk from one day to another. Certainly wages will not rise from one day to another or from one month to the next. But the road to independent, creative businesslike thought is open to everybody. . . .'[2]

Even during the XXth Congress, Polish Communist pre-war leaders who had either been executed or imprisoned

[1] Adam Schaff in *Przeglad Kulturalny*, Warsaw, November 3–9, 1955. Quoted from *News From Behind The Iron Curtain*, New York, March 1955.
[2] Quoted from *News From Behind The Iron Curtain*, April 1956, p. 47.

during the great purges were finally 'rehabilitated'. The Comintern had disbanded the Polish Communist Party in March 1938 under the pretext that it 'had been extensively infiltrated by enemy agents'. Those who had signed this Comintern resolution declared (according to *Trybuna Ludu*, Warsaw, February 19, 1956) that 'this charge was based on evidence falsified by *provocateurs* who have since been exposed', and 'the dissolution of the Communist Party was an unfounded act'. This 'provocation' was first described as one of 'Beria's criminal acts', but in the end Warsaw Radio bluntly said: 'Stalin himself approved the list of the members of the Polish Central Committee about to be arrested.'

Rehabilitation of pre-war leaders was intended to improve relations between the Polish and Soviet Communists. This 'family affair' did not, however, have any effect on the Polish people, among whom the Communists are an insignificant minority. But everyone was delighted at news of the rehabilitation of the soldiers of the Home Army (*Armia Krajowa*), who had courageously fought the Germans but had been described by the Communists after the war as a 'band of Fascists and reactionaries'. The newspaper *Poprostu* demanded that 'our schools should teach about the heroism of the A.K. (partisan) soldiers'.

The Poles then urged changes in the Communist leadership, and this became possible through the sudden death, from a heart attack in Moscow, of Boleslaw Bierut, First Party Secretary. He had been Poland's most outstanding defender of the Stalin line since the war. Khrushchev, who went to Warsaw for Bierut's funeral, was eager to see a man on whom Moscow could depend, taking over the First Secretary's post.

Edward Ochab was named but later on he disappointed the Russians by joining Gomulka. Eventually the Polish Communist leaders had to give way to the popular demand for a more congenial administrator. Gomulka, released from prison two years previously but still kept under house arrest, was finally rescued from disgrace. Ochab declared that 'Gomulka's arrest in 1951, which took place in the atmosphere created by

Beriaism, in the atmosphere of the Rajk trial, was unjustified and without foundation'. Even so, Ochab rejected the 'opportunistic and nationalistic deviations of Gomulka', which obviously sprang from his opposition to unnecessarily speedy collectivization of the land and to one-sided development of heavy industry, and from his defence of 'the Polish road to Socialism'. Several other Communists (and some Social Democrats) were released, and with them, twenty army officers who, according to Ochab, were arrested 'on faked charges of espionage'.

Communist leaders were accustomed to depending primarily (if not exclusively) on power. This prevented them from assessing fairly the volume of accumulated discontent and the intensity of the desire for change. So, when they were suddenly faced with the open revolt of the workers, the social class officially considered the pillar of the Communist regime, they were all the more surprised.

The strike among Poznan's workers on June 28, 1956, quickly developed into a general uprising. Placards carried by those in the procession said: 'Freedom and Bread!' 'Out with the Russians!' 'Down with false Communism!' The demonstrators asked the foreigners who watched the procession: 'Tell the world what you have seen. We want things to get better and the Russians to go home.'

The Government crushed the revolt relatively quickly, mainly because it remained an isolated incident limited to Poznan alone. There were 'sympathetic' strikes in some other towns, but these demonstrations were not co-ordinated and failed to make any impression.

The Poznan rising was crushed but its political significance could not be ignored. It revealed to the world not only the discontent of the Polish workers, but also their hatred of both the Communist administration in Warsaw and of the Russians. Poznan rioters expressed in simple but convincing slogans the desires of the entire Polish nation: an improvement in their standard of living, personal freedom and the departure of the Russians from their beloved land. They expressed, too, the chief aspirations of all the subjugated nations of East Central Europe. It is important to realize that at the first opportunity an oppressed people, led by the workers, rose against Communism. They did not demand merely the rectification of the errors and shortcomings of the regime, but the removal of the whole system. During a meeting of the Central Committee of the Polish Communists in October 1956, one of its members, Boleslav Ruminski, openly declared: 'After all, Poznan showed that there was neither party nor state authority.'

He did not exaggerate. The revolt proved that the police and even some Communist officials had nationalist sympathies. It was realized that the rebellion might have continued beyond the two days if Soviet tanks and troops had not surrounded Poznan. This Polish workers' revolution, quickly joined by people from other social classes, indicated the inevitable collapse of the entire Communist policy and emphasized the resistance of all social classes to an oppressive regime. In assessing the real feelings and true desires of the subjugated peoples behind the Iron Curtain, Poznan (and later the Hungarian revolution) is a far more important and dependable yard-stick than the so-called Polish October Revolution.

In the first moments of surprise and confusion, the Polish Government tried to blame the rising on the machinations of *provocateurs* and secret agents employed by the United States and West Germany. Cyrankiewicz, in a broadcast speech on June 29, spoke about 'criminal *provocateurs*' and 'imperialist centres' who 'wanted Poznan, site of the International Fair, to be made a centre of riots' and warned that 'all hands raised against the Socialist authority in Poland would be cut off'. He agreed that the dissatisfaction of a percentage of workers in Poznan was 'caused by the difficult material conditions of the working people,' and added, eloquently: 'The bloody events in Poznan will not, however, stop or weaken our efforts . . . for the democratization of our life . . . and the greatest possible care for a more rapid improvement in the living standard of the people of Poland.'

Some weeks later, Ochab, the First Party Secretary, who was considered a diehard 'Moscow' Communist, went even further, saying, at a Party Central Committee on July 18: 'In an appraisal of the reasons for the painful incidents in Poznan it would be erroneous to concentrate attention primarily on the machinations of *provocateurs* and imperialist agents. It is necessary to look first of all for the social roots of these incidents which have become for the whole of our Party a warning signal testifying to the existence of serious disturbances in the relations between the Party and various sections of the working class.' He admitted that the wages of the workers had fallen while the working norms had risen. 'About 75 per cent of the Poznan workers suffered from this,' he explained. The Government then hurried to increase wages, eager to suggest that they intended to improve social conditions generally.

This realistic evaluation of the reasons for the revolt and the Government's positive attitude to the workers' demands and recriminations prevented further outbursts of ill-feeling. It was important, too, that the 'Muscovite' Ochab joined forces with the 'liberal' Cyrankiewicz. The majority of the Polish Communist leaders realized that they could only save their administration by meeting (if only partially) the wishes of the people. They were compelled to do this by the steady increase in demands for 'liberalization' after the Poznan rising. The leaders also realized that their authority had been badly shaken. They were all the more anxious in the circumstances to create the impression that they were now prepared to follow their own 'Polish road' to Socialism. They tried to emphasize their intentions by electing to the Party leadership some 'liberal' or anti-Stalinist Communists and by restoring Party rights to Gomulka.

By their attitude to Poznan, the Polish leaders showed that they differed from the rest of the East European Communist hierarchy who saw in the rising the work of reactionaries and imperialist agents. Khrushchev was annoyed because the Poles disobeyed his orders 'to put all the blame for the Poznan events on Western agents and *provocateurs*',[1] and to show his displeasure he refused an invitation to attend a meeting of the Polish Central Committee. He sent Bulganin who, on July 21, 1956, declared in Warsaw: 'The recent events in Poznan, provoked by hostile agents, provide fresh evidence that international reaction has not yet discarded its plans made for the restoration of capitalism in the Socialist countries.' Bulganin's estimation of Poznan was clearly in conflict with the assessment of the Polish leaders and was not well received in Warsaw. The Soviet Prime Minister aroused still greater annoyance among the Poles by accusing their newspapers of falling under the influence of hostile elements. He added an emphatic warning: 'Every country should go its own way to Socialism, but we cannot permit this to be used to break up the solidarity of the peace camp . . . under the pretext of extending national peculiarities or democracy.' Bulganin's statement was considered by the Poles to be gross intervention by the Kremlin in the national affairs of Poland. It certainly contradicted the Soviet-Yugoslav Agreement which emphasized 'non-interference in internal affairs for any reason whatsoever'. Bulganin's visit to Warsaw merely increased anti-Soviet feeling in Poland, even among the Communists.

Prague, Bucharest, Sofia and Tirana accepted and repeated the Kremlin's interpretation of what happened in Poznan, and the Yugoslav Communists, still under the influence of Tito's triumphal return to Moscow, joined the others. Radio Belgrade called the rebellion the work of 'illegal reactionary circles'. But the official Party organ, *Borba*, admitted a few days later that 'Polish economic difficulties were the product of a wrong course', though it emphasized that 'Poznan provocation was a resistance to the positive orientation of the existing Polish Government which will gradually heal all those difficulties'. Yugoslav commentaries betrayed a certain embarrassment and uneasiness. It was not easy for Tito, who had just come to

[1] Stanislaw Mikolajczyk, 'Poland Today', *International Peasant Union Bulletin*, February–April 1957, p. 10.

terms again with the Russian Communists and the Soviet Government, to take sides against Moscow. And as a true Communist he could not admit that the workers might wish to overthrow a Communist regime. Yet he did not wish to anger the Polish Communists who were beginning to express their right to follow 'the Polish road to Socialism', for independence of this kind was his own pet idea. Tito found himself in much more serious difficulties after the Hungarian revolution. But he compromised on the Polish issue by laying the blame for Poznan on 'imperialist agents and the Stalinist wrong course'.

A PEACEFUL REVOLUTION

Internal disquiet continued in Poland. Wage increases, concessions to peasant and small private artisans, and similar social and economic measures failed to appease the discontented. When the Party Central Committee discussed the new Five Year Plan, it was evident that the Communist leaders wished to continue their existing economic policy, laying the main emphasis on heavy industry and giving industry priority over agriculture. This Polish Plan had been drafted before Poznan to fit in with the plans of the Soviet and the People's Democracies. To the Poles the plan offered no release from their slavery. The promises of Cyrankiewicz about improvements in the standard of living were received with increasing suspicion. The Government tried to soothe the people by allowing greater freedom for self-expression in Parliamentary debates and in the newspapers, non-Communists were also allowed to resume their activities to a limited extent, and further restrictions were placed on investigations by the Secret Police. Yet criticism of the Government policy increased. Even the Communist doctrine itself was questioned. The newspaper of the young intellectuals, *Poprostu*, talked about 'the twilight of Marxism'. Critics of a policy imitating the 'Soviet example' rapidly increased. The decline of Polish agriculture was identified with collectivization and with the adoption of the 'Stalinist method of village socialization'. In *Nowa Kultura* of September 9, 1956, the economist, Lipinski, rejecting the basic Leninist theory that an independent peasantry is a breeding ground of capitalism, wrote: 'On no account does Socialism . . . entail . . . nationalization of agriculture where previous capitalist development has not already organized agriculture in the form of great farm factories based on hired labour.'[1]

Julian Hochfeld, in *Zycie Warszawy* of September, wrote: 'It is my most profound conviction that the centre of gravity in the process of democratization lies not so much in opposing individual leadership with collective leadership as in opposing autocratic leadership with elective, controlled, responsible leadership, subject to recall. The thing that matters here is a *Sejm* (Parliament) which supervises the Government and a Government which is responsible to the *Sejm*.'[2] It was clear that the Polish administration could be maintained only by becoming less of a dictatorship.

The first trials of those accused of 'anti-Socialist' participation in the Poznan riots began at the end of September 1956. For the first time in Communist Poland, counsel and accused could defend themselves freely, and the Government found this situation extremely unpleasant. The trials offered an opportunity for public condemnation of a regime of violence and injustice. Sentences imposed were relatively mild. It was clear that the public sympathized with the accused. The Government finally announced in October that further trials would be postponed.

Even so, the frequent changes in the leadership of the Party, in the Government and in ministerial offices did not satisfy the people and provoked ever sharper comment in the newspapers. Rather than continue to face such increasing criticism, Hilary Minc, First Deputy Premier, 'resigned' on October 9. Minc, an economist, was said to be responsible for the catastrophic state of the Polish economy and for the poverty of the people, and it was thought that he was sacked to please Gomulka, with

[1] *News From Behind The Iron Curtain*, November 1956, pp. 47 and 48.
[2] *Op. cit.*, p. 43.

whom the Party leaders had been negotiating since his return to their midst in July. The more that internal tension developed the more urgent became the demand that Gomulka should become head of the administration. Discontented Communists, and even many non-Communists, had great faith in the man who had been a victim of Stalin's doctrinaire intolerance. Gomulka could never be blamed for the present misery of the country; it had been caused instead by Stalin's disciples. It was realized that the 'deviations' for which Gomulka had been imprisoned were merely justifiable attempts to avoid the catastrophic consequences of excessive, one-sided industrialization and farm collectivization. Everything confirmed that he had been right when he advocated a 'Polish road to Socialism'. It could never have been the same as the Soviet road, even though Stalin had believed otherwise. Gomulka, the man who had unjustly suffered for the truth, was soon recognized as a national leader who alone could save the country from a desperate situation.

In this way, favourable psychological conditions for Gomulka's return to power were created. He was helped because the authority of the Party leadership had been seriously undermined by the criticism of the intellectuals and by Poznan. His supporters acquired greater influence among the workers, among the intellectuals and among the Polish officers and soldiers who bore resentfully their humiliating subordination to the Soviet military hierarchy with Marshal Rokossovski at its head. Even the peasants expected Gomulka to improve their living conditions.

So the Central Committee of the Party met on October 19, 1956, to prepare for the installation of Gomulka as head of the Party. His election as First Party Secretary would probably have been carried through without difficulty had the Soviet leaders not staged a sudden dramatic intervention. While the Central Committee was electing Gomulka and General Spychalski (later appointed Deputy Minister of Defence) to the Politburo, Khrushchev, Molotov, Kaganovitch and Mikoyan, accompanied by several Soviet generals, walked in on them. At the same moment it was announced that the Red Army was indulging in threatening manœuvres, some units moving towards Warsaw.

It is not yet accurately known what happened between the Soviet and the Polish leaders. The scene was dramatic and the clash between them violent. All Warsaw, all Poland lived through a moment of the highest tension. Everybody realized the possibility of a conflict between the Soviet forces and the Polish Army and police, to whose side the workers came after quickly equipping themselves with arms. The Soviet leaders realized the importance of keeping Poland through Marshal Rokossovski and those Polish Communists who were blindly faithful to the Kremlin. But the Polish leaders who were grouped round Gomulka courageously defied the Russians to fulfil the threat of military intervention. Ochab stood up to Khrushchev, who had forced him upon the Polish Politburo as First Secretary in the spring, as energetically as the others. It is said that he was encouraged by the Chinese Communists, during his visit to Peking in September 1956, to win more independence from Moscow. The Soviet leaders were astounded. They realized that they could enforce their will only through the intervention of the Red Army. This would result in heavy fighting with the whole of the Polish nation ranged against them. Gomulka and his supporters knew that they could depend on the support of the factory workers, the peasants, students, bureaucracy, the army and a large part of the police force. Moscow had not been well informed about the true situation in Poland and the members of Khrushchev's delegation discovered the danger of a Polish rising against Soviet intervention only when they actually reached Warsaw.

They gave way. They guessed that a battle with the Polish nation would only encourage the other subjugated countries, particularly East Germany, to take similar action to embarrass Russia, and in making this retreat they took comfort from the knowledge that Gomulka and Ochab would be compelled to count on Soviet help in maintaining the Oder-Neisse frontier. Also they realized the importance to these men of the 'hard' Moscow Communists who had been united in the Natolin Group. (Natolin is a suburb of Warsaw.)

The day after the mission returned to Moscow the new Polish Politburo was elected. Gomulka and Ochab were triumphant; Rokossovski and six 'Stalinists' were ousted. Gomulka, unanimously elected First Secretary of the Party, became the new Communist leader of Poland. His victorious restoration appeared to be complete, and he knew that he could depend, even though he was a Communist, on the support of the non-Communists. The new Polish leadership started immediately to make changes in the Government, in the Army and in the Party. The most significant political event was the resignation of Rokossovski. As soon as the Marshal had left his post as Minister of Defence and Commander-in-Chief of the Polish Army to return to Moscow, he was appointed Deputy Minister of Defence in the Soviet Union. Moscow thus ostentatiously confirmed that Rokossovski, in the guise of a Pole, had been in Poland as the Soviet representative, controlling Poland in the tradition of the former Czarist governors. The new Polish Defence Minister was General Marian Spychalski, a Gomulka supporter who had also been a victim of Stalin's spite. Polish officers on whom the new regime could depend were appointed to leading positions in the Army.

'RAISON D'ETAT' POLICY

Gomulka was swept into power by the liberalizing movement both inside the Party and outside of it; a movement striving not only for greater internal freedom and better economic conditions but also for less dependence on Moscow. Right from the start the new Polish Government faced difficulties. It depended on the support of the members of the liberalizing movement, so it had to pay particular attention to their wishes. Yet it could not neglect the powerful Russian forces, from whom economic help was needed. Nor could it ignore the influence of the Moscow 'diehards' who, forced into the background, were still energetic opponents. All these factors persuaded Gomulka to take a 'middle course'. He tried to preserve a balance between the local extremists. And it is doubtful whether he would have succeeded in pacifying the anti-Soviet and anti-Communist elements had the Polish people not been intimidated by the tragedy of the Hungarian Revolution, so brutally crushed by the Red Army.

Gomulka's compromise was accepted from the beginning by those Poles who realized that, without the help of the Russians, they could never maintain their claim to the Oder-Neisse Line. Gomulka, speaking at a dramatic session of the Central Committee immediately after the departure of Khrushchev's mission from Moscow, declared categorically: 'If there is anyone who thinks it is possible to kindle an anti-Soviet mood in Poland then he is deeply mistaken. . . . Polish-Soviet relations based on the principles of equality and independence will create among the Polish people such a profound feeling of friendship for the Soviet Union that no attempt to sow distrust for the Soviet Union will find a response among the Polish people.'

Two days before the second Soviet intervention in Hungary, the Polish Central Committee, fearing that the anti-Soviet attitude of the Hungarian revolutionaries might find a response among anti-Soviet-minded Poles, published a forceful appeal 'to the Polish nation', laying particular emphasis on the fact that: 'The stay of Soviet troops in Poland . . . is necessary and indispensable, not only from the point of view of the security of the Soviet Union . . . until an agreement is reached . . . on the withdrawal of all occupation troops from the whole of Germany . . . but also, to an even greater degree, from the point of view of our own security and the inviolability of our frontiers against the schemes of German militarism. It is known that the Soviet Union is so far the only one of the Four Powers which has recognized and guaranteed our Western frontiers. . . . Demands for the removal of Soviet troops from

Poland in the present international situation are contrary to the most vital interests of the nation and of the Polish *raison d'état.*'

Appeals to the people to preserve 'calm, discipline and responsibility' were explained in this sense. The anti-Soviet demonstrations in Wroclaw and in Szczecin, where the Soviet consulate was attacked, and elsewhere, were severely condemned. Cardinal Stefan Wyszynski's appeal for 'national unity', on his release from prison on October 28, contributed to peace and quiet.

During the visit of Gomulka and Cyrankiewicz to Moscow in October 1956, the Poles achieved more favourable terms in the repayment of credits granted by Russia, a promise of delivery in 1957 of 1,400,000 tons of grain on a long-term credit basis and of commodities to the value of 700 million roubles, payable in 1958–60, and a pledge that Moscow would pay a higher price for Polish coal. In addition, the Soviet leaders said they would repatriate some of the 2,000,000 Poles detained in Russia. Cyrankiewicz, in a speech to Parliament on November 20, assured the deputies that 'the Moscow talks were conducted . . . on the basis of the recognition of the sovereignty and full equality of rights of the contracting parties'. This was understood to mean that Russia had decided to recognize the Gomulka regime. Finally, an agreement defining the new status of Soviet troops in Poland was signed on December 17. The withdrawal of Red Army units from Poland was out of the question. The Kremlin leaders would only pledge that the 'temporary stationing in Poland (of the Red Army) . . . cannot lead to interference in the internal affairs of the Polish People's Republic'. It was decreed that any movement of Soviet troops 'outside the places of their deployment will in every case require the consent' of the Polish Government. The size of the Soviet force and the construction of their military installations would also be subject to the approval of the Polish Government. This agreement formally respected the principle of Polish sovereignty and independence. But its fulfilment depends on the decision of the Soviet Government. The presence of Red Army units within their country is a warning to the Poles that they are constantly exposed to the possibility of Soviet intervention. They are reminded, too, that the Red Army does not stand only on their eastern frontiers but is also stationed in East Germany. Gomulka did not exaggerate when, immediately before the elections in January 1957, he said that if Poland adopted an anti-Soviet and anti-Communist policy she could quickly be wiped off the map of Europe. The Polish leaders have continually reminded the public since the October Revolution that Poland must preserve friendship and alliance with Russia if she is to continue to exist at all.

The October changes did not make any fundamental difference to Poland's dependence on Moscow. But they produced a lessening of the direct control of the Russians on all spheres of Polish public life. Poland may not be independent but she has acquired a certain measure of autonomy – less in foreign affairs but greater in domestic policy. And Gomulka is resolved to follow 'the Polish road to Socialism'. 'The roads to the achievement of this goal,' he said on October 20, 1956, 'can be, and are, different . . . the model of Socialism can also vary. It can be like that of the Soviet Union. It can be shaped in the manner seen in Yugoslavia. It can be different still.' Characteristically, he pointed out that 'after the Second World War the Soviet Union ceased to be the only country building Socialism. People's China and a number of the People's Democracies, including Poland . . . entered the arena.'

This means that the Polish Communist administration under Gomulka's leadership recognizes 'the principles of proletarian internationalism' and the necessity for co-operation among the Communist countries, but refuses to submit always and in everything to the wishes and the commands of Moscow, and tries to attend primarily to the particular needs of Poland.

The political orientation of the Gomulka regime was most clearly expressed in the Polish-Chinese Declaration signed at the end of Chou En Lai's visit to Warsaw in the early days of

1957. China's Prime Minister obviously warned the Poles against following Hungary if they wished to avoid provoking the Red Army. He failed to make them follow the example of other Communist satellites in condemning the Hungarians as the tools of counter-revolutionaries or in praising the Russians for thrashing these 'reactionaries'. The Polish delegate abstained when the other members of the Soviet bloc voted against the United Nations resolution condemning Soviet intervention in Hungary. But Gomulka agreed to a declaration in which Poland and China supported the Revolutionary Worker-Peasant Government of Hungary headed by Janos Kadar, and resolutely opposed 'all attempts of imperialist circles to intervene in the internal affairs of Hungary'. A few words expressing the conviction that 'the Hungarian nation will find adequate strength to overcome the consequences of past errors and present difficulties', clearly blamed the Stalin line followed by Rakosi for the crisis in Hungary.

Polish Communists differed from others, not only in their attitude towards the Hungarians but also in that they rejected the formula accepted by the others, even the Chinese, about the unity of the Communist camp under the 'leadership' of the Soviet Union. Instead, the Polish-Chinese Declaration recognized 'the principles of proletarian internationalism' and the 'common ideology and objectives' of the Socialist countries. It also emphasized that 'relations between Socialist countries which are sovereign and independent states should be based on the principles of respect for sovereignty, non-interference in internal affairs, equality and mutual benefit'.

Many of the declarations published by Gomulka's Government made abundantly clear Poland's desire for any measure of independence that could be won in face of the threatening superiority of Russia. It emphasized, too, the hope that the people would be allowed to follow their own road to Socialism.

The Poles were strengthened by the belief that they could depend on the support of China. But their desires were too audacious in the eyes of those Soviet leaders who, warned by the Hungarian Revolution, saw in 'special national' paths dangerous deviations that might threaten their domination of the satellite countries. Yet most Poles, yearning for real independence and for the removal of the Communist dictatorship, thought Gomulka was not expressing their hopes in terms that were sufficiently forthright.

GOMULKA'S MIDDLE COURSE

Right from the beginning, Gomulka's 'middle course' created suspicion and distrust, not only among Moscow's supporters in the Natolin group but also among Poland's liberal Communists, among the nationalists and, of course, among all the non-Communists. The difficulties in which the new Polish regime inevitably found itself were temporarily overcome, mainly through the great esteem in which Gomulka was held. Everyone in the end submitted to his authority. Poland could scarcely have avoided dangerous internal discontent and stormy demonstrations if this had not been so. Even so, Gomulka could not entirely ignore the demands of the liberal wing of his Party. 'Stalinists' were replaced by 'Gomulka-ites' in the leadership, in the Government, in the army, in the administration and in the trade unions. Moscow-dominated youth organizations were replaced by 'revolutionary' formations of industrial and rural youth. So-called 'workers' councils' were established to allow the people to take part directly in the administration of their industries. But the power of these workers' councils was never clearly defined. They were obviously intended to appease a popular demand for some kind of self-government; they revealed the general desire for a democratic way of life, but they never enjoyed such extensive economic autonomy as the workers' councils of Yugoslavia, and it was soon announced that they could only operate within the framework of directives from a central planning agency. Still, this was a step towards the vision of a workers' democracy.

Gomulka openly admitted that the collective farms, in spite of great outlay, had smaller results and greater production costs than the individual private farms. He promised that 'no threats or compulsion would be used' to form *kolkhozes*, but he demanded that inefficient and uneconomic collectives should be dissolved. Immediately the entire system of agricultural collectivization collapsed. Within not quite two months, according to Radio Warsaw, only 2,000 collective farms remained of the former 10,000, and of these (according to *Trybuna Wolnosci*) 'it is mainly the well-organized collectives which are being dissolved while the poor and inefficient ones are left'. The dissolution of the *kolkhozes* was, at least temporarily, the most important achievement of the Polish revolt. And to reverse the policy established by Gomulka could only draw the peasants into civil war. Anyway, according to what Gomulka said that October, only 8·6 per cent of the farm land was owned by the *kolkhozes* at the beginning of 1956, while 12·6 per cent was in the hands of the state farms and 78·8 per cent in the hands of individual farmers.

While the new Polish leaders pursued in the dissolution of collective farming and in the workers' councils, a policy on the whole similar to that of the Tito regime, they far surpassed the Yugoslavs in the political sphere. Gomulka permitted far greater political freedom. He also differed strikingly from Tito in admitting the necessity for religious freedom. Gomulka realized that he needed to be reconciled with the Roman Catholic Church, which, merely because it had been subject to monstrous persecution, had increased its influence and prestige. After the release of Cardinal Wyszynski from prison, a commission of representatives of the Church and the Government issued a proclamation revealing the terms of an agreement for the adjustment of relations between Church and State. It admitted an important step: that religious instruction would be allowed in schools for children whose parents wished it. It was characteristic of the mood of the country that complaints soon appeared in the newspapers that the Catholics were exerting pressure on children, even on atheists, to attend religious instruction.

Newspapers had freedom to criticize and many victims of the previous terrorist regime were rehabilitated. Proper legal procedure was restored to take the place of the former police despotism. Preparations were made for parliamentary elections on the basis of a new electoral law which – according to Gomulka's 1956 October promise – 'will allow the people to elect, not merely to vote'. But this right 'to elect' was very limited. On the voting slip were more candidates than the number of deputies decreed for each constituency – one deputy for 66,000 electors. A voter could cross out the candidates at the top of the list and thus give priority to the remaining candidates. The electoral lists were compiled by commissions of the National Front which was dominated by the Communist Party. It was only to be expected that the Communists should secure a worthwhile majority. Not many Stalinists figured among the candidates. Yet the Government feared that the people would either boycott the elections or would strike out the Communist names to the advantage of the non-Communist candidates. The electoral campaign was so lively that on the eve of the election (on January 19, 1957), Gomulka, still shaken by Chou En Lai's warning of the possibility of Soviet intervention, made a dramatic appeal to the electorate, explaining: 'The call for the deletion of Communist candidates from the voting lists is synonymous not only with the deletion of Socialism from Poland. The deletion of our Party's candidates is synonymous with the deletion of independence of our country. It is synonymous with the deletion of Poland from the map of Europe.' Gomulka's dramatic words betrayed the desperate anxiety of a man who realized that Polish Communism could be saved only by Polish patriotism. He depended on the Poles, the majority of whom are anti-Communist, to give priority to 'national Communism' over the hated Soviet domination.

The Polish hierarchy urged the people to vote. Bishop Choromandski, Episcopal Secretary, declared: 'Catholic citizens will have fulfilled their obligations of conscience by voting.' A Communist regime was saved in the election of January 20,

1957, as the lesser evil, by Polish patriotism, by the Polish Church and by the popularity of Gomulka, who appeared to many Poles as a patriot rather than a Communist. Voting was heavy. The leading candidates on the lists were elected in 111 districts out of 116. Yet, as well as responding to Gomulka's appeal, the electors displayed their leanings. Candidates known to be followers of the Stalin line received far fewer votes than the others. With the exception of Gomulka and General Spychalski (who took Rokossovski's place), the other Communist leaders (among them Premier Cyrankiewicz) did not receive such a high percentage of votes as the non-party candidates. But Eligiusz Lasota, editor of *Poprostu*, the militant paper of the liberal intellectuals, gained 98·43 per cent more votes than others who preceded him on the voting slip. These eloquent expressions of opinion did not alter the electoral result. The Communists were assured of a decisive position in Parliament. Two hundred and thirty-seven Communists were elected (51·7 per cent as against 65·4 per cent in the previous Parliament); 119 members of the United Peasant Party (26 per cent as against a previous 20·7 per cent); 39 members of the Democratic Party (8·5 per cent as against a previous 6·1 per cent); 67 non-Party, including 12 Catholic deputies (13·8 per cent as against a previous 7·8 per cent).

All the members of the Politburo, the Central Committee, the Party Secretariat and the members of the Government were elected deputies. And even though the Communist Party did not gain an electoral success through its own strength, it remained the decisive power in the country. It also remained the force that soon put the brake on democratic progress.

As soon as the new *Sejm* met in February 1957, the Communist leaders resolved to limit and control all tendencies towards liberalism. Cyrankiewicz argued that discipline was a 'necessary and prudent' procedure. 'The process of the changes,' he said, 'should not be too rapid.' He promised that the Government intended to extend the autonomy of local industry, but he definitely rejected proposals for the 'total liquidation of centralized planning'. He limited the effectiveness of the 'workers' democracy' because of the necessity for 'centralized planning', and demanded that the workers' councils should concentrate 'their main efforts on the internal affairs of the enterprise and the struggle for bigger, better and cheaper output'.

This meant that the workers were to remain subject to the decisions of the Party and Government. Because private trade had quickly begun to increase, Cyrankiewicz emphasized that private trade 'must amplify, help and develop, and not just exemplify a retreat from Socialist trade'. Deputy Kliszko spoke more openly, maintaining that the October resolution of the Central Committee in no way signified 'a turn away from the path of Socialism'. And, claiming that agricultural problems were not only economic, declared: 'We shall fight for the Socialist direction of the changes in the countryside . . . we shall always support the development of collectives.' No doubt about it: the Government had begun 'to turn away from the path of October'.

For the first time since the end of the war, criticism was heard from the opposition in the *Sejm* but, unlike the recent severe criticism in the Press, these voices were on the whole rather subdued. And considerable dissatisfaction was felt because the Natolinists, especially their militant leader Zenon Nowak, remained members of the old-new Government. Gomulka maintained that it was necessary to collaborate with them in the interest of the Party's unity and so the *Sejm*, with the exception of one solitary deputy, approved Cyrankiewicz's Government without any changes. When, a few months later, the radical 'liberalizing' editor of the *Trybuna Ludu* was replaced by a journalist who was in charge during the Stalinist period of persecution, it became evident that Gomulka was turning against the 'revisionists' with whose help he had come to power. Trends towards liberalization were increasingly played down by the Government. 'The first and chief reason,' claimed the *Trybuna Ludu* on April 1, 'for setting certain definite limits to democratic liberties is that both internationally and domestically, *bourgeoisie* forces are working . . . for a return to capitalism. . . . The dictatorship of the proletariat cannot grant democratic freedoms to the *bourgeoisie* and its organizations.' Yet by rejecting the 'revisionists', Gomulka did not pacify the opposition of the 'dogmatics', as the Stalinists of the Natolin group came to be known. On the contrary, they attempted by all means at their disposal to make the consolidation of Gomulka's regime impossible, accusing him of either having betrayed Communism or having been the cause of the economic difficulties which they themselves had created. They did not hesitate to foster anti-Semitic feelings, though originally these had been revived by their opponents because a few Jews such as Berman and Minc had played a leading part in the Stalinist regime. The Natolinists hoped that, should the Poles show their anti-Soviet feelings by rioting, a pretext might be found for Soviet intervention, which would put them back in power. In the end the Government was obliged to take energetic steps to prevent anti-Semitic excesses.

Gomulka was in a precarious position – not only for political reasons but also because he found himself unable rapidly to improve the economic and social situation. When blaming the policies of his Stalinist predecessors for the catastrophic state in which he found Poland's national economy, he also had the courage to declare publicly that it would take some time before wages and salaries could be raised to a satisfactory level.

Stefan Kurowski, the Polish economist, was ruthlessly critical of the Stalinist economy in the *Zycie Gospodarcze* of November 26, 1956. Coming from a Communist, these were hard words: 'The system of economic priorities of the Stalinist era became a theoretical foundation for the trend towards the militarization of the economy, and a kind of permanent militarization and economic militarization became the highest order and the final foundation of this system of priorities. . . . The rapid development of these privileged branches of the economy was achieved at tremendous costs, which found their expression in flagrant economic disproportions and in the low standard of living of the people.'

His advice was: 'Give priority to housing, Communist services and agriculture.' He also urged that 'outside aid' should be sought. Polish economists then believed that help could be expected from the United States and from other Western countries. The difficulties of raising coal production made the need for such aid all the more important. In the years of Communist oppression coal production had been kept reasonably high only by exceptionally harsh measures – such as Sunday work, very long working hours and by employing prisoners. A drop in coal exports was forecast for 1957, and Cyrankiewicz had pointed out in Parliament: 'The reduction in coal exports is not compensated for by the increased price we are receiving for this commodity.'

Gomulka did not even try to conceal that the critical situation in the country was being aggravated by inflationary trends. Striking for higher wages would be of no avail, he said, and added: 'A further increase in the wage fund in present conditions is impossible.' The economic plan put before the *Sejm* in March 1957 was more realistic than any previous plan: industrial production was to be raised by only 4 per cent (as against 9·9 per cent in 1956); agricultural production by a mere 3·4 per cent (compared with 6·3 per cent in 1956). An economic delegation was sent to Washington to ask for £70,000,000 of surplus farm commodities, especially wheat and cotton, to be bought for Polish zlotys, and a loan of £35,000,000 from the Export-Import Bank, with which to buy American machinery. In Washington the administration was not averse to giving such help, but Congressmen thought it unwise to subsidize a Communist Government closely allied with Moscow. Others, however, believed it advisable to succour Poland 'in its march towards independence'. Everywhere the question was considered one of outstanding political importance. Would not help of this kind profit the Communist regime rather than the people oppressed by that regime? Would not the West be easing the task of the Russians who would otherwise be forced to help a Communist administration that was in difficulties? Would not American dollars be used to consolidate the position of an otherwise shaky Communist regime, and thus strengthen the entire Soviet bloc? Western aid would undoubtedly help to improve the position of Gomulka's Government. It would also alleviate the suffering of the common people. But if it were to raise the Polish standard of living, would they, prompted by Western aid, demand further concessions from the Communist Government? Would their resistance to Soviet pressure increase in proportion? During the controversy in the Polish Council of National Unity in London, the Polish émigrés (under General Anders and Ambassador Raczynski) decided that aid ought to be granted. The chairman of the Executive Committee, Adam Ciolkosz, wrote at the time: 'Gomulka or no Gomulka, help should be given without hesitation and without delay, otherwise Moscow's attempt to put back the hands on the Polish clock would be facilitated.'

Another leader, the Polish exile Mikolajczyk, was much more reserved. He said that Gomulka was a staunch Communist who would not break his allegiance to Moscow. Even when it was granted, American aid was not enough to free Warsaw from the need to seek further help in Moscow. Poland will always need Russian cotton, corn, iron ore from Krivoi Rog, and other raw materials. Much more than £100,000,000 would be required to lessen Poland's dependence on Russia. Yet by appealing to Washington, Warsaw's Communist Government revealed that the Russians had only limited resources to contribute towards the prevention of an economic crisis which they had largely caused themselves by ruthless exploitation of Poland's raw materials; and by ill-advised and precipitous industrialization and collectivization. It was ironic that ten years after Poland was forced by Stalin to reject the benefits of the Marshall Plan, she was forced to seek help from the country that had produced this scheme for helping war-torn countries. Small wonder that Khrushchev should warn the Poles that they were now being 'wooed as a bride' by the United States, although only because the Americans hoped to 'find a lever to use against Socialism, against the Soviet Union'.

It was in the same speech at a Polish Embassy reception in Moscow in honour of the return of Cyrankiewicz from a tour of Asian countries, that Khrushchev warned the West: 'Don't try to test us as you did in Hungary. . . . You think of doing it . . . as in East Germany. Be careful. We are not saints and if necessary we can rap your knuckles.' At the same time, too, Khrushchev reminded Poland that it had no better friend than the Soviet Union. At least Russia was determined to defend the Oder-Neisse frontier. Having declared that the 'difficulties of the last few years are a matter of the past', he assured his audience: 'I believe in Gomulka because he is a Communist.' Yet according to the reports of many Western journalists, Khrushchev, on his sudden arrival in Warsaw in October 1956, angrily described Gomulka as 'a traitor to Socialism'.

But at the time of the Cyrankiewicz reception, the Russians were eager to improve relations with Gomulka's regime. They must have decided that, at least for a time, it would be advantageous to tolerate Gomulka, especially as he was gradually diverting the trend towards liberalization and proving his loyalty to Russia and other Communist countries. He still wisely refused to allow Russian interference in Polish internal affairs and Soviet newspapers continued to reproach the Poles for their 'national Communism' and 'revisionism', incompatible with the Moscow conception of Communism. Though time gradually softened the tone of these critics, distrust of Gomulka's policy flourished even after Khrushchev himself had done his best to establish confidence in him.

LIMITS OF 'POLITICAL REALISM'

Gomulka tried to overcome political and economic difficulties by taking a 'middle course'. He gradually exhausted the enthusiasm of those who wished Poland to be rid of Moscow's tyranny, and he also tried to restrain the opposition of the

Stalinite 'Natolinists'. Mainly, though, he tended to give way to the Stalinists at the expense of the more democratically minded Poles. He was at least successful at a meeting of the Central Committee of the Party in preventing the Stalinite 'dogmatists' from widening their influence. One reason for the violent attacks of the 'Natolinists' on his more liberal policy was that an overwhelming majority of the members of the Central Committee had decided to support his reconstruction programmes. The leaders of the Stalinites, Zenon Nowak and Klosiewicz, remained in the Government but they were unable to penetrate into the Politburo. Jacob Berman was expelled from the Party for three years. This was mild punishment for the leader of the Stalinite tyranny, but it showed that Gomulka was wavering lest he should arouse the anger of the Russians by being too touchy with their cherished 'Natolinists'.

When the Stalinites insisted that the Polish Party should recognize 'the Soviet leadership in building Socialism', and condemn 'the counter-revolution in Hungary', Gomulka said: 'Internationalism, yes; servility, no.' Gomulka thus proved himself an adept at keeping at bay the opposing forces with which he was surrounded. It was left to Ochab, who had already astonished Khrushchev with his courageous behaviour, to say bluntly to the Stalinists: 'We have had enough speeches written with imported ink. . . . We do not want foreign patterns and lectures. . . . Some people ask that the phrase "with the Soviet Union at the head" should always be used. This is not always a just principle. In some instances, when this has been unjustly used, it has cost us a great deal.'

Ochab and Gomulka, in defending their 'Polish way to Socialism', claimed, according to some reports, the approval of the Chinese Communists of their handling of the 'Muscovites' who were demanding subordination to Moscow. This allegedly aroused fresh anger among the Soviet leaders and Gomulka had to hasten to Moscow to reassure them of his good intentions. During his visit there, a resolution was accepted mentioning Russia as 'the first state of the dictatorship of the proletariat', and adding that it was the 'mechanical imitation' of Soviet practice during Stalin's reign that caused the 'ossification of Marxist thought'. Gomulka was forced to condemn Poland's 'liberalizing trend' and stressed the necessity of preserving the unity, discipline and leadership of the Communist Party.

It was significant that he again asked that workers' councils should be subordinated to the Party's organizations in the factories and that the country people who had disbanded most of the collective farms should be won over to other forms of co-operation – but without pressure.

Later, Warsaw's Central Committee confirmed Gomulka's conception of the 'Polish road to Socialism', but hastened, in the same breath, to reassure the Soviets with a remarkable appendix: 'The attitude of the Party has not and cannot have anything in common with the so-called national Communism which is an invention of imperialist propaganda, designed to sow discord among Socialist countries.'

The May decisions of the Central Committee of the Polish Communist Party retreated from the aspirations of the October revolution. Hopes that had flourished when the people showed their hatred of Moscow, remained unfulfilled. Red Army units remained to remind the Poznan rebels that their demands for freedom, even though supported by the whole nation, were being ignored. The grip in which Moscow held Warsaw was all too tight. The Poles prayed (and fought) for far greater independence. Gomulka's Poland definitely had more political and cultural freedom than Tito's Yugoslavia, but the dictatorship of the Communist Party remained, even if the methods it employed were more moderate than in other Communist countries.

Gomulka's regime was afraid of their workers becoming self-governing. Other Communist regimes suffered the same fear. Gomulka and his Cabinet colleagues obviously regretted the failure of the collective farms, and only the pressure of economic need forced them to permit, in restricted form, the restoration of small trades and handicrafts. Everything possible was done to prevent encouraging 'capitalist' elements in the national economy. To expect a different course from a regime that remained Communist would be foolish.

It is idle to discuss whether 'Gomulkism' is a 'national Communism'. Gomulka would have welcomed the widest possible autonomy for his country. Obviously he hoped to extend the economic co-operation of Poland and the West in order to solve, in the shortest possible time, his own economic problems. He did not hesitate to resist direct Soviet intervention, yet was anxious not to provoke the open enmity of Moscow, and as a sincere Communist he was convinced that Poland's place was in the Communist camp or, more precisely, that his special 'Polish brand of Communism' could not survive if he broke away from the Communist community. After the Hungarian revolution, even Tito was wary of breaking all links with the other Communist countries. Yet Tito was geographically out of reach of direct Russian intervention.

'Gomulkism', as far as it meant 'national Communism', depended on the good will of Moscow. Though Gomulka counted on the support of China (whose influence in the Communist camp was greatly enhanced by the October revolution), Mao Tse-Tung could protect him from Soviet interference only as long as Warsaw remained Communist and did not deviate basically from 'Leninist principles'. For this reason, Gomulka and his colleagues were determined to oppose every move that might appear to be directed against Lenin's programme for the dictatorship of the proletariat.

The Polish Party Secretary, Roman Zambrowski, arguing with the 'revisionists' and especially with the young intellectuals' paper, *Poprostu*, condemned the propaganda of 'integral democracy, freedom for everybody and the free play of all political forces'. In a speech published in *Zycie Partii*, Warsaw, March 1957,[1] he added: '. . . individual voices stating that our Party has compromised itself and that only the Polish *raison*

[1] Quoted in *East Europe*, New York, May 1957.

d'état and Poland's geographical position prevent us from proposing a dissolution of the Party, are glaring manifestations of alien, revisionist views.'

Gomulka's regime remained faithful to Communism, not only of necessity but also because of their own sincere convictions. Even if they wished to remedy the blatant errors and crimes of the previous Stalinite era, they wished even more to retain a dictatorship for their Party and to cling to all the main principles of Communism. Even so, the Poznan revolt that brought Gomulka to power was at least successful in freeing Poland from direct Russian tyranny. For many years the Russians had been treating the country as though it were a helpless colony to be mercilessly exploited. The revolution left the Poles worse off materially than before, but better off in civil and individual liberty than the people of any other Communist country. But that was as far as it went, or was likely to go as long as Communists dominated the Government.

A democratic administration, freely elected, may have been the dream of the majority of the workers and the peasants and the liberally minded Communist intellectuals too, but they all realized eventually that there is no Socialism in a land where 'a state wants all its citizens to have the same opinions in philosophy, foreign policy, economics, literature and ethics'; where 'a state does not mind being hated so long as it is feared'; where there is 'a system of government towards which most of the governed are hostile'; and where 'the workers have no influence on the Government'. . . .

This pithy summing-up of a Communist administration appeared in an article by the young philosopher, L. Kolakowski.[1] Attempts to have the article published in the newspaper *Poprostu* failed, so students posted it on their bulletin board in Warsaw University.

Gomulka's position became embarrassing. Not even a Communist could be happy about the tight-rope walking that became inevitable if he was to remain in power. The loyalty of

[1] Quoted in *The New Leader*, New York, February 18, 1957.

his devoted followers had to be risked. It was a calculated risk. He took it and lost. His fight against 'revisionism' was intended on the one hand to repulse the attacks of the Stalinite 'Natolinists'; on the other, to alleviate the suspicions of Moscow. It was too much for him. Gomulka finally became estranged, not only from the liberally minded section of the Communists but also from the majority of the Poles who had clearly and bravely shown their hatred of Soviet domination and Communism itself.

It was significant that the Catholic deputies of the new *Sejm*, collecting in a group under the name of *Znak* (The Banner), expressed the wishes of the Poles when they said that, according to their hopes, Gomulka represented the symbol of the true 'Polish political road' and not 'the Polish road to Socialism (i.e. Communism)'.[1]

During these months of crisis, the Poles proved their political maturity by exercising a remarkable reserve that was a complete contrast to their traditionally militant and hazardous romanticism. This new political realism was brought about to a great extent by the social changes of the post-war years in Polish society. Representatives of the working classes and intelligentsia had taken the place of the former militant and romantic *szlachta* (gentry). The Poles had realism forced on them. They learned in a tragic manner. Polish blood was shed in vain and Polish hopes that the West would give them effective and practical help in their fight against the Russians were dashed. Doubts about the possibilities of resolute Western action had increased when the Western Powers merely made disapproving sounds while the Red Army massacred the Hungarian rebels.

Lastly, but not least, the new realism came from the realization that the Oder-Neisse frontier would exist only as long as it suited Russia to keep it in existence. Every Pole fears the possibility of another Russo-German *rapprochement*. For clearly, Poland would again be the victim, just as she was when

[1] Quoted in *Polish Affairs*, London, April 1957.

she was decimated in the eighteenth century and later in 1939. All this explained why even the Catholic deputies proclaimed that the alliance with Soviet Russia was 'in the present situation an irrevocable condition of national existence'. Nationalism became the fundamental cause of Polish realism, a realism that astonished the world. And it was nationalism above all which persuaded the majority of Poles at home and in exile to tolerate Gomulka's regime, even when he showed he was abandoning the promises made to the Poznan rebels.

The new realism of the Polish Nationalists is limited. It is not appreciated by the whole nation. The traditional desires of the Nationalists are resilient and stubborn. They are not easily dismissed. Anger against Russia will always linger in Poland. Gomulka must continue to try to appease the undying love of a democratic way of life if he is to prevent reaching the point of another explosion. His sound reasons for the alliance with Soviet Russia may still act as a powerful brake, but even this brake may fail if the shadow of tyranny does not diminish and the economic situation does not improve. Another revolutionary outburst in Poland is still possible. And in Moscow, with its traditional dislike of Warsaw, there would be the strongest temptation to intervene, even more brutally than in Hungary.

CHAPTER VI

The Hungarian Revolution

THE INTELLECTUAL PIONEERS OF FREEDOM

Had the Red Army not intervened at the very beginning of the
demonstrations in Budapest in the last days of October 1956,
some kind of 'Gomulkism' might, quite conceivably, have also
been established in Hungary. Until that time at least, events in
Hungary, a satellite that – since the Poznan rising – was considerably influenced by Poland, were not dissimilar to the
pattern of political evolution in Poland.

Brutal Soviet intervention was only one reason why the
revolution spread like fire throughout Hungary. As early as
1955, the regime in Poland was making reluctant concessions
to the ever-increasing pressure of the liberals. These concessions became more frequent in Poland after Khrushchev's
attack on Stalin, but Rakosi continued to impose his harsh rule
in Hungary. His Stalinist line was made all the more unbearable
because the Hungarians – unlike other enslaved nations – had
enjoyed, from the middle of 1953 to the beginning of 1955,
certain advantages from the 'softer' policies introduced by
Imre Nagy. Rakosi came to be loathed more and more,
especially by Communist intellectuals and students. Finally,
the Hungarian intelligentsia, Communist and non-Communist,
became the chief advocates of a return to democracy. Spurred
on by their consuming desire for freedom from tyranny, they
prepared the way for revolt. While Rakosi became more cruelly
inflexible, they grew proportionally more radical.

After the dethronement of Stalin, the only course left to this
intractable Stalinist was to appear to conform to the new policy
line. Rakosi began to learn that lip-service was not enough
when Moscow rehabilitated the notorious Bela Kun, on its own

responsibility. He had formed a Communist Government in Hungary in 1919 (it was the only one outside Russia to last for several months), but he was a victim of one of Stalin's purges in the thirties, and was at this time living in exile in Russia.

With obvious reluctance, Rakosi was then forced to rehabilitate Rajk and those of his comrades who had been either executed or sentenced to life imprisonment in 1949. To prove, too, that he was not defying Moscow, he ordered that 'anti-Stalinist' or 'Titoist' Communists – including Janos Kadar – and a few Social Democrats, should be released from gaol. Among these were Miss Anna Kethly and Gyorgy Marosan who, as a member of Kadar's Government, eventually distinguished himself by his brutal severity. Freedom was ultimately granted to all Hungarian Social Democrats (and to some from other enslaved countries), whose continued confinement was denounced by members of the Labour Party during a dinner given to Khrushchev on his visit to London. Rakosi, still under pressure, also freed some members of other Hungarian political parties, notably Bela Kovacs, the extremely popular leader of the Smallholders' Party, who had spent ten years in Soviet gaols. Though Archbishop Groesz was amnestied in May 1956, Cardinal Mindszenty was not released.

These half-hearted concessions, granted by Rakosi's government with extreme unwillingness, aimed at appeasing the people, but they merely provoked more discontent. The Government started to weaken and its members grew more and more embarrassed by the changing political climate of Communism. Writers and students made dramatic use of the official programme of 'deStalinization' to discuss and emphasize their increasingly radical demands. The 'Petofi Circle', founded by Communist students in the spring of 1956, became, with the help of the Writers' Union, a rallying point for the new, unofficial opposition to the Government. It was symptomatic that young intellectuals should wish to continue in the tradition of Alexander Petofi, the poet who was a hero of the national-liberal revolution led by Lajos Kossuth in 1848. This 1848 revolution, a Hungarian struggle against Habsburg absolutism that was then supported by Russia's autocratic Czar Nicholas I, became a source of infinite inspiration to the Hungarian revolutionaries of 1956. The importance of national tradition as an ineradicable force in every nation was proved once more.

When, under the new policy of the Kremlin, it became safe to criticize not only Stalin but also the 'personality cult' too, the whole Rakosi regime was bitterly attacked. Students, under the leadership of such nonconformist writers as Tibor Déri, Gyula Háy and Tibor Tardos, demanded that the teaching of Russian should no longer be compulsory, that Marxist indoctrination classes should be reduced, that academic freedom should be granted to universities, that Hungarians should be free to meet the people of the Western Powers, that non-Communists should be allowed to arrange meetings and to take part in political life. They also wanted speakers and writers to be free from censorship.

All these coincided with the demands being made by Czech students and Polish intellectuals. Rakosi's government merely added to the venom of the 'Petofi Circle' by temporarily forbidding their meetings. The Communist writer, Gyula Háy, then opened a 'truth campaign' in *Irodalmi Ujság*, a writers' journal which, because of the way it criticized the Government, attained an unusually high circulation. 'We know', he wrote, 'the terrifying consequences of all forms of the personality cult, the wrong and harmful resolutions passed without opposition, the thoughtless servility, the establishment of smaller or larger associations of yes-men, the persecution of criticism, the whitewashing of liars, the crushing of human rights and law. . . . The time has come for us to convert to the truth, the overall, unconditional, profound truth which serves the people and the Party.'

Such implied criticism of the Hungarian Government was encouraged when the Poles of Poznan staged their riots. During the summer of 1956, students, professors and writers urgently demanded, at a succession of meetings, that Rakosi should resign and Imre Nagy be allowed to resume his political activities. The advocates of freedom scored their first, if limited, success, when Rakosi offered his resignation as the First Secretary of the Party, admitting at the same time that he had committed 'grave errors'.

The Russian leaders realized then that they could no longer support Rakosi, and Tito made up their minds for them. During successful negotiations to establish a fresh basis for collaboration between Russia and Yugoslavia, he insisted on the 'removal' of the 'Stalinist' who, foremost among the satellite Communists, had been most relentless in the struggle against him. But the flame of revolution was kindled when Rakosi was replaced by his closest friend, Erno Gero, an equally brutal and hated 'Muscovite'. Tito, speaking on the Hungarian revolution at Pula on November 11, 1956, said: 'The Soviet leaders . . . committed a mistake by not also allowing the removal of Gero and other Rakosi followers.'

Tito felt it necessary at the same time to explain why he had made agreements with Gero when the Hungarian leaders visited Belgrade immediately before the outbreak of the revolution. 'When we were in the Crimea,' he said, 'Gero happened to be there and we happened to meet. . . . We wanted to show that we were not vindictive. . . . But things had already gone too far. . . . Gero's visit to Yugoslavia and our joint declaration would no longer help.' Tito was merely confirming the adage about those in power seldom understanding the necessity of timely concessions. He was equally clumsy. By imprisoning Djilas, the Yugoslav dictator showed himself to be as inflexible in the exercising of power as those whom he wanted to teach a lesson.

Gero was incapable of stemming the tide of discontent that was threatening to engulf Hungary. The concessions he granted, reluctantly and under pressure, were too few, too poor and too late. It was not enough to appoint new members of the Politburo, Kadar among them. The articulate Hungarians demanded that Imre Nagy should be returned to power. Slight wage increases and fresh help for farmers were inadequate gestures. The Government obviously wanted agricultural collectivization, considerably accelerated during the previous months, to go on. Hungarian leaders were not even enthusiastic about the negligible modifications that they were forced to make in their Second Five Year Plan, which had been drafted according to the old directives.

In these circumstances, the Hungarian opposition quickly gained strength. Even before Rakosi's fall, Gyorgy Lukacs, the eminent Marxist theoretician, had admitted that Marxism 'had never fared worse' than at that time. 'In the Horthy era,' he said, 'people, if only a small group, risked their lives to obtain works by Marx or Lenin. . . . The past seven or eight years have been such that this attitude was destroyed.' Marxism no longer appealed to the people. It seemed decadent. Even Communist intellectuals were turning away from it, mostly without realizing why they had lost faith. Local writers were attacking Gero's regime with growing sharpness, and their clamour for greater civic liberty grew louder. Gyula Háy wrote in *Irodalmi Ujság* on September 8: 'The writer must not be permitted . . . to incite to murder, to arson, to robbery and larceny, to the overthrow of the People's Democracy. . . . On the other hand, the writer, like everyone else, must have unlimited freedom to tell the truth, to criticize anyone or anything . . . to believe in Almighty God and to deny God . . . to think in a non-Marxist way . . . to find unjust something that is still considered officially as just.'

Such 'unlimited freedom' was incompatible, not only with practical policy but also with Communist doctrine itself. In fact, the nonconformist Communists who were advocating the introduction of the principles of a liberal democracy, were undermining the autocratic one-party rule that is the foundation of a Communist state.

The spirit of revolt revealed itself most clearly at the congress of the Writers' Union in the middle of September 1956. A secret vote for the new Presidium rejected all those who had even passively supported Rakosi's regime, but Communist rebels and even non-Communist writers were elected and speaker after speaker sharply criticized the 'regime of tyranny', declared that 'the central issue was literary freedom which is inseparable from the people's freedom', and demanded the rehabilitation of Imre Nagy. The writers were asked dramatically to 'form a defensive and offensive alliance to tell the truth'. In sincere self-criticism it was admitted by Háy that Communist writers, 'having submitted to the spiritual leadership of the Party Secretariat, let themselves be led astray on to the path of mendacity'. 'The best of us', he continued, 'suffered horribly in this atmosphere of lying . . . and paid dearly for the lie . . . with the lowering of the standard of our work. . . .'

The poet Konya cried out: 'The traditional imperatives of literature, its very nature and honour, the interests of the people, social and political progress, make it incumbent on the writer to speak the truth and nothing but the truth.' And this insurgent Communist asked poignantly: 'In the name of what morality do the Communists consider themselves justified in committing arbitrary acts against their former allies, in staging witch trials, in persecuting innocent people, in treating genuine revolutionaries as if they were traitors, in gaoling and killing them? In the name of what morality? Certainly not in the name of a revolutionary movement.'

Thus these Hungarian intellectuals revealed their agony of mind. They were taking part in a moral insurrection against violence, untruth and hypocrisy. Their ardent desire for truth (and the courage to speak the truth) was one of the deepest sources of the Hungarian Revolution. Something approaching mysticism lay in this exhilarating zeal for truth. The speeches and the writings of the Hungarian intellectuals and young students show that they conceived 'truth' as a 'categorical imperative' that should govern the life of an individual and the whole of society. In this they came near to the views of the old Russian revolutionary intelligentsia who identified the concept of 'truth' with that of 'justice'. It will always be the glory of the intellectual élite to have infused the Hungarian national revolution with moral pathos.

The writers' congress increased the tension. The Government, eager to win sympathy and avoid trouble, organized a state funeral for Laszlo Rajk and three of his comrades who, it was admitted, 'were innocently condemned and executed'. It was a cruel farce that the same people who had agreed to the executions (stage-managed by Rakosi) now pretended to be indignant that Rajk should have been 'slandered'. They deceived no one. About 200,000 people attended the funeral and gave all their sympathetic attention to Rajk's recently released widow. They obviously rejoiced when they saw Imre Nagy emerge from the crowd and embrace this courageous woman. Gero could no longer resist the pressure and Nagy was re-admitted to the Party, though not to its leading ranks.

The opposition movement, led by the intellectuals, inspired the workers to raise their demands. The trade union council, though still under the control of the Party, demanded a broadening of 'trade union democracy', the establishment of 'workers' control' and a 'prominent part for the unions in solving production and management problems'. The plant manager could retain his 'full right' to make decisions, but in questions concerning wages and workers' welfare he should consult a union committee.

The workers themselves, asking even more than this, considered their union demands to be very moderate. They wished to press for genuine 'workers' self-government' in the factories. Eventually the Government's agricultural policy was criticized. The whole pattern of events was gradually preparing the country for the psychological moment at which there would be a radical change of regime. As soon as it became known that Gomulka had thwarted the Russian leaders in their efforts to preserve the existing Polish regime under the control of Rokossovski, the Petofi Circle in Budapest began calling for the restoration of Imre Nagy, the expulsion of Rakosi from the Communist Party and the public trial of General Mahily

Farkas, who had been arrested on charges of brutal persecution. They also demanded 'equality' in Hungary's relations with the Soviet Union and the publication of all commercial agreements with Moscow, including the trade pact that enabled the Russians to exploit the rich deposits of uranium, found a few months previously at Pecs.

At the same time the Hungarian Government was asked to pass the administration of the factories over to the workers, and to revise the Second Five Year Plan. The Petofi Circle finally announced that it would organize a mass demonstration on October 23 to express the deep sympathy and solidarity of Hungarian youth with events in Poland. Nobody expected this demonstration to end in a bloody rising. The Hungarian revolution was not premeditated. It did not even follow a plan. It sprang from a spontaneous uprising of a people, provoked by the intellectuals, to protest against the conditions under which they were existing. Finally, it should be realized that conflict started, not at the planned instigation of the demonstrators but because of the violent reactions of a panicky government.

A ban on student demonstrations was withdrawn when the rest of the people began to show their displeasure at such a prohibition. But it was too late to stop thousands of people assembling at the Petofi statue and marching to the statue of General Bem, a Polish patriot who fought with the Hungarians during the 'umbrella revolution' in 1848. Peter Veres, the Hungarian writer, read to the multitude assembled round General Bem a list of 'demands' which, even though radical, did not, on the whole, surpass those accepted by Khrushchev in Warsaw. The Hungarian resolution merely asked for 'an independent national policy based on the principles of Socialism'; 'equality in relations with the U.S.S.R. and the People's Democracies'; 'a revision of economic agreements in the spirit of the equality of national rights' (in other words, an end to Russian exploitation of Hungary); the management of factories by workers and specialists; the right of peasants 'freely to decide

their own fate'; the removal of Rakosi's clique and the appointment to the Government of Imre Nagy, who was described as
'a pure and brave Communist enjoying the confidence of the
Hungarian people'. The resolution also advocated a 'resolute
stand . . . against all counter-revolutionary attempts and
aspirations', and 'a free and secret ballot in the elections to
Parliament and to all autonomous organs of administration'.

NATIONAL UPRISING

Having expressed their enthusiatic agreement with the resolution, the demonstrators began to disperse. But most of them,
without any special reason or appeal, started to march towards
Parliament. Soon, more than 100,000 people were waiting hope-
fully for the announcement that Imre Nagy had been appointed
Prime Minister. Instead, they heard Gero, returning only that
day from Belgrade, deliver a provocative speech over the
wireless, condemning the student demonstrations as nationalistic and chauvinistic and stressing that the Government
would defend the achievements of the People's Democracy
from whatever quarters they might be threatened. He complained that any suggestion that the Russians were not respect-
ing the equality of Hungary (or were exploiting trade with
Hungary for their own benefit) was a 'barefaced lie, a hostile
slander without a grain of truth'.

People were shocked by the insolence of Gero's speech.
His intransigent attitude and his arrogant lies made them
angry. Russian exploitation of Hungary was obvious to everyone. Some of the crowd suggested marching to the Radio
Building to insist on a wireless programme being devoted to
their demands for a new Government policy. While the
majority moved towards the Radio Building, several thousands
of demonstrators went to the city park where, cheering as they
marched, they pulled down an enormous statue of Stalin. In
an hour it was broken to pieces.

The municipal police so far watched with passive forebear-
ance. But the Radio Building was guarded by detachments of

the Secret Security Police (the notorious AVO), who attacked the demonstrators as soon as they tried to enter the building. The first shots, fired by the Secret Police, acted as the signal that released the temper of the rebels. Demonstrators obtained weapons from the police and soldiers. Workers brought further weapons from the factories. Gero aggravated the situation by repeating his provocative (and untrue) assertion on the wireless that 'the Fascist, reactionary elements had launched an armed attack on public buildings and on armed security units'. His ban on all meetings and marches was simply ignored. It might even have been possible to prevent the Budapest riots from developing into a general rising, had Gero resigned and Nagy been placed at the head of the Government. But by his behaviour Gero provoked an explosion. Although eventually he made a concession asking Imre Nagy to become Prime Minister on October 23, he obviously intended to remain First Secretary of the Party.

At the same time, without the knowledge of Nagy, he made an arrangement with the local Red Army Commander, General Thikonov, that his soldiers would help to suppress the riots in Budapest. George Mikes, in his excellently documented book, *The Hungarian Revolution*, says Gero did not go directly to Moscow but only to General Thikonov. It is not known whether Thikonov subsequently acted on his own without first obtaining the consent of Moscow. Anyway, Gero was only too sure that as soon as the first Red Army tanks appeared, all rioting would end. Everybody would be too frightened to go on fighting. Who would have expected the Hungarian people to rush into an unequal fight against tremendous Soviet superiority? But there are situations that cannot be assessed by realists, thinking coldly only in terms of power. Hungarians had been living for years in a state of latent revolt. A full realization of their dissatisfactions and their hopes had been brought about by the critical speeches of the intellectuals. A single spark was enough to start their blaze of rebellion. And a brief Government announcement broadcast at 8 a.m. on

October 24, 1956, formed such an incendiary spark. It said:
'The Government was unprepared for the bloody, dastardly
attack by counter-revolutionary gangs, and applied for help,
in accordance with the terms of the Warsaw Treaty, to the
Soviet formations stationed in Hungary. The Soviet formations, in compliance with the Government's request, are taking
part in the restoration of order.' At the same time a state of
emergency was proclaimed.

At first the Hungarians were confused. Imre Nagy became
head of the Government, but Andres Hegedus, a willing
stooge of Rakosi and Gero (and who, until the previous day,
had been Prime Minister), became First Deputy Chairman.
Gero's position as First Secretary of the Party was, according
to an official communiqué, strengthened by the Central Committee. And it was obvious from this that Rakosi's clique was
intent on maintaining its hold on the country.

The announcement that the Government itself had asked the
Red Army for help could at the time only be interpreted to
mean that it was Nagy who had made the request. The people
felt they had been shamefully betrayed by him. It was not until
some days later that they learned Gero had contrived to
obtain Red Army help without Nagy knowing. Gero's machinations caused Nagy to lose the people's confidence and for
this reason his pathetic appeals that the fighting should stop
had no effect. At this time Nagy had no influence, even on his
followers.

George Mikes quotes in *The Hungarian Revolution* a report
from a dependable witness (whose identity is concealed to
prevent exposing him to Communist persecution) saying that
at dawn on Wednesday, October 24, Suslov and Mikoyan
appeared unexpectedly in Budapest. Mikoyan blamed Gero for
all that had happened and reproached him especially for calling
on Russian troops. Mikoyan was equally angry with General
Thikonov. Gero was relieved of his post and packed off to
Russia, and the job of First Secretary to the Party was entrusted
to Janos Kadar, who was trusted by the Russians as a

dependable Communist. This seemed at the time to be an excellent choice because Kadar had been one of Rakosi's victims.

Nagy wanted to tell the people that it was Gero who had called in the Russians but Mikoyan 'advised' him to refrain from making such a revelation. He reminded Nagy that order would easily be restored by Russian tanks. Once order had been restored, Mikoyan continued, the Russians would leave the country, provided certain conditions were fulfilled. Mikoyan and Suslov then left for Moscow, believing that the rebels would soon be brought to heel. Nagy was in the end prevented from telling the Hungarians about Gero's request for Red Army help by two Russian officers, members of a counter-espionage unit, who threatened him with revolvers. 'While he was making his first broadcast, the two Russians stood behind him, their hands deep in their pockets,' it was reported. In the Western comments on Mr Nagy's first broadcast, it was generally remarked that he seemed to be 'speaking under great stress and with deep emotion'.

The information given by Mr Mikes is probably true. Mikoyan obviously realized that the Russian intervention was a mistake but was himself wrong in believing that Red Army tanks could stop the Hungarians giving vent to their feelings. If he had allowed Nagy to tell the full story, the need for Russian intervention for the second time might have been unnecessary. As it was, Nagy's appeal for an end to the fighting and for the restoration of peace and order (broadcast early on October 24) had no effect. Having lost faith in Nagy, the Hungarians did not believe him when he promised at long last to fulfil the programme he produced in 1953, aimed at 'the systematic democratization of the country'.

Despite the forecasts made by the politicians, the angry Hungarians threw themselves against the Red Army tanks with a courage that has few parallels in history. What the Communist leaders (Hungarian and Russian) least expected, happened. The first civilians to resist Soviet tanks were workers.

To the amazement of the Russians, the army of revolutionaries increased hour by hour and they were joined by units of the Hungarian army and police. Only 40,000 men of the Secret Security Police force (AVO) – most of them being either criminals or former members of disbanded Fascist organizations – fought with the Russians against their own people. They fought for their own skins, knowing they were hated for cruelties perpetrated over years of Communist tyranny. They knew that a victorious revolution would only lead to their being liquidated. The revolutionaries dealt with them without mercy.

Intervention by the Red Army abruptly changed a rising against oppressive dictatorship into a national revolution against the tyrannical rule of a hated foreign power. Traditional anti-Russian feelings, kept alive in recent years by enforced and disgusting glorification of the 'Soviet example', exploded with full force. The brutality of the Red Army's intervention recalled a similar episode when Czar Nicholas I sent troops to Hungary to suppress Kossuth's revolution. In the same way a hundred years later, a 'People's Government' in Moscow was despatching military units to stamp out fresh trends towards democracy and cruelly to crush those who questioned Russia's right to exploit another country. That is why even Communist army officers such as General Maleter joined the revolution without hesitation; that is why people of all classes swiftly arraigned themselves in a united fighting front; that is why the Communist Party crumbled into ruins almost overnight.

Within two days the whole country was engulfed in revolution. People everywhere – children and their elders – fought the Red Army with incomparable courage. Russian soldiers were surprised and bewildered. They obeyed their officers without enthusiasm. Young people who had been forced to study Russian explained to them that they were fighting the workers, the common people – not 'Fascists'. Russian soldiers soon realized this for themselves. Many carried out their appalling task only half-heartedly. Some even gave their weapons to the rebels. Hundreds (perhaps thousands) rebelled themselves and joined the fighting Hungarians. The hesitant attitude of the Red Army units enabled the revolutionaries to organize their forces during the first days of the struggle.

It was significant that the Russians started using Red Army units that had not been stationed in Hungary. They drafted Russian soldiers who had not been 'democratized' by contact with Hungarians. It would be idle to draw conclusions only for the behaviour of the Red Army in the October risings, but it would seem that the Russian soldier, capable of exceptional sacrifice in the defence of his own land, is less resolute and dependable when faced with a campaign of expansion in another country.

The Hungarians embarked, in the middle of the fighting, on a programme of radical and political social changes. This was a spontaneous development. There were no governmental directives or any central leadership. One commentator remarked that this reorganization was 'inspired by the practice of the Bolshevik revolution but with the object of fighting against the Bolshevik regime; the result of ten years' Communist indoctrination was a refusal of the dogma while applying some of the method'.

Administrative councils, composed of Communists and non-Communists were formed everywhere to represent the workers, peasants, soldiers, intellectuals and youth. Workers' councils took over the management of the factories. The Government lacked authority and power, so it was local, worker or peasant self-government bodies that in some places organized the fighting against the Red Army and prevented the country from sinking into anarchy. The 'soviets' (or workers' councils) had long lost their significance. They had deteriorated in Russia into useless instruments of centralist autocracy. In Hungary they were born of a spontaneous popular movement, and they soon became the living organs of a rising democracy and the effective instruments of a fighting revolution.

Their most important and remarkable feature was the similarity of their objectives and aims. Though a variety of different programmes had been proclaimed by individual Hungarian 'soviets', they all agreed on the basic demands: political and civil liberty; free and secret elections; free competition among political parties; parliamentary democracy; independent trade unions; the right of workers to run factories; abolition of the compulsory agricultural co-operatives; abolition of the Secret Security Police.

Basically, these were the claims on which the writers and students had agreed before the revolution. They were now more precise – and more radical. Everywhere it was being stressed in different ways: 'This is not a counter-revolution, but the national movement of Hungarian working people. They do not want the manufacturers and the landlords to be restored; the national revolution is not aimed at the restoration of the old regime.'

Similarly, it was being emphasized that Hungary would remain a Socialist democracy. The principle aim of the revolutionaries was a liberal parliamentary democracy based on local and professional self-government, with the preservation of public ownership of industry and voluntary agricultural co-operatives administered solely by the peasants. Individual ownership of land was to exist side by side with these.

This programme and the paramount part played in the revolution by workers and progressive intelligentsia completely refute Russian allegations that the revolt was the work of Fascists and reactionary counter-revolutionaries. Many conservatives and reactionaries did take part in the revolution and if a new democracy had been established they would probably have used their freedom to advocate their ideas. But they did not start the revolution and had no influence on its development.

Cardinal Mindszenty said on the wireless during his temporary spell of freedom: '. . . We do not oppose the justified development of our country . . . we only desire that this development should be sound.' He also stated explicitly: 'We have a classless society and a state where law prevails; we support private ownership which is rightly and justly limited by social interests.' He also stated that 'we want to live in friendship with all the people of Europe'. As well as America he expressly named 'the powerful Russian Empire', and all Hungary's neighbours.

It is possible that the Cardinal did not satisfy everybody and his speech could not, at that time, cause general enthusiasm. But there was nothing reactionary in it. Reports that he had asked for the return of Church property were unfounded. And it must be remembered that Cardinal Mindszenty never excelled in the political realism that was natural to the Polish Cardinal Wyszynski or the Czechoslovakian Archbishop Beran. He is simply a dignitary of the Church, convinced of the superiority of Church over State. Once, when asked by an American journalist whether he would consent to be Prime Minister, Mindszenty proudly replied: 'I have a higher position; I am Prince Primate of Hungary; but of course I shall always be glad to offer guidance to the Prime Ministers.' It is understandable that the brutal tortures to which he was subject while held prisoner by the Communists did not make him any more keen on Marxist principles. Yet he said: 'Personal revenge must be avoided and eliminated.'

The programme for liberty produced by the Hungarians (and formulated with less clarity by the Poles) is undoubtedly shared by other subject nations. The great and lasting achievement of the Hungarian revolution was the production of a clear programme of comprehensive reconstruction, not only for Hungary but also for all the countries of Eastern and Central Europe after their liberation.

Bitter fighting continued in defiance of all official appeals for a cease-fire and a return to normality. Workers went on strike. Peasants willingly supplied the rebels with food. Whole districts were under the control of the revolutionary national councils. The whole army – with small exception – fought against the Red Army. Nagy realized that at any moment a national Government, possibly proclaimed in Gyor in western Hungary, could gain the support of the whole country. Every day it became more and more obvious that the Hungarians were turning against even such liberal Communists as Nagy himself, and that they were determined to fight for the introduction of parliamentary democracy. Nagy feverishly discussed with the political and military representatives of the Kremlin in his efforts to have the Red Army withdrawn. Members of the Hungarian High Command themselves distributed hundreds of thousands of leaflets, asking not only for 'the immediate withdrawal of Soviet troops from our motherland' but also for 'the immediate cancellation of the Warsaw Agreement'.

Possibly Russia's envoys in Hungary advised their masters in Moscow to recall the Red Army. Towards the end of October the Russian units began to leave Budapest's streets. Nagy then announced over the wireless that his reorganized Government would ask for the withdrawal of all Russian troops.

NATIONAL INDEPENDENCE

The departure of the Red Army, emphasized by Nagy's promise, suggested to the Hungarians that their struggle had gained its immediate objective. General rejoicing in Budapest was increased and Nagy's popularity restored when Nagy finally admitted that Gero had asked for Soviet help without his being told. The Hungarians felt they had gained a victory and regained a hero. The adoration of Nagy reached its peak on October 30, when he announced: 'The Cabinet has abolished the one-party system of government and has decided that we should return to a system of government based on the democratic co-operation of the coalition parties as they existed in 1945.'

The members of the new Government were to include three Communists and two representatives of the Smallholders Party – Zoltan Tildy and Bela Kovacs. It was his courageous stand against Fascism and later against Communism that gained Kovacs his high respect as one of Hungary's great democrats. Finally, Anna Kethly, an old Socialist fighter with an impeccable record that earned her great popularity, and Guyla Kelemen also joined Nagy's team.

The appearance of his liberal administration filled everyone with hope. Hungary had embarked on the road to political democracy. As soon as the Russian troops left, the country would at last have real independence. Rejoicing increased when the Kremlin declared, in a formal proclamation, that the relations of Socialist nations could be built 'only on the principle of full equality, respect for territorial integrity, state independence and sovereignty and non-interference in each other's domestic affairs'.

The Russian announcement admitted that 'in establishing new regimes in the People's Democracies there were many difficulties . . . violations and mistakes that infringed upon principles of equality in relations among Socialist states'. Yet it stressed at the same time that the XXth Congress of the Soviet Communist Party in February 1956 – at which the ghost of Stalin was dethroned – 'condemned these violations'. So the Soviet Government proclaimed its readiness to discuss the recalling of Soviet 'advisers' from the People's Democracies and to examine, together with other parties to the Warsaw Pact, the need for keeping Soviet troops stationed in these countries . . . on the basis of an agreement among all the Pact's participants.

The Russian Government claimed that 'the just and progressive movement of the Hungarian working people' was misdirected 'by forces of black reaction and counter-revolution' and that the Soviet troops had acted 'on the request of the Hungarian people's Government'. The declaration went on: 'Believing that the further presence of Red Army units in Hungary can serve only as a cause for even greater deterioration of the situation, the Soviet Government has given instructions to its military command to withdraw from Budapest. At the same time, the Soviet Government is ready to enter into relevant negotiations with the Hungarian Government and other participants of the Warsaw Pact on the question of the presence of Soviet troops in Hungary.'

This was all very important. Moscow seemed ready to repair the unfortunate consequences of her military intervention and reach a compromise agreement with Hungary – probably on the Polish pattern. Not even the most militant Russian leaders seemed to oppose a settlement; presumably they hoped a solution would be found that need not necessarily jeopardize the strategic position of the Red Army. Some people claim that the Russian declaration was only a cunning manœuvre to gain time to move all Red Army divisions needed to crush the Hungarian rising mercilessly. Lack of genuine information prevents anyone on this side of the Iron Curtain from proving this assertion, but such an interpretation of the Soviet declaration might seem justified by subsequent developments. Probably the Russian leaders decided at one time on a partial retreat in the hope that this would enable them to retain a decisive influence in Hungary.

This might be supported by the following sentence in the Soviet declaration: 'The Soviet Government express confidence that the people of the Socialist countries will not permit foreign and internal reactionary forces to undermine the basis of the people's democratic regimes.' In these words is a hidden warning to those who might endanger Communism in Hungary. As soon as they issued their declaration, the Russians had to face the probability that Communism might be swept out of Hungary. For it was then that Nagy announced the abolition of the one-party system and the establishment of a coalition Government with a Communist minority. The Kremlin bosses knew that the Communist Party would be defeated in free elections. They suddenly realized, too, that many workers' councils, revolutionary committees of the Army, students' councils and local national councils were demanding, not only the withdrawl of the Red Army but also the revision or abolition of the Warsaw Pact. This was alarming news. It caused a sudden change in Soviet policy. The Russian leaders met again to decide that they must crush Hungary until nothing was left of the revolutionary spirit. The second Russian intervention was the consequence.

In the light of these events it might be argued that the Russians were finally provoked to take drastic action by the Hungarian Government's declaration of neutrality. But Nagy did not announce his intentions until November 1, and on that day fresh Red Army units had already occupied Szolnok. Almost simultaneously with the withdrawal of the Russian soldiers in Budapest, extra Soviet divisions poured into the country and, under the pretext of covering withdrawal, they began to occupy one place after another. From then on the movements of the Red Army confirm that the Kremlin's leaders had decided to use decisive force against the Hungarians rather than risk the establishment of a non-Communist government, with the subsequent loss to the Soviet empire of this important satellite.

At this time the British and French Governments announced their intention of intervening in the conflict between Egypt and Israel, and it has been argued that the Russians only threw the whole dreadful weight of the Red Army into Hungary because they realized that the Anglo-French expedition would keep the Western Powers pre-occupied with Suez. It is much more likely that the Russians decided to crush the Hungarian revolution irrespective of anything that might be happening in the Middle East. They could not afford to allow Hungary to slip from their grasp if it started on the road towards real democracy. Moscow quite naturally exploited the general disapproval of the Anglo-French intervention in Egypt. Beside this crisis Soviet intervention in Hungary was, they felt, hardly worth mentioning. And it became obvious that the reaction of Asian nations to Soviet attacks in Hungary would probably have been more condemning had not 'the colonial aggression of the British and French Imperialists' absorbed all their interests. The Anglo-French action in Suez made it easy for the Soviets to divert attention from their bloody massacres in Hungary.

Yet, in spite of all this, it remains doubtful whether, even without trouble in the Middle East, the Western Powers would have done anything to prevent the Russians from lashing so angrily at the Hungarians.

Considerable energy would have been required, and there were fears that a more resolute move by the West might start a war. The Hungarians continued to cherish the hope that the revolution would be successful in restoring a democratic way of life. New political parties were being formed; old parties were restored. Anyone with anything to say seemed to be able to publish a newspaper. Censorship was abolished. The atmosphere was primed with the intoxicating spirit of freedom. Workers' councils took over the management of factories. Peasants began to disband the collective farms. Officers and soldiers, remembering that the rebels who defied the might of the Habsburgs in 1848 were called Honveds, prepared for the re-emergence of a national Honved army.

The Communist Party, compromised by these revolutionary changes, disintegrated to such an extent that Kadar, now First Secretary, tried to prevent complete devastation by giving the old gang the new title of the 'Socialist Workers' Party'. To restore confidence in the Party he announced that the new organization was being formed only by Communists who had fought against Rakosi's despotism. The executive committee, he explained, was composed of himself, Imre Nagy and five others. But he and Nagy were already quarrelling. Nagy was eagerly trying to win back the support of the revolutionaries, determined to meet their wishes for democracy. Despite all that he had suffered in Rakosi's prisons, Kadar remained a staunch Communist. Deep Marxist convictions prevented his agreeing to the introduction of a political system that favoured the existence of more than one party. He saw the danger to his own party and realized that without the armed support of the Russians the Communists in Hungary were doomed. In the past they had always been in an insignificant minority. If the revolution were successful, Communism would again be at a low ebb. Kadar believed that Hungarians, like the Poles, should be allowed to follow their own road to Socialism. This would still leave the Communists in control. Nagy, politically much more shrewd than the rather naïve Kadar, realized the full implication of what was happening.

The momentum of the revolution was pushing the Hungarians towards liberty, and national independence seemed so important to the people that the more they were opposed, the more bitter would be their struggle. He realized that Gomulka had kept the Polish rising within limits mainly because there were no bloody clashes with the Red Army. The Hungarians became impatient. They were asking, with growing insistence, for an immediate withdrawal of all Russian soldiers. Encouraged by the news that President Eisenhower had condemned Soviet intervention and that the United Nations had begun discussing their struggle for freedom, they began to have confidence. Then Peter Kos, Hungary's representative at the United Nations, followed Russian instructions and said that it was a domestic issue that did not concern the United Nations. He was recalled by the Government in Budapest because he had 'betrayed the cause'. And now the Hungarians, bewildered and suspicious because Red Army units that left their country were quickly replaced by fresh contingents, began to feel a new surge of hatred against Moscow. The Hungarian revolutionary trade union council proclaimed a general strike, to last until every Russian soldier had left the country. This defiance seems to have been too much for the men in the Kremlin. They decided to end the revolution as swiftly as possible – on their terms.

Mikoyan flew to Budapest in November and summoned Kadar, Apro, Marosan and Munnich (but not Nagy) to the Soviet Embassy. They vanished for three days and emerged again only when they had officially been acclaimed by the Russians as representatives of the new Government. Even so, they appeared only under the protection of Soviet guards. By the time Mikoyan reached Budapest, Soviet troops were pushing into the heart of Hungary. When they began to close in on

Budapest, Nagy urgently proclaimed 'the neutrality of the Hungarian People's Republic'. Budapest's Radio announcer reported that Nagy had demanded an immediate withdrawal of the Russian military units that were being sent into the country. 'He has told the Soviet ambassador', it was said, 'that the Hungarian Government is giving immediate notice of the termination of the Warsaw Pact and is declaring Hungary's neutrality. He has added that the Hungarian Government is appealing to the United Nations and the four Great Powers to safeguard the nation's neutrality.'

Nagy then asked the Secretary-General of the United Nations by telegram to put the case of Hungary on the agenda of the next session of the General Assembly.

SOVIET AGGRESSION

The die was cast. Nagy has since been criticized for this action. It is argued that he merely aggravated the situation, provoking the Russians to take more drastic action. It was obvious that the Kremlin would refuse to countenance Hungary's attempt to quit the Warsaw Alliance and establish herself as neutral.

Russia's high command could not tolerate such a display of independence. If it had succeeded, the whole satellite system would have been endangered. General revolt might have followed. Yet Nagy could not have acted in any other way. Everything indicates that he was making a desperate attempt to save the country at the last moment by provoking international action. The people believed that the Russians were leaving, but Nagy knew that fresh Red Army units were rushing into Hungary. He was fully aware, too, that Budapest was encircled and that the airports on the outskirts of the capital were occupied by Russian troops. Another attack on Budapest could be expected at any moment.

In such terrifying circumstances, Nagy could only hope that by putting Hungary's plight before the world he might persuade the United States and other Western Powers to announce their readiness to guarantee Hungary's neutrality. Dependable witnesses have reported that he hoped the West would ask the Soviet Government to start negotiations to establish Hungary's new status. For Nagy it was a cruel predicament. He knew the worst of both sides. He had been under pressure from the Hungarian revolutionary movement from the moment the Red Army opened fire on the rebels. He realized the irresistible desire of his people to liberate their country from Russian bondage. No one in the surge of revolutionary ardour believed the Warsaw Pact could be invoked to justify Russian intervention. And the Hungarians became all the more incensed because there was nothing in the published articles of the pact that gave Russia the right to send troops into Hungary to save a Communist government.

Most people believed the pact expressly rejected interference with the domestic affairs of a member. Every day fresh voices were heard advocating the termination of the pact. In the days preceding Nagy's proclamation, the demand was repeated again and again in the resolutions of different revolutionary councils, particularly the military council organized by the followers of General Maleter, who, until the beginning of the rising, had been a resolute Communist.

Intensive pressure from the revolutionary units that were constantly fighting the Russians, and the belief that the West would organize diplomatic help, combined to convince Nagy that he should break with the Kremlin and proclaim his country's neutrality. His courageous decision expressed the wishes of the whole Hungarian nation (with the exception of a few Muscovites and members of AVO), but it made the Soviet leaders realize the danger of the Communist empire disintegrating. Stalin had succeeded (with the help of both Hitler and the Western Allies) in creating an empire about which the greatest of the Czars had only dreamt. Now they were in danger of losing it.

If the Hungarians broke loose, the Poles would try to follow them, for Gomulka had yet to be taught the value of keeping

Red Army units in Poland. For the Russians, drastic and immediate suppression of the Hungarian Revolution was essential. Moscow's generals had probably realized this when they started sending new divisions into Hungary while pretending to withdraw troops from Budapest. No matter what the men in the Kremlin may have thought, the Red Army realized that the Hungarian Communist Party must not lose power. Budapest must be forced, despite anything that Nagy might say, to accept their supremacy. Nagy's repudiation of the pact merely convinced them that the Hungarians must not be treated as leniently as the Poles. They must be taught a lesson that would be obvious to all the satellites – a lesson that meant 'no concessions'.

The outcome of the Hungarian rising could have been less tragic had the Western Powers replied more positively to Nagy's declaration of neutrality, especially if they had pressed Moscow to recognize Hungary's desire to be rid of the Warsaw Pact. Such Western diplomatic initiative would have prevented the Hungarian rebels from feeling that they had been abandoned. Possibly it would have caused the other enslaved nations to show a similar desire for neutrality. It was a golden moment for the West. The Allies had the opportunity of mobilizing world opinion, within and outside the United Nations, against the Communists, and of coupling the withdrawal of British, French and Israeli troops from Egypt with the withdrawal of Russian troops from Hungary. In the beginning the situation in Egypt may have helped the Russians, but it could have been used in the end to put pressure on them. It was possible for the Allies to say to Russia: 'We are willing to pull our troops out of Egypt at the request of the United Nations. You do the same in Hungary.'

Energetic and imaginative diplomacy could have prevented Nasser's boastful claim that he had triumphed and at the same time have mitigated the terrible suffering caused by Russian intervention in Hungary. Soviet influence in Hungary might not have been eliminated, but it could have been substantially reduced. The Western Powers did not realize the unique opportunity offered by Nagy's declaration. Yet it was an opportunity that will not easily repeat itself. The Allies became too preoccupied with Suez. The United Nations demanded that Britain, France and Israel withdraw their troops, but forgot to apply the same principles to Russia. The Soviet leaders saw, probably with surprise, that the Western Powers behaved in the United Nations as though they had no firm convictions about the Red Army's massacres of Hungarians. It became obvious that strong words of protest were not to be accompanied by energetic action. The will was lacking. Only irresolution and delay marked Western policy. Right at the start Moscow gambled on the conviction that the West would restrict itself to protests – and protests alone. The Russians guessed they could crush the Hungarian struggle for freedom without the rebels receiving any effective help from the West, particularly from the United States. Small and entirely isolated, Hungary was at their mercy.

When the Hungarians were going to bed on November 3, to enjoy the first real quiet and peaceful night they had known since the revolution began, the Red Army's commanders were making final preparations for a massive attack on an unsuspecting population. First, they ensured that the rebellious Hungarian military leaders were moved out of the way. Pretending that they wished to discuss the 'withdrawal of the Soviet troops', the Russians invited General Pal Maleter, Minister of Defence, and General Kovacs, Chief of the General Staff, to a meeting at midnight on November 3. They were arrested.

Fifteen Russian divisions, equipped with 6,000 tanks, began an all-out onslaught on Budapest and other towns at 4 o'clock on the morning of November 4. Imre Nagy announced over the wireless in an excited voice: 'Soviet troops have launched an attack against our capital city with the obvious intention of overthrowing the lawful, democratic Hungarian Government. Our troops are fighting. The Government is in its place. I

178

hereby inform the people of Hungary and world opinion of the situation.'

But Nagy's Government could not remain in its place for long. Soon after seven in the morning, Russian tanks closed in on the Parliament building and Red Army officers rushed in to arrest the members of the Government. Nagy, with fifteen colleagues and their families, asked for asylum in the Yugoslav Embassy. Cardinal Mindszenty took refuge in the United States Embassy.

The Red Army attacked ruthlessly, but despite the savagery of the Russian gunners, they met with unexpected resistance. The Hungarians defended themselves literally to the last available cartridge. Workers, soldiers, students, young men and even children fought with incomparable bravery. Only a great writer could celebrate this epic of matchless heroism against an overwhelmingly powerful enemy. From the beginning, these gallant defenders of their country's freedom were broadcasting desperate appeals over the radio. But their pleas for help were in vain. No help came. The Western Powers were paralysed by fear of a world war. They did not intervene in this terrible drama by taking any energetic or even diplomatic action, though the fighting went on for nearly ten days. Lone Hungarian heroes could not continue to resist the Red Army's might. But they held out desperately, earning glory that will always inspire individuals and nations who yearn for liberty. Sporadic fighting went on in many places until nearly the end of December. But the general strike was broken by hunger and finally the leaders of the workers' councils were all captured.

Only the shortsighted could think the sacrifice of the Hungarians was useless. The revolutionaries were crushed by Russian tanks. The Hungarian revolution remained unvanquished. Its ideas and heritage of courage will one day destroy the whole gigantic Soviet menace.

Hungary's martyrdom was cruel. Indian observers estimated that 25,000 Hungarians and 7,000 Russians were killed. Others say the Hungarian losses were between 30,000 and 50,000 dead.

Many rebels, mainly young people, were carried off to Russia. How many, we do not know. And about 2 per cent of the whole population, mostly youths, fled to Austria and to Yugoslavia, among them a number of industrial workers and technicians. To the vast number of victims of Soviet violence must be added the thousands executed or arrested after the rebellion had been crushed. Some estimates suggest that there have been 2,000 to 5,000 executions in Hungary since the end of the revolution. More than 20,000 were imprisoned. Most of the 13,000 political prisoners released during the revolution were subsequently rearrested, according to Mr Andrew Martin, a member of the International Commission of Jurists.

Prodigious damage was caused when public houses and buildings were shelled. In places, more of Budapest was destroyed in 1956 than in 1945. Fighting and strikes reduced industrial and agricultural production until, after the revolution, the country was left with nothing but sorrow and hardship. Yet the most serious loss was freedom. Hungary was thrust into a worse state of slavery than ever. The vengeful Russians established a new Government led by Kadar who, with Munnich and several others, fled from Budapest during the worst days and took refuge in Szolnok, which was occupied by Russian troops throughout the fighting. The circumstances in which this Government was formed have never been revealed. This much is certain: the Russians dissolved Nagy's legal Government, which enjoyed the confidence of the Hungarian people, and in defiance of every international principle and agreement, put in its place by brute force the Kadar Government which was opposed to everything the Hungarians desired. Kadar's puppet Government was illegal, but its Foreign Minister, Imre Horwath, was admitted to the United Nations as Hungary's legal representative. He remained until he left of his own accord.

Kadar's first declaration as ostensible head of the new Government revealed that he had asked the Soviet Government for 'help in liquidating the counter-revolutionary forces and restoring order'. The Hungarians, of course, realized that the Red Army had launched its attacks before the Kadar Government was formed. Further, Kadar was not formally sworn in as Prime Minister by President Doby, the head of state, until three days later. It was the same fraudulent Communist farce, similar in circumstances to the first Soviet intervention when it was said that the Red Army was fighting Hungarians at the request of the Hungarian Government. In both instances the Russians intervened without even consulting the Hungarians, thus flagrantly breaking all the pledges they had given, and their solemn promise in the Warsaw Pact itself, that they would not interfere with the domestic affairs of another state.

INDIGNATION AND PASSIVITY OF THE WEST

Russia's attack on the Hungarians caused anger and indignation in Western Europe and in North and South America. In many countries, mass demonstrations were arranged to demand that action should be taken to stop the Soviet brutality. In countries with strong Communist Parties (particularly France and Italy), demonstrators showed their contempt for the Russians by attacking their own countrymen. Never before had the people of the free world shown so violently their hatred for Soviet tyranny. Russian brutality was shown in stark contrast to the heroism of the Hungarians. The rebels won admiration and sympathy. Food and medical supplies were sent to the Hungarians and sanctuary was promised for the refugees who were pouring out of Hungary in daily increasing numbers. Though strictly neutral, Austria welcomed the victims of the Red Army's violence with unsurpassed zeal. The kindly, hospitable Austrians set an example to all democracies. This was practical, genuine sympathy.

Even the fellow-travelling Asian countries showed their horror at the inhumanity of the Russians. But these nations were mainly pre-occupied with British and French 'colonial aggression' in Egypt and their interest in the Russian aggression was not so keen as it might have been. Nehru, when his henchman, Krishna Menon, took the Communist side in the United Nations, finally uttered, under the pressure of world opinion, a cautious condemnation of the Red Army intervention in Hungary.

The uncommitted nations realized that, even though paying lip-service to 'anti-colonialism', Russia was following her own crude imperialist policy. Moscow became more and more suspect. Communist Parties were dangerously weakened. The confidence of the Party rank and file was undermined and many intellectuals resigned. Even those dedicated characters who wanted to remain Communist strongly criticized Soviet brutality. The indignation was general but only in rare instances did anyone show signs of wishing to take action against the Russians. Other Governments were obviously embarrassed, and as time passed, their embarrassment increased. Four days after the first Russian move against the rebels, the Security Council decided, in spite of Soviet protests, to put consideration of 'the situation in Hungary' on the agenda. But it was left to the chairman to decide if and when a meeting should be convened to discuss this breach of the United Nations principles. It was significant that other Powers carefully avoided putting 'Soviet aggression in Hungary' on the agenda, in this way avoiding having to discuss possible sanctions against the aggressor.

When Nagy told the Secretary-General of the United Nations that Hungary wished to quit the Warsaw Pact Alliance and become a neutral, he asked that the matter of Hungary's neutrality and the whole question of his country's future status should be discussed at the forthcoming session of the General Assembly. It would seem that he still believed it possible to put enough pressure on the Russians to make them agree with the Western Powers to guarantee Hungary's neutrality.

But two or three days elapsed before the Security Council returned to 'the situation in Hungary', and the United States proposed a resolution expressing the hope that the Russians would recall the Red Army from Hungary without delay. When the Soviet delegate shamelessly lied to the Council by pretending that his Government was discussing with the Hungarians the withdrawal of Russian troops, no vote was taken and the meeting adjourned for two days.

The delegates to the United Nations were wavering and temporizing on Hungary's plight, but at the same time they were exerting pressure on Britain, France and Israel to take their troops out of Egypt. The news that the Red Army, reinforced by troops from Russia, had launched a massive, concerted attack on Hungarian civilians, reached New York on the morning of November 4. The Security Council met in the afternoon but the Soviet representative vetoed a resolution condemning his country's action.

An emergency session of the General Assembly's Political Committee was called immediately and a resolution proposed by the United States was accepted by 50 votes to 8. These were the eight members of the Communist bloc. Fifteen countries abstained – among them the delegates of the Asian countries (including India) and Yugoslavia and Finland. The resolution asked the Soviets to 'desist from any form of intervention in the internal affairs of Hungary' and to 'withdraw all its forces from the Hungarian territory' without delay. Furthermore, the United Nations acknowledged 'the rights of the Hungarian people to a government responsive to its national aspirations and dedicated to its independence and well-being'.

The Secretary-General was asked to 'investigate the situation, to observe directly through a representative, named by him, the situation in Hungary, and to report thereon to the General Assembly . . . and to suggest as soon as possible a method of bringing to an end the foreign intervention in Hungary'. (France had asked that this wording be used instead of 'the existing situation'.)

The Hungarian and Russian Governments were asked to allow United Nations observers into Hungary so they could report to the Secretary-General. And, pathetically enough, members of the United Nations were asked to help the Hungarians with food, medicine and other supplies.

In defiance of the United Nations, the Russians continued their brutal suppression of the Hungarians. Yet the United Nations (or, to be more precise, the Western Powers with America at their head) made no attempt to exert effective pressure on Russia to obey the demands of the resolution. The Hungarian revolutionaries, dying by their thousands, continued to make desperate appeals to the free world.

'Why cannot you hear the call for help of our murdered women and children?' asked Radio Rakoczy. 'Hear the call for help of a small nation. We are not Fascists. We will prove this to an independent international committee but not . . . to those who reply to us with phosphorus bombs. . . . Take urgent action. If necessary, we shall keep on fighting for the freedom of Hungary up to the last drop of blood against the foreign occupiers.'

Next Radio Rakoczy repeated its appeals even more poignantly: 'We ask you in the name of all that is dear to you, to help us. This is our message today when, as far as we know, the extraordinary session of the United Nations will meet. Don't you think the United Nations have it in their power to stop further bloodshed? . . . Or do you want us to lose all faith in the world's conscience and decency for ever, when we are fighting for the freedom of the whole world? . . .

'This is our message to President Eisenhower on the day of his election: If he will stand by the oppressed and by those who are fighting for freedom, a blessing shall fall upon him. . . . In Egypt it has been possible to carry out the United Nations resolution. . . . There is a cease· fire and the police of the United Nations . . . are . . . in the zone. We ask for similar measures to be taken in Hungary. Please forward this appeal to President Eisenhower. We ask for immediate intervention. We ask for immediate intervention.'

These brave, despairing cries were never answered. Day after day passed but the United Nations took no action. Eventually, the Secretary-General, Mr Hammarskjold, asked the representative of Kadar's illegal administration, as he sat placidly in the General Assembly, whether his Government was willing to admit observers. Eventually, an emergency special session passed, on November 9, a resolution drafted by Cuba, Ireland, Italy, Pakistan and Peru condemning Soviet intervention as a 'violation of the Charter and the Peace Treaty'. The Cuban delegate, Nunez-Portuondo, originally proposed that 'the violation of the Genocide Convention' should also be emphasized. This point was, in the end, omitted from the text. The Cuban tried harder than any other delegate to ensure that the United Nations resolutions were carried out, and made another attempt to have genocide mentioned in a further resolution at the end of November. This resolution also strongly condemned the deportation of Hungarians to Russia. It was passed on November 21.

All efforts at the beginning of November to have free elections under United Nations auspices, mentioned in a resolution, proved fruitless, but a more moderate resolution proposed by the United States was accepted, appealing to Russia 'to cease immediately actions against the Hungarian population which are in violation of the accepted standards and principles of international law, justice and morality'.

None of these resolutions (or those subsequently accepted by the United Nations) meant anything. The Kadar Government did not reply to the United Nations representations until after the Red Army had already crushed the main centres of resistance. Kadar asserted that the Hungarian and Soviet Governments were 'exclusively competent' to handle the withdrawal of the Russian troops. The presence of United Nations observers was not warranted. Soviet troops were in Hungary at the request of the Hungarian Government. The arrangement of free elections was 'entirely within the competence of the Hungarian authorities'. The Kremlin scornfully rejected all messages from the Secretary-General and the Hungarian Government refused to invite him to

Budapest. Kadar said merely he was willing to invite him to Rome.

News of the mass deportations from Hungary led the United Nations General Assembly (at the instigation of Ceylon, India and Indonesia) to urge Kadar again 'to accede to the request made by the Secretary-General, without prejudice to its sovereignty' to permit observers to enter Hungary. But this appeal met with the same dismal fate as the others. It had no effect whatever. All these United Nations resolutions were voted too late and with too much hesitation. No indication was given that the United States or any other Western Power was ready to enforce them. The Assembly of Captive European Nations, in which nine enslaved peoples are represented by prominent exiles, asked the United Nations to refuse 'recognition of the pseudo-Government created in Hungary by Soviet force' and 'to refuse to accommodate in the United Nations . . . any representative . . . designated by this so-called Hungarian Government'. It also asked for 'an international United Nations force to secure and supervise the withdrawal of Soviet troops from Hungary and the establishment, through democratic processes, of a Hungarian Government responsive to the will of the people'.

These requests had the sympathy of some delegations (especially Latin-American representatives) but they were not considered officially by the Great Powers of the United Nations. Suggestions from the Assembly of Captive Nations that consideration should be given to political and economic sanctions against the Soviet Union (in accordance with the corresponding articles of the United Nations Charter), if Russia continued to ignore the General Assembly, were completely disregarded. Other similar suggestions were considered dangerous provocation.

The United Nations proved helpless against a great Power that cynically ignored them. They were helpless because the other big Powers lacked the will to act energetically against the Russian Communists. It is impossible to accept the argument

advanced at the time that there was no effective means of forcing the Russians to climb down. War must be avoided, it was
said. And so, apart from general protests against Soviet intervention and the passing of resolutions in the United Nations, no
kind of pressure, either political or economic, was applied.

Yet Bulganin did not hesitate to threaten Britain and France
with guided missiles. When the Russians began to organize
Muslim 'volunteers' for Egypt, the West should have been free
to organize true volunteer groups to help the Hungarian
people. France alone had thousands of young men ready to go
to Hungary. If action of this kind was considered too risky,
why did not the American, British and French Governments
solemnly warn the Soviet Government that it was contemptuously breaking international pledges? Why not threaten to
sever diplomatic relations? Such political gestures would have
greatly influenced Moscow. The Russian leaders were not united
and the Western Powers could have shown more eagerness
to guarantee Hungary's neutrality. Why did not the Secretary-
General go to Budapest or at least send his observers there,
irrespective of the attitude of the illegal Kadar Government?
Russian guards would probably have prevented United Nations
envoys from entering Hungary, but such action would have
helped to emphasize the despicable behaviour of the Soviet
Government.

The Hungarians did not expect military help from the United
States and other Western Powers, but they at least expected
the assistance of effective political action. The reporter of the
commission of inquiry established by the General Assembly in
January 1957, wrote that while some 'freedom fighters' did not
expect 'United Nations troops to come marching over the
border (They said: 'Our revolution was not worth a Third
World War'), they did hope for some sort of help from the
United Nations – perhaps a visit to Budapest by the Secretary-
General, Mr Hammarskjold.'

Had the United Nations or the Western Powers alone given
'some sort of help' the Hungarian revolutionaries might have

been able to continue in their resistance against the Red Army units; unrest would have spread to other enslaved countries. Probably this would have forced the Russians eventually to make some concessions. It would have meant the Hungarian revolution had not been in vain. As it was, the revolution ended in a total defeat for democracy only because the Russians were left to do as they wished.

Western action of any kind involved a certain amount of risk, but the West cautiously avoided even the smallest risks, not only helping the Russians to gain a victory but also giving the impression that the democracies had no intention of interfering in the Communist sphere of influence in Eastern and Central Europe. Lack of an effective Western policy during the Polish and Hungarian revolutions helped the Russians to regain, in a relatively short time, their mastery of an empire that was about to disintegrate.

The five members of a special committee on Hungary, created by the General Assembly – they were Australia, Ceylon, Denmark, Tunisia and Uruguay – reported in June 1957 that they had interviewed 111 Hungarian refugees in New York and Europe, but they were not allowed to visit Hungary and both the Soviet Government and the Kadar administration refused to co-operate with them.

In a report of nearly 400 shattering pages, the five-member committee established beyond doubt that the Hungarian revolt was 'a spontaneous national uprising', inspired by a desire for national independence and democratic freedom, and that the Soviet intervention was solely the result of Soviet decision, a gross interference with the internal affairs of a second state and a clear case of aggression. The Committee found no foundation for the assertion that the Russians intervened 'at the request of the Hungarian Government' and they concluded that 'until further information comes to light, it would be wise to suspend judgment about whether such an invitation was issued at all'.

The report also revealed that the Russians – probably forewarned by events in Poland – began moving troops three days before the Hungarian demonstrations started. Red Army units that went into action against the rebels a day later, were not part of the occupation force. They had been drafted into Hungary, probably because the Russians decided that trouble was inevitable. This proves that Moscow intended to crush any attempt to overthrow the Communist administration, regardless of a request from the Hungarian Government.

The United Nations found abundant evidence that Soviet preparations for further intervention, including the movement of troops and arms, had been under way since the last days of October. Documentary evidence also showed how baseless were Soviet assertions that the rising was provoked by Hungarian reactionaries and by 'Western Imperialists'. United Nations investigators confirmed that, from start to finish, the rebellion was led by students, workers, soldiers and intellectuals, many of them Communists or former Communists. The rebels emphasized that democratic Socialism should be the basis of the future Hungarian political structure and that such social achievements as land reform should be safeguarded.

The Committee established that the Kadar regime had no popular support. It confirmed that the basic human rights of the Hungarian people were violated by various Governments before October 23, and that such violations had continued after November 4. Lastly, there was proof that many Hungarian rebels (men, women and youths) were deported to Russia. The Committee decided that 'a massive, armed intervention by one Power on the territory of another, with the avowed intention of interfering with the internal affairs of that country, must, by Russia's own definition of aggression, be a matter of international concern'.

MUSCOVITE COUNTER-REVOLUTION

Hungarian resistance was much stronger and of longer duration than the Russians expected. The people continued fighting and the workers refused to return to work despite all the appeals of the Kadar Government. Eventually the Russian adviser in Budapest told Kadar to try to pacify the rebels by making false promises in negotiations with a workers' delegation. Kadar subsequently promised elections in which several parties would be represented. He also pledged co-operation with non-Communists and on one occasion admitted that the Communist Party might be thoroughly beaten in a free General Election.

This was a significant admission, yet Stalin had expressed the view at Potsdam in 1945 that free elections in the Central European countries would mean the decisive defeat of the Communists. Most of the Communist leaders seem to be aware of this danger, yet Khrushchev, in an interview televised in the United States, said that the Kadar Government would survive even the withdrawal of the Red Army.

Hungarians refused to believe Kadar when he talked of fulfilling the main requests of the workers' councils – withdrawal of Soviet troops, free elections and the return of Imre Nagy to power. The Hungarian strikes went on and in many places, particularly in the mountains, guerrillas never ceased to harass the Russian troops. Their sporadic attacks interfered with supplies for Russian garrisons. Red Army morale began to sink. The crisis became acute when Nagy and his friends, enticed from the Yugoslav Embassy by a false promise of a safe-conduct, were immediately arrested by Russian security officers. The protests of the Yugoslav Government were in vain. It was officially stated by the Russians that Nagy and his friends, Mrs Julia Rajk among them, went to Rumania 'at their own request'.

Soon afterwards Nagy was proclaimed a 'traitor' and the 'agent of counter-revolution', and we now know that, with General Maleter and others, he was executed. Fresh demonstrations were started by the women of Budapest at the beginning of December. They lasted several days, the crowds shouting: 'Out with the Russians. Down with Kadar!' 'We want Imre Nagy!' The factory workers went on strike again and there were renewed clashes between the Soviet soldiers or members of the AVO and the Hungarians. Finally, the Government declared martial law on December 9 and ordered workers' councils to be dissolved.

A series of mass arrests began. Leaders of workers' councils and student groups were among the first to be rounded up by the Secret Police. A general strike again started to spread through the country. This was an expression of the tenacity and courage of the Hungarian workers, but in the circumstances it was doomed. Terror once again ruled Hungary.

The death penalty was introduced for striking or actively opposing the regime, and Jozsef Dudas, the popular chairman of the Budapest National Revolutionary Committee, and another rebel, Janos Szabo, were executed six days later. On the same day, several writers were arrested, among them Gyula Háy, one of the intellectual leaders of the rising. The arrests of Tibor Déri, Zoltan Zelk and others soon followed. From then onwards, arrests of writers, students, workers, officers and peasant leaders became a daily occurrence.

Arrests numbered 15,000 by the beginning of April 1957. Thousands were executed or beaten to death. Deportations to Russia continued. The Writers' Union, the Petofi Club, the Journalists' Association and the workers' councils were banned. Trades unions and similar organizations were reorganized under the leadership of veteran Communists. The Secret Police (AVO) was revived.

During the revolution, 55 per cent of the collective farms had been disbanded. Now they were restored by order of Kadar. The Hungarian Communist Party was reorganized – though only with difficulty. Kadar had promised Parliamentary elections in May, but he explained at the last minute that they would have to be postponed. It was necessary, he said, to concentrate instead on restoring the economic damage caused by the revolt. He broke another promise by saying that a multi-party system would destroy Hungary's 'national unity'. Earlier, *Nepszabadsag*, the official organ of the Communist Party, had prepared the way for this contemptuous rejection of democratic principles by saying: 'The creation of other political parties would have served only one purpose: the concentration of anti-Socialist forces, legal cover for their activities, and a sharpening of discord.'

Kadar confirmed the fears of the Hungarians: he broke all the pledges made to placate the rebels. Using such slogans as 'Return to Communism', 'Fight the Nagy revisionism', the Kadar regime (or, more precisely, the Russians, working through the Kadar Government) restored their violent dictatorship in Hungary. They kept themselves in power by similar (if not worse) methods to those of the tyrannical Rakosi.

Insignificant concessions were granted to peasants or minor trade unions. Some of the lesser intellectuals were pardoned. The Marxist philosopher, Gyorgy Lukacs, a man of great in telligence but of weak character who was Minister of Culture in the Nagy Government, was allowed to return to Hungary. But such tactical manœuvres changed nothing in the basic reality, that the Russians had enforced a strict Communist dictatorship on Stalinist lines on their Hungarian satellite. Educational courses in Marx-Leninism and the teaching of Russian in schools again became compulsory.

The complete enslavement of Hungary was confirmed when Kadar visited Moscow at the end of March. In an attempt to make people forget his former Titoist inclinations, Kadar condemned with bitter sarcasm the Yugoslav Communists for the so-called 'national Communism' for which they used 'de-Stalinization' or other catchwords. He pilloried 'the traitor Nagy' and called his brand of national Communism 'a twin of Hitlerite National Socialism'.

A joint Soviet-Hungarian declaration described the Hungarian 'counter-revolution' as a machination of the American 'imperialists'. The rebellion, it was said, was the outcome of 'the treacherous policy of the Nagy-Losonczy group', which 'long before the October rising, had been negotiating with secret counter-revolutionary elements'.

The declaration admitted that Rakosi and Gero had committed 'grave errors', but Kadar had already said that such 'mistakes' of the past were of secondary importance. The declaration asserted solemnly that 'with the brotherly help of the Red Army (which had fulfilled its international duty) the Hungarian people saved the national independence of their country and the achievements of the people's democratic regime'.

No less provocative was the revelation that Russian troops were remaining in Hungary 'only to safeguard the freedom of the Hungarian people against the aggressive plans of international reactionaries'. After categorically condemning national Communism, the declaration proclaimed that the 'building of Socialism in different countries must advance along *a common road*, on the basis of the social laws discovered by Marx-Leninist science', or, in other words, according to the policy of Moscow. The stressing of 'proletarian internationalism' had a similar meaning – greater obedience to Moscow. Finally, the Soviet and Hungarian Governments declared 'their resolve to support and reinforce the Warsaw Pact'.

Through this declaration, Khrushchev let it be known that Moscow was the boss and Hungary again a mere slave. Kadar confirmed his acceptance of this situation by his boundless servility. The Russians had to help the administration they had established in Budapest. Hungarian economy was disrupted. Khrushchev granted Hungary, during Kadar's visit to Moscow, another long-term loan and wrote off the old Hungarian debt that accrued through the transfer of German assets to Hungary and through the Russians claiming a share of former mixed Soviet-Hungarian companies.

By the grandiose dismissal of this colossal sum of money, the Russians were only partly returning something they had previously snatched. The payment of another Hungarian debt was 'deferred for a long time', and it was agreed that 'once the mining of uranium ore had been organized, Hungary would deliver to the Soviet Union, at equitable, mutually profitable prices, whatever ore was not needed for Hungary's national economy'.

This reference to uranium was inserted because, during the revolution, the Hungarians had protested against Soviet exploitation of their mineral resources. Everyone realized that the Russians would continue to dispose of Hungarian uranium according to their own terms.

But at least in the immediate future, the Russians would be forced to give the Hungarians more than they could possibly extract from them. Some help was given after the rebellion by other Communist countries, including China. The Red Army wanted Russia's supremacy over humiliated but undaunted Hungary, while the Kremlin had to pay for their own arrogance by sending supplies and making loans to a puppet Government that existed solely on their charity.

CHAPTER VII

Challenge to Soviet Hegemony

A THREATENED UNITY

The Russians also had to prepare to maintain large armed forces in Hungary in order to stop fresh outbursts of revolution, for they realized that discontent was still smouldering under the hot ashes. Propaganda and security police were used to prevent the revolutionary contagion from spreading to other enslaved countries. Signs of unrest appeared everywhere. Feverish attacks on 'revisionism', 'liberalism', 'bourgeois nationalism' and 'national Communism' by Communist leaders in these satellite countries, and constant appeals for increased 'vigilance' against 'counter-revolutionary centres' were evidence enough of their fear of the hidden force of democracy. Even inside Russia there were signs of trouble. Moscow's spokesmen admitted that there was unrest in Lithuania but dared not add that it had also occurred in the Ukraine. Lithuania's discontent suggested that there was desire for freedom in all the Baltic nations.

The Moscow intelligentsia, especially the younger members, doubted the official explanation that the Hungarian rising was a 'reactionary, Fascist, counter-revolution'. They were tormented by the belief that the Red Army's intervention was neither necessary nor justified. The men in the Kremlin were sufficiently shrewd to recognize these danger signals. The Hungarian rising and, to some extent, the Polish rebellion, had endangered their hegemony in an empire stretching from the Baltic to the Mediterranean. Their primitive reaction, based entirely on power politics, was to call for even greater rigidity of Marxist-Leninist orthodoxy. They rehabilitated Stalin. Khrushchev said: 'To make no concessions and to continue fighting until the final victory of the working people. . . . If by this is meant Stalinism, then we are Stalinists. . . . God grant that every Communist should be able to fight like Stalin.'

They decided that Party discipline should be stiffened. In 'the name of proletarian internationalism' they unconditionally rejected 'national Communism' and proclaimed the absolute need of the 'unity of the Communist bloc under the leadership of the U.S.S.R.' They brutally dammed up the liberalizing streams, which they themselves had released by their anti-Stalin campaign. To re-establish Soviet domination in the vast territory over which they ruled, the Kremlin leaders decided that the Red Army must be the weapon used to crush any move by any subject towards democracy. They made it clear that the Red Army would be used again as mercilessly as it was used in Hungary if there was provocation.

Moscow at this time opened an intensive propaganda campaign against American and Western 'imperialists' who had inspired the Hungarian rising. This was a fraudulent attempt to 'undermine the unity of the Socialist camp'. Monstrous, patently untrue assertions were shamelessly repeated. The United States had condemned Anglo-French intervention in Egypt as bitterly and as vigorously as the Soviet Union itself, but the Russians suddenly began to accuse the Americans of having secretly engineered the action. Shepilov, then the Soviet Foreign Minister, declared: 'The aggression against Egypt and . . . the counter-revolutionary putsch in Hungary . . . were part and parcel of one and the same broadly conceived strategic plan.'

Soviet propaganda hastened to interpret the Eisenhower Middle East doctrine as evidence of America's imperialist and colonialist ambitions. Euratom and the European Common Market agreement were attacked as further proof of the aggressive intentions of the Western imperialists and German militarists.

These wild lies were repeated with due solemnity to the

Czech, Rumanian, Bulgarian and Albanian Communist Governments. For them, the Hungarian and Polish risings had brought nothing but fear. Moscow was their only hope of salvation if their regimes, too, were threatened by their unhappy, enslaved countrymen. Polish Communists, with Gomulka at their head, treated with reserve, if not contempt, the Soviet attempts to blame the West for engineering the Hungarian rising. Some Poles said quite openly that the main reason for the rising was the wretched condition into which Hungary had fallen during the evil days of the Rakosi-Gero administration. The Yugoslav Communists soon became involved in a fresh ideological conflict with the Russians.

NEW QUARRELS WITH TITO

Agreements between Moscow and Belgrade, published with a great flourish in June 1956, proved to be short-lived. Fresh differences of opinion soon became obvious. Only a few weeks after the signing of the joint declaration, Moscow, in a secret circular (the details have never been officially revealed), warned the Communist parties everywhere against Titoist 'deviations'.

Khrushchev went unheralded to Belgrade in September and persuaded Tito to go to the Crimea with him. Little of what they said to each other became known, but there were indications that they could not agree on the policy adopted by Russia towards the satellites. It is possible that the Poznan rising in Poland strengthened the critics of 'liberalization' and forced the Moscow leaders to issue warnings against the dangers of 'Tito-ization'. Even the Crimea talks failed to reconcile the views of Tito and the die-hards in Moscow. Undoubtedly, the Hungarian revolution emphasized the tension between Moscow and Belgrade.

Yugoslav Communists were embarrassed by events in Hungary. On principle, they could not agree with Nagy's democratic programme promising a multi-party political system and free elections, so they welcomed the formation of a

Kadar Government, knowing it would mean the continuation of a Communist regime.

Tanyug, the official Yugoslav news agency, said: 'There can be no peace, progress or independence in the East European countries except on the basis of Socialism.' Yet Yugoslavs could not approve Soviet intervention. After some obvious hesitation, Tito, at Pula on November 11, declared that the Hungarian rising had been the result of Stalinism and added that the Soviet leaders had 'wrongly considered the whole thing as a question of the cult of personality and not as a question of the system'. Tito then revealed that during his visit to the Crimea he found the Russian leaders to be divided amongst themselves.

The division lay, he said, between the 'Stalinists' and those who 'stand for . . . a more rapid development in the direction of democratization . . . and the creation of new relations among Socialist states'. The Soviet leaders, he continued, feared that 'reactionary forces' would grasp power if 'liberalization' became excessive in Eastern Europe.

He explained that in Poland, despite the persecution and the Stalinist methods of destructive *cadres*, a nucleus, headed by Gomulka, had survived and 'reactionary forces could not find expression, although such forces certainly did exist'. Referring to East Germany, to other satellite countries and to the French Communist Party, Tito said: 'I cannot say that this positive development in Poland, which is very similar to ours, has been welcomed in the other countries of the so-called Socialist camp. No. They criticize it secretly and among themselves, but also to a certain extent publicly.' He asserted that 'it was a fatal mistake for Gero to call in the Soviet Army', and continued: 'This justified the Hungarian revolt and an uprising against a clique was transformed into a revolt of the entire people against Socialism and the Soviet Union' – in favour of reaction.

Tito reproached Nagy with 'having done nothing to prevent this', and declared: 'It is clear, we have said it and we will always say it, that we are against intervention and the use of foreign military force. Which is now the lesser evil? Chaos, civil war, counter-revolution and a new World War, or the intervention of Soviet troops? . . . The former is a catastrophe and the latter is an error. It is understood that if the latter saves Socialism in Hungary, then, comrades, we can say, although we are against intervention, that the Soviet intervention was necessary. . . . I can only say that the establishment of a bourgeois and reactionary system is the worst thing that could have happened. . . .'

Yet Tito also admitted: 'It is our tragedy, the tragedy of all of us together, that a terrible blow has been dealt to Socialism: it has been compromised.' His speech was outstandingly important. It revealed the painful embarrassment and scarcely reconcilable contradictions faced by all Communists who deviate from Stalinism. Under the pressure of growing social and political discontent and difficulties, they feel (and even acknowledge) the need for a more lenient dictatorship, the need to grant economic and social concessions, and to permit a certain amount of criticism to act as a safety valve for accumulated dissatisfaction.

But the Communists in transition also fear that the 'liberalizing process' might go so far as to sweep away Communism itself. Tito was right when he blamed Russia for having 'failed to see and correct the errors of Rakosi's rule beforehand . . . and to make it possible for those people to come forward whom the working class and the entire people trusted'.

As soon as the Hungarians began to destroy their Communist administration in order to establish a true democracy, Tito, despite all his dislike of foreign intervention, thought Red Army tanks preferable to democratic freedom. No doubt Mikoyan, Khrushchev and all those who stood for controlled deStalinization and a certain measure of 'desatellization' among the Central European countries, found themselves in a similar quandary. When they found that, through Hungary's example, the whole Soviet hegemony (and Communism, too) was at stake, they decided, possibly with reluctance, that democracy was not to be introduced in Hungary. 'Stalinist' methods of brute force were the alternative.

I do not agree with those who argue that the Russians were determined from the very start to crush Hungary's national aspirations so cruelly. At that time the Russians themselves were in favour of a measure of liberalization. It is obvious that Moscow, made uneasy by events in Poland, took precautions against similar demonstrations getting out of hand in Hungary. This does not mean that all the Russian leaders were already planning ruthless aggression against a few Hungarian nationalists. All that is known about Mikoyan's unexpected visit to Budapest on October 24 indicates that some of the Soviet leaders were still inclined to compromise with Nagy as they had done with Gomulka. But they wrongly believed that the Hungarians could be frightened out of making further demonstrations.

The evidence – the extraordinary way Russian army units were 'coming and going', and the declaration promising negotiations 'concerning the presence of Soviet troops in Hungary' – proves that the Russians were not unanimously decided on the best method to deal with the situation in Hungary. Only when Nagy pledged his support of a multi-party system, a coalition government, free elections and finally the termination of Hungary's membership of the Warsaw Pact and the country's neutrality, did the Kremlin's leaders agree on the brutal suppression of the Hungarian dreams of democracy and independence.

The dyed-in-the-wool Moscow 'Stalinists' never had any misgivings. They were always convinced that harsh dictatorship alone could keep Communism in power in the satellite countries – or anywhere else. That is why they were unyielding and aggressive in home and foreign policy. They insisted uncompromisingly on doctrine remaining orthodox. They believed only in force. Their intractability was more in harmony with the needs and conditions of true Communism than a policy that might allow concessions to mitigate the rigours of dictatorship. Yet they face increasing difficulties. Their only answer to changing circumstances is to intensify their stubbornness and brutality. This in turn can only increase domestic and foreign tension. Stalinism creates the possibility of ultimate rebellion by stiffening the slave's yoke, but 'deStalinization' also unleashes revolutionary forces to threaten the whole Communist system.

The choice is not, as Tito believes, between Stalinism and some kind of more liberal Marx-Leninism, but between Communism (Stalinist or Leninist) and a new, liberal social democracy. For this reason, Tito finally agreed that Red Army intervention in Hungary was 'necessary'. The triumph of democracy (or, in the terminology used by Tito and Moscow, 'the establishment of a bourgeois and reactionary system') would be for him 'the worst thing that could have happened'. The collapse of a Communist administration in a neighbouring country would have endangered his own dictatorship in Yugoslavia.

Milovan Djilas, in an article for which he was sentenced to many years in prison, said: 'Yugoslavia supported this discontent in the other East European countries dominated by Moscow as long as it was conducted by the Communist leaders, but turned against it – as in Hungary – as soon as it went further. The fact that Yugoslavia abstained in the United Nations on the question of Soviet intervention revealed that Yugoslav national Communism was unable in its foreign policy to depart from its narrow ideological and bureaucratic class interests and that, furthermore, it was ready to yield even those principles of equality and non-interference in internal affairs on which all its successes in the struggle with Moscow had been based.'

Tito's approach to the Hungarian revolution was shared by Gomulka and, to some extent, by Chou En Lai. And it showed the limitations of so-called 'national Communism'. Tito, like Gomulka, refused to submit in all things to the *diktat* of Moscow. Yet, while rejecting Soviet interference, especially military intervention, in his affairs, he feared above all a victory of democratic principles in East Central Europe. This was why, despite all their resistance to Soviet domination, the other Communist leaders were determined to see Russia maintain Communism as the dominating, dictatorial ideology in that part of the world.

Tito and Gomulka may have appeared more enlightened by cultivating extensively friendly relations with the West, but basically they had to agree with the Russians on the main points of international policy. They could not endanger themselves by doing anything else. Even 'national Communist' regimes need not only the preservation of Soviet power in Russia but also the preponderant influence of Moscow in East Central Europe.

The Russians must have realized this, yet in their vehement campaign against 'national Communism' they fiercely repudiated Tito's Pula speech. *Pravda* criticized certain statements 'which, both in form and substance, are opposed to the principles of proletarian internationalism and the international co-operation of workers'.

In other words, they were fighting over the question of Soviet dominance of the Communist camp. Sharper still were the attacks on Tito by the satellite Communists. They all realized that without Soviet help their regimes, menaced by the example of the Polish and Hungarian risings, would collapse if solidly attacked by a united opposition. Albanian attacks on Tito were the most violent; they refuted his 'anti-Soviet lies' and accused him of his own 'brutal' interference in the internal affairs of Albania, Bulgaria and other countries.

Albanian Communists also accused Tito of maltreating the Albanian minority in Yugoslavia, and hinted that they would like to see the existing Albanian-Yugoslav frontier altered in favour of Albania. When the Bulgarians criticized Tito at the same time, it looked as though Moscow wanted to warn Yugoslavia in this fashion that it was vulnerable from attack by both the Bulgarians (with their grievance about Macedonia) and the Albanians.

Only in Poland, to the annoyance of Moscow, did Tito's

opinions find sympathy. Fresh diatribes against Tito were heard when Kadar visited Moscow. Kadar rejected Tito's interpretations of the Hungarian crisis. Yugoslav Communists, he argued, 'are adopting a view that happens to be identical with the non-Marxist assessment of Dulles and Radio Free Europe'. Yet Kadar's rejection of the Yugoslav evaluation sounded strange on the lips of a Marxist. He was shocked, he said, by the idea that his regime 'should build the Hungarian People's Republic on the so-called central and district workers' councils, the very bodies which had attacked the people's (the Communists') power by armed provocation'.

In this statement Kadar unwittingly confirmed that the workers had risen against the Communist regime, and admitted at the same time that a Communist government cannot depend on the support of the workers' elected representatives.

Bulganin agreed that the Yugoslav leaders did not differ 'from the imperialists in their analysis of the situation in Hungary'. Recalling that Nagy had found sanctuary at the Yugoslav Embassy, Bulganin added: 'Everybody knows that Imre Nagy and his group received practical support from Yugoslavia's leaders. All these facts could not fail to lead to a sharpening of the ideological differences that exist between Yugoslavia and the countries of the Soviet camp.'

'National Communism' was once more categorically rejected. Soviet leaders renounced, after the October risings, their conciliatory ideas on 'individual roads to Socialism' on which the agreement with Tito had been based. They returned to the Stalinist conception that there is but one 'common road' leading to Socialism, a road trodden under the generally recognized leadership of the Soviet Union. 'National Communism' again became a dangerous heresy, merely because, after October 1956, the Kremlin advisers were seized with a fear that this could become a step towards the total extermination of Communism. Satellite Communists were terrified for the same reason. It could mean the loss of their jobs, their power and even their heads.

So antagonism between Moscow and Belgrade emerged again in a more acute form. The much-publicized agreements made before the rebellions were forgotten. The Russians stopped the financial aid about which there had been negotiations. Promises of a resumption of limited trade with Yugoslavia were never fulfilled. Yet neither the Kremlin nor the Yugoslav dictator was eager to renew the violent hostilities that had followed the break between them in 1948. Indeed, Bulganin ended the speech in which he severely censured the Yugoslav Communists on a conciliatory note: 'We . . . will continue to do everything possible to lessen these differences, and to eliminate them completely.'

Belgrade's answers showed an equal desire to avoid another exchange of acrimonious polemics with Moscow. Communism generally had been weakened by the risings in Poland and Hungary. The Yugoslavs and the Russians realized the consequences of a quarrel that could only emphasize their inability to work together. But although they disagreed on many things, they were at least agreed on protecting their own dictatorships. Also, the Yugoslavs, thoroughly alarmed by the punishment inflicted by the Red Army on Hungary, realized that although Soviet power might be unpleasant, it did, after all, afford some protection for any Communist dictatorship.

Trade negotiations between Russia and Yugoslavia were renewed in the spring of 1957. And both Moscow and Belgrade formally commemorated the first anniversary of their 1956 reconciliation when the Soviet Minister of Defence visited Tito in June. Marshal Zhukov was considered over-optimistic when he had expressed the hope, in the comforting glow of early reconciliation, that, if there were a war, the Soviet and Yugoslav armies would fight side by side. And the Polish and Hungarian troubles showed that as long as Tito remains in power, Yugoslav forces will never be among those who take up arms against Red Russia. But this does not prevent the personal unfriendliness that causes tension between Moscow and Belgrade from persisting, and the Hungarian revolution showed how difficult it was to reconcile nationalist ideals with an international overlordship even among Communist dictators.

Khrushchev and Tito tried once more to reconcile their ideas at a secret conference in Rumania in August. Eventually a communiqué announced that they had met and explained, too, that they had agreed 'to work for a further all-round development of relations and for the removal of obstacles hindering this development'. In these revealing words lay a hint that the obstacles to complete and friendly co-operation had not been swept away; that Tito had not changed his fundamental position of independence. But he had agreed with Khrushchev on the need for 'maintaining constant ties by the exchange of party delegations, mutual information and publications . . .' to 'strengthen in every way the unity and fraternal co-operation of the Communist and workers' parties and the peoples of all the Socialist countries and of peace-loving and progressive forces throughout the world'.

This vague phrasing was said to indicate Tito's readiness to help in the creation of another Cominform to replace the one disbanded in April 1956. Khrushchev, hearing that the Czech, East German and French Communists had been pleading for a new Cominform as a precaution against further Polish and Hungarian risings, said during a visit to Prague that the collaboration of the Yugoslavs in building a new international Communist body would be most desirable.

Although Khrushchev and Tito remain reluctant partners, they continue to recognize the need to help each other in trade, and the Russians eventually fulfilled their promise to give Yugoslavia the money with which to build aluminium and fertilizer plants during a seven-year reconstruction programme. But, despite his efforts, Khrushchev was unable to persuade Yugoslavia to accept the Kremlin's leadership.

CHINA'S GROWING PRESTIGE

The Polish and Hungarian risings weakened Russia's position in another way. China used this European crisis to claim for herself a place as an equal partner of Russia in the world of Communism. She even began to interfere in European affairs. China studied every move in the Polish and Hungarian incidents. Chinese newspapers, especially the *Jen-Min-Jih-Pao*, indicated that the Peking Communists accepted Moscow's declaration of October 30, 1956, as proof that the Russians wished to make amends for the way the other Communist states had been treated since the end of the war. At the same time, the Chinese believed that the demands made by the Polish and Hungarian people were justified. Peking emphasized that it was necessary to distinguish between such nationalist aspirations and the activities of small groups of reactionaries.

Relations between Communist countries should be based, according to Peking, on a genuine respect for the sovereignty, independence and equality of each state. Interference in the domestic affairs of another Communist country should not be tolerated. 'Great Power chauvinism' – this was evidently a criticism of Soviet foreign policy – must at all costs be avoided.

When the Red Army went into action in Hungary, Chinese newspapers said that, by making mistakes in the past, Russia had helped to bring the trouble on herself. Yet the Chinese also reproached the Hungarians for endangering the unity of the Communist world. They accused Nagy and his Government colleagues of betraying 'the cause of Socialism'. The Chinese Communists emphasized that Red Army intervention was necessary and inevitable to ensure that a counter-revolutionary (or anti-Communist) administration was not established to threaten the independence and security of all European Communist states. (Tito's arguments were the same.) Peking agreed that the unity of the Communist states grouped around Russia should be preserved, no matter what the cost – in lives or principles.

For this reason, too, the Chinese said that the 'whole Socialist camp' must be made aware of the need to strengthen and maintain the Warsaw Pact. Once the Hungarian crisis had passed, the Chinese Communist newspapers began to explain that not only Fascist groups had been responsible. The rebels came 'from various classes', it was explained. This led the Chinese to point out that military intervention in a foreign country [such as Tibet?] always created an exceptional situation and caused 'certain misunderstandings'.

Jen-Min-Jih-Pao again stressed that it was necessary for the stronger states to avoid making mistakes of Great Power chauvinism while smaller countries should fight against the dangers of reactionary nationalism. Presumably the Chinese Communists agreed with Soviet intervention in Hungary because they realized, with Tito (and Gomulka), that any sign of disintegration in the Communist world would endanger their own position and benefit the capitalist world. At the same time, they supported Russia's action, only on condition that Moscow renounced 'Great Power chauvinism' and collaborated with other Communist states, especially with China, without imposing her will on them. In other words, China demanded equality.

Chou En Lai's visits to Poland and to Hungary showed China's increased importance in the Communist world. Possibly Moscow's leaders themselves asked the Chinese Prime Minister to help in restoring the unity and the morale of the Communist states. But the Chinese shrewdly decided to exploit Moscow's embarrassments in order to strengthen their own position in the Communist world.

Chou En Lai was unable to persuade Gomulka to recognize Russia as the head of the Communist camp; nor could he make him publicly declare his whole-hearted approval of Red Army intervention in Hungary. A Sino-Polish declaration in January 1957 merely stated: 'The common idea of Socialism closely binds the U.S.S.R., the Chinese People's Republic, the Polish People's Republic and the other Socialist countries.' In this document, Russia is left on the same level as other Communist states. No less significant was the way in which the declaration emphasized that 'the basic principles of Marx-Leninism should be applied, taking into consideration the concrete conditions prevailing in different countries'. Such recognition of the principle of 'different roads to Socialism' – replaced by the Russians with the principle of a common road to Socialism under the leadership of Moscow – was not incorporated in the Sino-Polish declaration on Hungary. Chou En Lai and Gomulka agreed 'to support' the Kadar Government and 'resolutely to oppose all attempts on the part of Imperialists to intervene in the internal affairs of Hungary'.

Moscow could hardly feel gratified by Gomulka's diffident attitude to the Red Army intervention in Hungary, and the Russian leaders must have been very conscious of the danger of Gomulka and Tito sharing the same opinion of the way Moscow handled Nagy. Yet Chou En Lai must have helped considerably in making the Poles understand the necessity of remaining friendly with Moscow if they, too, wished to avoid Red Army interference.

One paragraph of the Sino-Polish declaration was never given its proper value. The Chinese showed for the first time a direct interest in European affairs. They said: 'The present western frontier of Poland on the Oder-Neisse line constitutes a frontier of peace between Poland and Germany, in accordance with the interests of European security.' The same term was used in a declaration signed by the Poles and the East Germans during Gomulka's visit to Berlin. The Oder-Neisse frontier which East (but not West) Germany considered to be permanent, was described as 'a substantial element of peace and security in Europe'.

The Sino-Polish statement added: 'The Governments of the two countries support each other's desire to guarantee the sovereignty, territorial integrity and security of their countries.' This significant political intervention of Communist China in European affairs showed Peking's willingness to guarantee the western frontier of Poland, and prepared the ground for China's taking part in important settlements in Europe or at least in East Central Europe.

Poland had strengthened her position, having found in China

a second Great Power which, like Russia, recognized her frontiers. Poland could now summon Chinese help to protect her sovereignty and security, even if threatened by Russia. For the Poles, China was a welcome ally and protector of their interests, the more so as the Peking Communists, in spite of their formal recognition of Russia as 'the head' of the Communist camp, insist on the equality of the Communist states and the principle of non-intervention in their internal affairs, and advocate a doctrine of 'different roads to Socialism' according to 'concrete conditions prevailing in the different countries'.

Sino-Polish friendship showed itself again during a visit of Polish Ministers to Peking in 1957. This Polish delegation visited seven Asian countries, India among them. Everywhere they tried to gain understanding for 'the Polish road to Socialism' and support for the Oder-Neisse line as 'the frontier of peace against the Western imperialists and militarists'.

When a Czech Government delegation visited China, North Vietnam, North Korea and Outer Mongolia, and signed treaties 'of friendship and co-operation' with China and Mongolia, a Sino-Czech communiqué stressed 'the unity of the Socialist camp headed by the Soviet Union'. From a reference to Russia in communiqués signed with other Asian Communist countries, it is evident that, unlike the Poles, the Czech leaders consider that Moscow alone is the Socialist Mecca. They did not even give undue prominence to their delegation's visit to Peking.

Cyrankiewicz, however, on his return to Warsaw, said: 'Our views on building Socialism are close to those of China. In our country, the expression of these views was the Eight Plenum [when Gomulka came to power on his own terms despite Russia's antagonism], and in China it was the thesis of the blossoming of all flowers.'

He left no doubt that Poland appreciated China's support for a policy based on a 'national road to Socialism' – a policy condemned by Moscow's Stalinists.

The Chinese, eager to influence European diplomacy, saw

Gomulka's Poland as a convenient stepping-stone to a new world of greatness. And it was a stepping-stone they could use without having to submit to Kremlin policies. They could still maintain their own brand of Communism. During a brief visit to Budapest, Chou En Lai showed that he shared the Russian view of the Hungarian revolution. Yet a joint declaration published at the end of his talks with Kadar twice mentioned 'the great mistakes of the previous leadership'.

This communiqué, full of bitterness about the activities of American imperialists and foreign and Hungarian counter-revolutionaries, stressed the 'closeness and friendly co-operation among the countries in the Socialist camp, led by the Soviet Union', and recalled Moscow's promise to rectify previous 'violations and mistakes' in her relations with other Communist states, in accordance with the Leninist principle that these states should be equal.

It was not only the need to maintain the unity of the Communist states against the 'Western imperialists' that led China to show such interest in the Hungarian rising. In a speech made on February 27, 1957 (but not published until June 18), Mao Tse-Tung admitted that the Hungarian revolution had raised considerable interest in China. He said that certain people, rejoicing in the Hungarian crisis, hoped something similar would happen in China; that thousands of people would demonstrate in the streets against the People's Government. Such hopes were contrary to the interests of the masses and could 'find no support among them'.

Some people under Hungarian influence, he explained, believed there was 'too little freedom in our People's Democracy and more freedom in Western Parliamentary democracies'. He added that they 'demanded the establishment of the Western bipartisan system with one party in power and the other outside the Government'. But as leader of the Chinese Communists he naturally rejected the two-party system because, as he said, it was nothing but 'a means by which a bourgeois dictatorship can be kept in power'.

Mao Tse-Tung condemned the Hungarian revolution as a counter-revolution, but he showed a greater appreciation than either the Russians or their satellite Governments of the experience that had been so painful and so ominous for Communism. He submitted a new political programme in which he acknowledged that many conflicts must exist in a Communist society. He suggested that it was difficult for the Government and the people always to agree in detail. He stressed that Marxism could not be inculcated by force but only by patient education and persuasion, though, at the same time, he advocated the use of force against 'reactionaries' who tried to destroy the 'Socialist structure of a state'.

Peking showed greater understanding than Moscow of the Hungarian and Polish calls for freedom. And Mao Tse-Tung and Chou En Lai at least indicated that the Hungarian Revolution had shaken Communism's complacency. Indeed, Chou En Lai, speaking at a meeting of the Chinese People's Congress, condemned 'rightish deviations' and hinted that the Hungarians had greatly increased the desire for freedom in all Communist countries – particularly in China.

Peking may have helped Moscow to overcome the immediate difficulties caused by the Hungarian crisis, and to restore at least the appearance of co-operation within the Communist camp. But at the same time, using this opportunity to interfere in Russia's sphere of influence in East Central Europe, Mao Tse-Tung revealed his desire to be the ideological leader of the Communist world.

UNREST IN THE SATELLITE COUNTRIES

The October risings weakened the position of Russia as the undisputed master of the Communist world. The men in the Kremlin had to reconcile themselves to a considerable increase in China's influence. They had to agree to the Poles having their own brand of Communism and they had to face fresh tension in their relations with Tito. Nor was it easy to restore (and to maintain) Russian prestige in other satellite countries.

The Communist leaders of these states fell over themselves to prove their dedication to Moscow (and to condemn the 'Hungarian counter-revolution'), but the exaggerated zeal with which they tried to emphasize their loyalty only proved that they too were terrified that their people might be affected by the Hungarian example. This was revealed not only by their hysterical campaign against 'revisionism', 'national Communism' and all species of 'liberalism' but also by their persecution of the real or imagined enemies of the 'People's Democracy'. A strengthening of their dictatorial methods was inevitable, yet they tried to appease their people by reducing prices, increasing wages and making concessions to factory workers. They also applied less pressure in exacting compulsory deliveries of food from the peasants.

Moscow invited Communist delegations to the Soviet capital, sent their own representatives to the enslaved countries and encouraged visits among the satellite leaders. Never before, within a few months, were there so many official visits of Party delegations or Government leaders to Moscow, Budapest, Berlin, Prague, Warsaw and other capitals of the Communist countries. Never before was there such a flood of declarations of all kinds, of such long, grandiloquent and drearily uniform utterances. In each of these, the firm co-operation of the Communists and the leadership of the Soviet Union was stressed. They all contained diatribes against the foreign and internal enemies of 'Socialism' and the 'People's Democracy'; all fiercely attacked the United States and the 'other Western imperialists'; all condemned in strong terms any deviation from Kremlin orthodoxy.

Tito was censured and there was much criticism of Gomulka. The painfully monotonous insistence on the leadership of Russia in the Communist world showed that this was an uncertain supremacy. Constant exhortations for vigilance as well as such terrorist methods as trials of 'spies' and 'agents' were the unmistakable signs of nervousness among the Communists. Impassioned condemnation of 'national Communism' was also proof of the weakness of the satellite regimes. All the minor Communist dictators realized that without the protection of Moscow and the Red Army they would be swept away. Czech Communists were particularly frightened. They saw their only salvation in a Stalinist policy. Unlike the Polish Communists, they rejected Mao Tse-Tung's tendency to allow any criticism at all.

Jiri Hendrych, Secretary of the Czech Communist's Central Committee, explained that Mao Tse-Tung was striving for 'the conquest of bourgeois ideology in an open clash of opinions'. This was important in Asian and African countries whose 'national *bourgeoisie* was a fundamental force in the fight against imperialism'. But Czechoslovakia lay on the frontier of that capitalist world in which nowadays the most aggressive ideas were being developed . . . and there was no room for compromise with a 'class enemy' or for toleration of alien ideas.

Prague's Vice-Premier, Vaclav Kopecký, attacking with extraordinary virulence 'writers who had learned nothing from Poland and Hungary', declared that the Party would not tolerate the propagation of 'revisionist, nationalist and bourgeois liberal opinion' or permit 'opposition policies' to be discussed. He was adamant about the Communist Party not allowing 'Western bourgeois decadence' to blossom in its garden. In the following months many state trials were staged in Prague, and at least ten people, accused of espionage and anti-state activities, were executed. Of the unknown number sent to prison, some (including Catholic priests) received very long sentences. It was significant that the Czech Communist leaders should have been so openly apprehensive, for the people themselves showed very few signs of unrest.

Students and young workers demonstrated during the critical days of the Hungarian Revolution, but their protest meetings were quietly and effectively handled by the security police. The members of the Government, having full control of the newspapers, did not allow a word of criticism of their administration. A strict censorship was applied, and in the few instances in which mildly reproachful articles were published, resolute official action was taken at once. Discontent among the Czechs was neither greater nor less than the unrest in other slave states, but the local Communists, rigidly disciplined by a tough leadership, were not allowed to develop the kind of individual thoughts that led to splits in the Party in Poland and Hungary.

The economic situation in Czechoslovakia, always the richest of the Central European countries, was not as bad as in neighbouring Communist states, despite many shortages. But the main reason why the Czechs remained passive was the tragic fate of Hungary's rebels, crushed so ruthlessly by Red Army tanks without being given any help at all. Memories of the fate that overtook Czechoslovakia when Hitler's tanks and armoured divisions rumbled over the frontier and into Prague were revived in the minds of many people. A highly developed sense of political realism, though not always blameless, warned them against risky action or a futile struggle, at least while the existing balance of Communist power was maintained. Yet the Czech Communists behaved as though they were menaced by rebels, partly because they wished to demonstrate that they would be ruthless if endangered, and partly because – as one foreign observer put it – they were living 'in an atmosphere of undefinable internal tension'.

The visit of Khrushchev and Bulganin to Czechoslovakia in July 1957 was welcomed by the Czech Communist leaders because this spectacular backing from the Kremlin's masters for their 'faithful Leninist policy strengthened them against bourgeois trends'. Khrushchev, fully approving the firm policy of the Czechoslovak Communists, detected signs of deviation and his speeches came as a warning to all who dared to oppose Prague's Government or endanger the 'eternal Soviet-Czechoslovak friendship'. Even so, the Communist leaders began to realize that they were more and more hated by the people. The more they became isolated from the masses and from the rank and file of their own party, the more they became dependent on

Moscow's support. For the Kremlin, Czechoslovakia is vital because of its situation in the midst of volcanic Germany, undependable Poland and restless Hungary.

Prague's Communist leaders were haunted by the fear of revolutionary movements in East Germany. If trouble started in Communist Germany the Czechs would also rebel, it was thought, in the hope that West Germany and the other Western Powers might then take action.

Moscow shared these apprehensions. They sent impressive numbers of Red Army reinforcements to East Germany, not simply to frighten Poland but to insure against the possibility of a German rising. The East German Communist leaders were never suspect. They watched the Polish and Hungarian risings with even more disfavour than the Russians themselves. Of all the Communist parties, the East German remained the most Stalinist in character, probably because it was the weakest. The Hungarian revolution had a much stronger influence on East German intellectuals and students (and also on a considerable section of the workers) than the Polish revolt, because there is a traditional nationalist enmity between the Germans and the Poles, despite the official friendship of their Communist Governments.

It was not always possible even for the German and Polish Communist leaders to hide their feelings for each other. Walter Ulbricht, the true ruler of East Germany, brutally suppressed all expressions of sympathy for 'revisionism' and 'nationalism'. (Professor Wolfgang Harich, the young Communist 'heretic' who wished to 'liberate Marxism-Leninism from Stalinism and dogmatism, and to restore its basis of humanist, non-dogmatic thought', was sentence to ten years' imprisonment.) And Ulbricht's ruthlessness undoubtedly stopped a dangerous trend towards liberalism in East Germany. In a way he was helped by the West Germans urgently exhorting their East German countrymen to keep calm. They, too, feared the unfathomable consequences of a rising in East Germany.

The Russians had to succour Ulbricht's puppet Government

when Poland reduced its coal exports. The Kremlin gave East Germany a handsome loan and increased deliveries of Soviet coal. They also increased the prestige of East Germany – a satellite that had so far been treated as a second-rate member of the Communist alliance. An East German delegation was invited to Moscow, to be received with great pomp, and immediately after the suppression of the Hungarian rising the Russians suggested an exchange of visits between the East German and other Central European Communists. Delegations from the Czech and East German parties met in December 1956. They easily came to an agreement because both had the same servile devotion to Moscow. They condemned the Hungarian 'counter-revolution', Gomulka's deviationism and the attitude of Tito. The two Parties jointly declared that they 'decisively opposed all attempts to split the Marxist workers' movement by a division into Stalinists and non-Stalinists – these ideas originating only in the arsenal of imperialist propaganda'.

They pledged 'their firm determination not to allow any violation of the principles of proletarian internationalism, and to combat all nationalist and anti-Soviet tendencies'. The declaration asserted that 'all talk about alleged "national Communism" conflicts with Marxism-Leninism'. They upheld 'unwavering friendship with Russia as a prerequisite for the victory of Socialism'. The 'lesson of Hungary' was the 'need to increase political and ideological vigilance . . . to thwart in good time the intentions of our enemies, particularly NATO'.

Finally, they emphasized the need to strengthen the Warsaw Pact, and their declaration became a pattern for all those that followed. Most important politically was the agreement between Gomulka and Ulbricht during a visit of a Polish delegation to East Berlin. Although Ulbricht was unable to persuade Gomulka to abandon his 'soft middle-way line' or to acknowledge explicitly the Soviet leadership, the Communist leaders agreed on the necessity of fostering the 'solidarity of the Socialist camp' and of strengthening the Warsaw alliance against the militarists of NATO and West Germany who presented 'a menace to the German Democratic Republic, Poland and other countries'.

Gomulka fully supported the Russian ideas for German unification. Despite his apparent willingness to co-operate with East Germany, he showed quite openly that he would not be averse also to a similar *rapprochement* with West Germany. At the same time, he succeeded in obtaining from Ulbricht fresh recognition of the Oder-Neisse line as a 'substantial element of security and peace in Europe'. The significance of the joint declaration was that the Polish Communists had the same views on all the principal questions dividing the West from the East as the Russians and the other Communist countries.

One of the most significant effects of the Polish and Hungarian risings on Soviet diplomacy was the immediate recognition by Russia of East Germany as 'an equal and especially cherished member of the Communist block alliance'. The Chinese Communists commended the wisdom of this Soviet move, and by recognizing East Germany's sovereignty they grasped another opportunity of exercising their influence in Europe. The closer association between Ulbricht and Khrushchev meant that East Germany became even more enslaved in the true Stalinist spirit. Moscow thus put a tighter ring around Poland and shattered Polish hopes for gaining more independence. And by this move the Russians planned to stop the disintegration or deterioration of their whole empire.

At one time it was thought that the liberation of Central Europe could come only after East and West Germany had been united under a freely elected Government. But the Hungarian rebellion, though unsuccessful, at least showed that East Germany itself could become free to choose its own future through one of the Middle European satellites breaking away from Russia's grip. Soviet diplomats realized far more quickly than Western experts the dangerous possibilities in the restlessness of the satellite people. This was another reason why Hungary had to be taught a lesson, and also why East Germany should be drawn closer than ever before to the Warsaw Pact allies.

In a joint declaration, the Speakers of the Polish, Czech and East German Parliaments declared: 'The security and integrity of the German Democratic Republic are an indispensable condition of the maintenance of peace in Europe . . . the existence of the German Democratic Republic is a guarantee that the platform of the progressive elements of the German people will be able to exert its full influence during the settlement of the German problem.' The three delegations underlined in the same declaration that the 'existing frontiers of Poland and Czechoslovakia are definitely fixed and are unalterable'. This is the price East Germany paid for equality within the Communist empire.

During a visit to East Germany in the first half of August 1957, Khrushchev emphasized that he was solidly behind Walter Ulbricht, a staunch Stalinist opponent of any kind of political relaxation or leniency. This confirmed the belief that the Russians favoured an iron-fist policy in maintaining their control over East Germany. Khrushchev, categorically refusing all Western suggestions for German reunification, unreservedly backed Ulbricht's proposal for a loose confederation of East and West Germany. Moscow's open hostility to Chancellor Adenauer indicated that it still hoped to solve the German problem on its own terms or, at least, to secure as much influence as possible in the future German settlement. Time and again the Russian and East German leaders repeated their willingness to co-operate over zones of limited (and inspected) arms in Europe, thus making it all the more clear that Moscow was eager to disarm and neutralize Germany while keeping intact Communist outposts in East Central Europe.

By establishing East Germany as a fully fledged member of the Communist alliance, the Kremlin's masters, paradoxically enough, strengthened their grip on this slave state, but at the same time they increased the risk of further rebellion. They enabled Ulbricht to make the most of a ruthless tyranny. And when Khrushchev ostentatiously approved this cruel dictatorial policy, the disgust and hostility of the East Germans was dangerously increased. They probably refrained from further demonstrations against the Communist rule only because they believed that unification (probably by becoming neutral) might be achieved more readily if they remained subservient. Probably the Russians realized that they were taking a calculated risk. But there was no doubt that Khrushchev, with his zigzag policy, was playing a far more hazardous game than Stalin or the Stalinists. He was gambling on keeping this resentment bottled up until he had a chance of trying to persuade the West to accept his plans (at least in part) for Germany's future.

But in their eagerness to repair the damage done to their empire by the Polish and Hungarian risings, the Soviet leaders took risks with contradictory policies. They made many dubious decisions, and it was not accidental that East German and Czech Communists, terrified by the possibility of fresh outbursts of rebellion, accepted the necessity of reinforcing the Warsaw Pact which to them was 'a mighty bulwark against the dark plots of the members of the Atlantic alliance'.

The Russians learned a lot from the Polish and Hungarian risings. The swiftness with which they made use of the knowledge acquired should be a lesson to the West. One of the first Soviet moves was to make new agreements about stationing Red Army units in the enslaved countries. A new arrangement, necessary after the treaty with Poland signed in December 1956, showed some respect for Polish sovereignty. Ostensibly, Soviet troops could be stationed in Poland only by the consent of the Warsaw Government. Similar agreements with East Germany, Rumania and, finally, Hungary stressed that the presence of Russian units on the territory of these countries 'in no way affected their sovereignty'.

In reality the agreements gave these Governments even less authority than was granted to the Poles. But in Poland, as everywhere else, everything depends on the willingness of the

Soviet Government to fulfil contractual obligations. The presence of Russian troops in these countries may constitute a constant danger, but it also facilitates Red Army intervention if there is trouble among the people. All the satellite Governments, with the possible exception of that of Poland, would anyway ask for Soviet intervention should they find themselves threatened by internal unrest. Or at least, the Russians would soon be able to find a Gero or a Kadar to ask for help.

Because at that time the Russians felt the situation in East Germany to be particularly delicate, they stipulated in their agreement with Ulbricht that the Russian Commander could, if the security of his troops was endangered, 'take all necessary steps to avert this danger'.

This clause reveals the true meaning of Moscow's efforts to 'strengthen the Warsaw Pact'. The Kremlin dictators, including the military leaders, no longer had any illusions about the dependability of the satellite armies. If the Warsaw Pact did not increase the Soviet military potential by including the armed forces of the enslaved nations, it at least justified maintaining Russian troops and Red Army bases in these countries. In an emergency the Russians had the 'legal' pretext they needed to intervene against anti-Communist upheavals. This put them in the right with the United Nations (another lesson they had learned). Finally, the Russians, under pressure from liberalizing forces, made the Warsaw Pact a valuable political instrument in bargaining with the Western Powers.

In this manner the Russians, in the first half of 1957, restored their domination of the captive nations and, by deft diplomacy and even shrewder pressure, maintained considerable influence, even in Poland. Only Hungary was subject to the brutal terror that was characteristic of Stalin's era. But the Russians had to start paying heavily for their 'benign' overlordship.

Until the Polish and Hungarian revolutions they exploited the satellites, but in the last ten years they have been forced to help them economically and financially. This was the only way they could maintain the local Communist leaders in power.

Millions of roubles flowed from Moscow into the satellite capitals. Costly loans, trade credits and the cancellation of old debts were also part of the price paid by Moscow for the doubtful security of being protectively ringed by slave states. The extra cost of keeping Red Army units in these countries must have been formidable. From time to time the Russians announced that they had, in fulfilment of one promise or another, cut their army by so many hundreds of thousands. This may have been prompted by the need for economy as much as the need for showing peaceful intentions. But they could not risk reducing their occupation beyond a number considered adequate for an emergency such as a revolution. These troops were a safeguard, not against Western aggression so much as against nationalist risings. But that did not make them any less costly.

Of course, under the terms of the Warsaw Pact, the satellites had to help to pay for the Russian defence forces billeted on them, even though they realized these Russian soldiers were in reality their gaolers. East Germany paid least of all – only half of the total cost. Even so, the Germans faced an annual bill of probably £20 million – quite as much as the other less wealthy satellites.

By having a double value for the rouble the Russians always made the satellites pay dearly for their 'trade' with the dominating country in the Communist empire. To the superficial glance the exchange seemed reasonable. In reality it was overwhelmingly in favour of Russia. But even this did not help when Poland decided to cut by 7 million tons the coal she had been sending each year to Czechoslovakia and East Germany. To prevent a domestic squabble among the satellites, Russia was forced to supply the deficit. But the Hungarian decision to cut exports of bauxite hit the Czech aluminium industry, and the Russians could do nothing about it.

The ambitious Five Year Plans aimed at the economic integration of the Communist countries had to be drastically revised at the time when they were to start showing the wonderful results of a division of labour among members of the Warsaw alliance. Also, at the very moment when the frightened Communist leaders were trying to prevent unrest by promising a better standard of living, they were forced to make heavy cuts in capital investment and to increase the money needed to develop the production of food and consumer goods at the expense of heavy industry. Yet according to Soviet principles, heavy industry should always have priority.

Czechoslovakia's President, Zápotocký, explained it all away by saying: 'Because of recent international events which have not been without effect on our economy, we also have to adjust and change our economic development in some directions.' Rumanian and Bulgarian Communist leaders also made similar speeches, and the Kadar Government had to admit that it was being forced to abandon the old (pre-revolutionary) Five Year Plan and prepare another. But then (to the satisfaction of the Polish and Hungarian rebels) even Russia herself was obliged to revise her Five Year Plan, adjusting her sights to more modest targets.

Some reports suggested that instead of producing about 593 million tons of coal in 1960 as planned, the Russians would settle for 550; and 8 million tons was knocked off the target of 68 million tons of steel. The electricity programme was also substantially reduced.

It is doubtful whether the Russians ever thought that to maintain Central Europe they would be forced to support (as though they were colonies) the slave states they had hitherto exploited. This unexpected burden would have caused less embarrassment if they did not have other obligations. But the Russians were obliged to try to satisfy what Khrushchev had called the insatiability of the Chinese Communists. The increasing demands of the Chinese, eager for the industrial development of their agricultural lands, were so great that some economists argued that Russia's alliance with China might become a burden rather than an asset. The unexpected calls on Russia's economy also came at a difficult time. Moscow was trying to compete with the United States in winning, by economic means, the favours of the Asian and Middle East countries. The Russians were left in the position of having to strain their own economy to the limit. This could only add further embarrassment, for they dare not risk unrest at home by cutting down the long-awaited and long-promised production of consumer goods.

The October eruptions caused the enslaved countries of East Central Europe to become a 'colonial problem' for Russia, far more dangerous than the colonial challenge facing the Western Powers. They could 'liberate' their colonies without placing any risk on their leadership in their own country, but the Russians had to go on paying or lose their dictatorial power in a fresh wave of national liberation.

CHAPTER VIII

World in Transition

THE HISTORICAL MEANING OF THE
HUNGARIAN REVOLUTION

The Red Army crushed the Hungarian rising; the Kadar regime, enforced on the defeated people, was established by terror in the shadow of the Soviet tanks. The Poles, afraid that their state might be erased from the map of Europe, became chary of liberalizing tendencies. This helped Gomulka to preserve a Communist regime of 'its own kind'. A threat of a merciless military intervention, hanging over all the captive nations, persuaded them to refrain from any action that might incite the anger of Moscow. After seeing what happened in Hungary, they were, at the same time, inclined to dismiss the possibility of any practical help from the Western Powers. The Soviets were able to continue holding East Central Europe in their thrall.

Yet it would be wrong to suppose that the October rebellions in Poland and Hungary were but passing episodes. They brought significant changes, not only in the Soviet empire but also in the whole Communist world. Organized Communism had been severely shaken; Soviet power had been seriously weakened.

It was only natural that Poland, under Gomulka, should subsequently play the more important role. Hungary could only speak to the world's conscience through her martyrdom. But the impact of the Hungarian revolution on the future will be more far-reaching than that of 'Gomulkism'. Its heroic cry for freedom could never be silenced. It will always have a lasting and ever-growing influence. For this was a real revolution, a great history-making event. It was a national protest, a blow for national independence against foreign hegemony. A social revolution – for social justice, a better life and autonomy of the social classes – against oppression, exploitation and misery. A political revolution – for freedom, the rule of law, and personal safety – against dictatorship. A spiritual and ethical revolution – for truth, freedom of conscience and spiritual independence – against lies and fraud, against forced moulding of the soul.

The Yugoslav Communist, Milovan Djilas, wrote in an article in the American weekly *The New Leader* on November 19, 1956:

'If the events in Poland encouraged the aspirations of Communist parties . . . for equality with Moscow, the Hungarian Revolution made a gigantic leap and placed on the agenda the problem of freedom in Communism, that is to say, the replacement of the Communist system itself by a new social system. . . . The changes in Poland mean the triumph of national Communism which in a different form we have already seen in Yugoslavia. The Hungarian uprising is something more, a new phenomenon, perhaps no less meaningful than the French or Russian Revolution.'

Djilas hardly exaggerates in his evaluation. The Hungarian Revolution was, despite its tragic ending, a historical event foreshadowing the disintegration of the Soviet Empire and the fall of Communism. The Hungarians finally destroyed the belief that ultimately Communism must be victorious. This belief in inevitable victory, predestined by history and inescapable, was systematically encouraged by the Russians. They kept it alive as though it were the word of a prophet. They realized that it had a hypnotic influence, even on anti-Communists themselves. Many of them, confused in mind, almost asked to be excused for not joining the movement that, sooner or later, must inevitably engulf the whole world.

Launched by intellectuals and workers, the Hungarian Revolution swept away this, the most dangerous political myth of our time and has raised again to a place of honour in every man's mind the eternal ideals of liberty and truth. Nothing could be as significant as the realization that these ideals finally won the unhesitating support of many Communist intellectuals and workers and inspired them to rebel against Moscow's domination. The Communist leaders realized that the very substance of Communism was threatened. They could not admit that it was the workers, the 'popular masses' who revolted against Communism. To do this would be to admit the failure of Communism and reveal its transient character, conditioned by temporary political and social circumstances. This is why they all – not only Khrushchev but also Mao Tse-Tung, Tito and Gomulka – cling desperately to the fiction that the Hungarian revolt was the work of the 'imperialist counter-revolutionaries' who had beguiled 'the popular masses' and led them astray.

The top Communists still possessed the means of coercion needed to preserve their hegemony. But once the Hungarian Revolution had sprung spontaneously from a popular movement, they no longer possessed the power to arouse the enthusiasm or create the driving force that was so characteristic of Communism in the past. They could not rekindle faith in the final and inevitable victory of Communism when this faith was swept away by a revolutionary movement of workers and many former Communists themselves.

Where lies the irresistible force of Communism if the masses, led not by the *bourgeoisie* but by workers and socialist-minded intellectuals, revolt against it? What is the future of Communism if a march of defenceless masses, inspired by the desire for freedom and justice, is brutally dispersed by the Red Army, pride and joy of the Communists themselves?

Tanks had replaced ideals. That was obvious. It was no longer the revolutionary Marx but his contemporary, the reactionary Czar Nicholas I who had become the model for his Communist successors in the Kremlin. Revolutionary troops of Koshut were defeated by Czarist forces, but the ideals of Koshut defeated the ideals of the imperial autocracy and the

Romanovs and the Habsburgs, just as today they are in the process of defeating Communist despotism. Khrushchev crushed Hungarian insurgents, but at the same time he destroyed the Communist belief on which his own empire was built.

If words still possess their accepted meaning, it is not an exaggeration to say that Moscow is now the centre of counter-revolution, determined to suppress any revolutionary movement inspired by the desire for liberty for individuals and for nations. It is the Communist dictators – Mao Tse-Tung no less than Khrushchev – who try to stem the rising tide of those liberal forces to which the future belongs. If they support liberation movements in Asia and Africa, they do it only to serve their own interests: they hope that after having pushed the Western Powers from those areas, they themselves will be able to take their place. But they intend to dominate (economically and politically), not to encourage independence.

Nothing is more symptomatic of the reactionary character of Soviet policy than its absolute lack of fresh ideas. Soviet leaders continue to repeat tired, old slogans that have long ago lost their effectiveness. The Russians have become bores with the soulless vacuousness of their diatribes. They are so unimaginative that they condemn liberalizing tendencies in the very words used by their Csarist predecessors to revile the revolutionary Russian intelligentsia. They denounce them as 'nihilism' or 'anarchism'.[1]

The 'Workers' Government' refuses any real autonomy to

[1] James H. Billington, in a remarkable article, 'The Renaissance of the Russian Intelligentsia', *Foreign Affairs*, April 1957, said: 'In 1863 as now, a cruel Russian repression of an uprising in Eastern Europe (in Poland) created a deep sense of mortification among Russian students and a sense of identity with the common victims of the oppressive Russian state. One even senses that the current [Soviet] student generation shares the implausible confidence felt by the radicals of the 1860: that the only real contending forces were themselves and virtually everyone in authority, "we" and "they".'

the workers; the 'workers' councils' introduced in Yugoslavia – with very limited powers – are condemned as 'anarcho-syndicalism' with a contempt which barely disguises Tito's mistrust of the workers. Because workers' councils were among the main and most effective organs of the revolution, Kadar disbanded them and imprisoned their representatives.

The ideological emptiness and dogmatic rigidity of Moscow made it possible for Peking to try to take over first the ideological and then the political leadership of Communism. With Mao Tse-Tung's alluring theory of a 'hundred flowers', Moscow's leaders showed with spiteful displeasure how much they resented this characteristically poetic attempt to make Communist doctrine attractive. Prague rejected it, asserting that it could be dangerous in a country bordered by 'imperialists'. This antagonism of Moscow's reactionaries and their friends in East Central Europe to the more elastic tactics of the Chinese Communists was all the more significant when one realizes (as a detailed analysis of speeches made by Mao Tse-Tung and Chou En Lai clearly shows) that the Chinese were continuing to advocate with their customary stubbornness the dictatorship of the Communist Party. They were willing to allow only very limited criticism within the rigid framework of any Communist regime.

The Chinese leaders merely emphasized the dangers that threaten a Communist regime as soon as the leaders begin to ease even slightly the rigours of dictatorship. Gomulka had the same experience. Moscow's distrust of his moderate course, recommended by Peking, testified to the fear of liberalization, especially after the shock of the Hungarian Revolution. Even Poland was watched with extreme vigilance. Although Molotov and his companions were banished to allow Khrushchev more elasticity in his policies, the same distrust and cautiousness continued to dominate all Moscow's manœuvres.

Tito admitted that the Hungarian Revolution 'dealt a terrible blow to Socialism', and by 'Socialism' he meant Communism. The ruthless use of violence had succeeded in suppressing revolution, but ruthless expedients can never prevent the inevitable crisis for Communism. The Hungarian Revolution revealed the writing on the wall. Ultimately, the work started by the Hungarians will be finished triumphantly. Meantime the effects of the revolt cannot be assessed fully. In spite of the terror of the Kadar regime (and because of it), Hungary lives in a state of latent revolt. Neither persecution nor intimidation could prevent the ominous unrest among the people in the subjugated countries. Conscience and scepticism torment not only the Soviet intelligentsia but also the officers and soldiers who had to murder Hungarian workers. The Hungarian Revolution caused Mao Tse-Tung to be faced by fresh demands for new liberalization. Tito became doubly beset by the 'neo-Stalinist' reaction of Moscow to the October revolts, and by his fears of what the 'Hungarian contagion' might do to Yugoslavs. Gomulka, forced to yield to the demands of the Moscow and Polish Stalinists, quickly lost the sympathy of the Liberals who supported him during the revolution. His action merely revived the distrust of Poland's non-Communists. The Kadar regime, officially supported by the Polish government, was considered contemptible by the very people who brought Gomulka to power. Most Poles, including even the Communists, continued to praise the Hungarian revolutionaries. Never before had the Communist leaders encountered so many difficulties.

The Hungarian Revolution of October 1956 sharpened enormously all the 'contradictions' in the Communist societies (of which Mao Tse-Tung spoke in detail when still under the immediate influence of shock); and the contradiction between the rulers and the ruled that led to the explosions in Hungary and in Poland were the most significant of all.

Tito admitted that Communism 'had been compromised', not only by brutal Soviet intervention but also in the beginning by the revolt of the workers. Soviet tanks had to confirm that Communism, no longer attractive to the people in all the countries where it was all-powerful, was being maintained by the autocratic means of oppression at the disposal of the dictators. The ideological and moral bankruptcy of Communism, confirmed by the October rising, was a body blow for the Communist dictatorship.

FORCES OF NATIONALISM AND LIBERALISM

How will the 'proletarian internationalism' be able to resist the dynamic thrust of nationalism – apparently a much stronger force than Communism? During the worst period of danger for Russia, Stalin organized the defence of the country in the name of nationalism and not Communism. The Poles and Hungarians rose against foreign hegemony. Feeling was so strong that it carried along the majority of Polish and Hungarian Communists. Gomulka was lifted to power by a wave of Polish nationalism that united the whole nation, both the non-Communists, with Cardinal Wyszynski at their head, and the Communists. All classes of society, led by the workers, united under the Hungarian national flag. Men in the Kremlin recognize that they too are menaced by nationalism, for they condemn 'national Communism'. Tito was successful in overcoming many internal difficulties for the very reason that he was the defender of Yugoslav independence against Moscow. The Chinese Communists, aware of the strength of nationalism, warn with characteristic guile against the 'nationalism of small states' and the 'chauvinism of great powers'. When speaking of such chauvinism they have Soviet Russia in mind.

Moscow and Peking try to increase their influence in Asia and Africa by inciting local nationalist movements, while they support the local Communist movements only in secret or very discreetly. How can proletarian internationalism continue to resist the spontaneous forces of nationalism, especially when it is generally known that this outworn slogan is but a disguise for Soviet hegemony? It is this hegemony to which all the nations of East Central Europe are opposed. Even Peking recognizes Soviet leadership only formally. Nationalist conflicts between Russians and non-Russians constantly threaten

the cohesion of Soviet Russia herself. The outburst of
nationalism that culminated in the October rising was a
reminder that this emotional force is much more powerful
than Communism.

While Soviet colonial domination provoked violent nationalist reactions, Communist tyranny revived a belief in liberalism
that was no less strong. During the October rising, nationalism
was firmly linked with liberalism, just as a hundred years ago
'young Italy', 'young Germany' and 'young Europe' rebelled
against the reactionary absolutism of the Holy Alliance. Polish
and Hungarian rebels strove for the national independence of
their countries as well as for civic freedom and human rights.
Documentary evidence proves that nothing was further from
their thoughts than an attempt to restore the *ancien régime*,
even less did they wish to introduce fascism. It is significant
that the Hungarian revolutionaries, without directives from any
centre and without any discussion among themselves, spontaneously formulated identical demands. Different revolutionary committees all asked identically for suppression of
the secret political police, for a revival of political and civil
liberties, for free elections, for a multi-party system, for
parliamentary democracy, for autonomous workers' councils
controlling the factories, and for free associations of farmers
with the right to form free co-operatives or to leave them and
cultivate their own land independently.

The revolutionaries clearly rejected any thought of returning
to capitalism or landowner feudalism. But they also rejected
Communism. Their aim was to create a new political order,
based on freedom, the rule of law and social security. Many
intellectuals, particularly those who had been (or still considered themselves to be) Communists, talked about 'humani-
tarian Socialism'. Basically, the political programme, with
which the Hungarians hoped to replace Communism, was
liberal Socialism or social liberalism.

Moscow and her satellites began a widespread campaign
against 'liberalism' which they identify with 'reaction' or

'Fascism'. This campaign, a Communist exhortation against 'liberalism' everywhere, was particularly noticeable in Czechoslovakia, where liberal traditions, thanks to the influence of Masaryk, were particularly strong. The Communists used the word 'liberalism' in the mistaken belief that it had painful associations, particularly for the workers who confused liberalism with capitalism. Communists well realize that, apart from religion, the liberal idea constitutes the most dangerous challenge to Communism.

And it was the liberal idea, born of their conception of liberalism, that the Hungarian revolutionaries had in mind. Liberalism as a political movement has been, since the nineteenth century, linked with capitalism. For this reason it became a target for the attacks of Marxists and other socialists. In his design for the dictatorship of the proletariat, Marx not only rejected capitalism but also put an end to freedom. This was essentially the cause of a Socialist crisis that has not yet been overcome. The ideal of freedom sharply divides the Democratic Socialists from the Communists. But as long as Socialists see the main goal of their efforts in the nationalization of economy, they will not escape the danger of ultimate centralized regimentation. This of necessity means the suppression of freedom. On the other hand, liberalism would stand definitively condemned if it were to insist on the exclusiveness of capitalist free enterprise.

The Hungarian revolution showed the way to a new social order: political democracy, safeguarding civic freedom and rule of law, should be based on the free associations of workers, peasants and other professions and on a mixed economic system with both collective and private ownership. The epoch-making importance of the Hungarian revolution lay in that it was not only a revolt against Communist tyranny but also that it established at the same time the positive aims of a new social order. Because of that its influence on any new organization of society should be permanent. Today its ideas operate in the first place as forces undermining Communist regimes; tomorrow the influence of its ideas may manifest itself even in the free world.

THE CRUMBLING OF THE MONOLITH

The October risings not only compromised Communism. They also caused ominous cracks in the Soviet bloc. Even Moscow's position was weakened. Though Russia managed to retain the strongest position in the Communist camp, the Kremlin's domination over other members, hitherto unquestioned, was left seriously impaired.

Now Peking is on the way to becoming a second centre of the Communist world, insisting on equality with Moscow. Poland, leaning on China and entertaining friendship with Yugoslavia, tries to follow her own road. Despite all the efforts to force her into a fresh alliance with Russia, she can no longer be considered a dependable ally. Yugoslavia is constantly involved in controversy with Russia and her Communist pawns. Tito, jealously guarding his independence, shows no sign of leaping at any time to the support of the Kremlin.

The development of Chinese influence is no less important than the crumbling of Russian prestige in East Central Europe. It would be futile to expect a conflict between Peking and Moscow. Communist China needs Soviet Russia for international, military and economic reasons. But as China's economic strength increases, her independence (especially where Russia is concerned) will also increase: as her power increases so will her aspirations and ambitions. The original unification of Communist Russia and Communist China was based on the relative weakness of China. Indeed, all Soviet domination has been based on the weakness of those on whom Russia imposed herself. When industrialization raised living standards in Russia, creating a new, rapidly increasing middle class, even the dictatorship at home began to experience difficulties. The oppressed became more exigent.

Russia and China became allies because of the circumstances

in which they found themselves. But they are also potential antagonists. Moscow is undoubtedly concerned about the growing political prestige of Peking. Soviet reaction to Mao Tse-Tung's theories of 'contradictions' in Communist society was unfavourable. The Kremlin insisted, after October 1956, on its 'leadership' in the Communist camp. It was realized that dualism or even polymorphism of power would lead to the disintegration of the Soviet empire and to heretical divergence among Communist movements in the world. In the division of power between Rome and Byzantium lay the reason for the disintegration of the Roman Empire. History never need repeat itself, but analogous causes sometimes have analogous consequences.

Moscow is justifiably worried, realizing that its exclusive supremacy over the Communist camp has been seriously challenged. Its authority has sunk low in East Central Europe. The subjugated countries can no longer be trusted. Communist rulers may swear allegiance to Moscow with great servility, but they speak only for themselves. And by trying to enforce this loyalty to Moscow by persecution, they themselves are merely admitting the poverty of their leadership. Czech Communists live in a permanent panic. Ulbricht would be swept away if the Soviet soldiers were to leave East Germany. Belgrade alone at present rejects Soviet supremacy, but elsewhere Communist regimes remain in power only because of the general fear of Soviet military intervention. The tasks imposed on the Red Army have grown monstrously. During the October rising it became evident that the satellite armies, created at great cost to everyone concerned, were of no use to Russia. The effort to win the Polish army over to Russia, by putting in charge the Polish-born Red Army Marshal Rokossovski, failed dismally. The Polish army seemed almost eager to fight against Soviet units. Hungarian soldiers joined the revolution against Moscow at the very beginning. The Communist general, Maleter, organized the defence in Budapest against attacking Soviet divisions. Even officers hitherto considered loyal Communists gave themselves to the service of the revolutionaries.

In an emergency the eighty satellite divisions would form a kernel of revolt rather than an auxiliary force of the Red Army. Partisans would harass the Soviet military machine over the whole wide area between the Baltic and the Mediterranean. This would cause Soviet divisions to be pinned down in all the regions now oppressed by the Russian dictatorship. Unless they believe in deluding themselves, the rulers in the Kremlin cannot fail to realize the proven undependability of the satellite armies, as well as the danger of revolt and sabotage if there were a war. The so-called 'strengthening' of the Warsaw alliance, stressed in all the declarations issued by the Communist Governments since the Hungarian rising, has no other practical meaning than to supply the Russian Government with a dubious legal pretext for maintaining garrisons and bases for aircraft, naval units and guided missiles in the captive countries. The Red Army is the only force in East Central Europe on which Moscow can depend. And it is significant that not only was there a purge of Czech and Bulgarian army officers in the spring of 1957 but also the numbers of Soviet instructors and controllers attached to the Czech General Staff increased by an unknown figure.

RUSSIA'S ASSETS AND LIABILITIES

All the facts confirm that the October risings shook Communism in all its forms: 'international', 'national' and 'Titoist', and it is obvious that the commotion in all Communist countries – from East Germany to China – continues.

The crisis in the Kremlin, apparent since the death of Stalin, becomes more and more significant. Yet even if this decline indicates the inevitable collapse of the Communist empire, it is impossible to say when the disintegration is likely to be completed – or how.

The resources at the disposal of the Kremlin are enormous. Russia is still the second strongest world power. Moscow's dictators may be subject to many internal difficulties and growing pressures that force them to make concessions. Because of this they behave in a most bewildering manner, virtually contradicting each other. Yet the inner discontent within Russia is not, for the time being, enough to endanger the regime. Similarly, the Chinese dictatorship is not yet threatened by any serious crisis, even though it often has to face considerable inner difficulties. Only in the subjugated countries of East Central Europe is the lid kept on revolt by the brutal pressure of the Red Army.

The knowledge that Russia could lose her supremacy over her European satellites makes it easier for the Kremlin to gain support from the Russians themselves, especially from the nationalistic army officers and economic managers who are proud of Soviet expansion. These Soviet nationalists are not suffering from 'the crisis of conscience' that attacked the Soviet intellectuals and students after the bloody suppression of the Hungarians.

Moscow exploits the knowledge that neither the United States nor her allies would provide military intervention if there were further risings. During the Polish and Hungarian Revolutions the Americans clearly indicated that they did not contemplate providing military aid in any form to rebels behind the Iron Curtain. Fear of provoking a world war paralysed the feeble attempts that were made by the Western Powers to undertake effective political or diplomatic action. The Russians were not disturbed when they began venting their fury on Hungary. The Poles had no other choice but to continue to accept dependence on Moscow. The others submitted with resignation to their fate, realizing that they, too, would be left without help. Many people behind the Iron Curtain, especially those in Poland, Czechoslovakia, Hungary and Rumania, began to wonder anxiously whether the Yalta conception of the distribution of 'spheres of influence' among the Great Powers was not still in existence. But neither the Western Powers nor the Communists seemed willing to remember that pledges were given about free elections. Meantime, Russian power, not yet encountering any serious challenge from the West, retains threatening proportions. And the Russian leaders themselves are still strong enough to wage a political offensive against the Western Powers in Asia, in the Near East and in Africa. As long as they hold their positions on the Elbe, the Vltava and the Danube, the men in the Kremlin will not relinquish the hope that they might one day add a united Germany to their sphere of domination and thus start spreading their influence to the rest of Western Europe. The Soviet threat to Europe has not been removed by the growing realization that nuclear war seems hardly probable. War is not the only means by which the strong can gain supremacy over the weak. Soviet Russia, in contradiction to the Wilhelmite or Hitlerite imperialists, is not likely to start a major war, though she would have no hesitation in provoking, engineering and maintaining, if necessary, local wars. By holding the centre of Europe, Russia manages to keep the whole of Europe in the shadow of her menace. Her position in Central Europe also enables her to maintain a beachhead for the operations needed for spreading over the whole of Europe her dangerous political doctrines. This could be invaluable if she decided on a campaign of political expansion.

Despite everything that has happened it is probable that Western diplomatists will again under-estimate the importance of East Central Europe. The danger of this happening is all the greater because of the feeling of security created by the un-doubted lessening of the likelihood of a war. Public interest is concentrated on preventing any conflict in which nuclear weapons would be used. Public opinion insists on disarmament. But most people do not yet realize the terrible consequences of continuing Soviet hegemony over East Central Europe.

Too many Western diplomatists and politicians feel that the present position, with Germany divided, and Russia dominat-ing East Central Europe, is more beneficial than harmful. They feel it helps to maintain the security of the Western world. But in reality it only helps Russia. These two problems should never be separated. The first that is likely to arise is the re-unification of Germany. It is dangerous to under-estimate Germany's desire to become a united nation once again. The greater the obstacles placed in the way of German reunification the greater will be the risk of dangerous complications. It is doubtful whether Soviet dictators can continue to prevent another revolutionary explosion in this region if they insist on holding East Germany in subjection. And if the Western Powers, co-operating with Adenauer's Bonn Government, maintain their present attitude towards feeling in Germany, they are only likely to help those West Germans who advocate reunification through direct negotiations with the Communists. The Western Powers must in the end recognize that the Russians are implacably opposed to their terms for re-unification.

Only the strong personality of Dr Adenauer has guaranteed West German membership of the Atlantic Alliance. Social Democrats, Liberals and others resolutely anti-Communist, all lean towards Western political and social ideas. But this does not mean that they also see in the North Atlantic Treaty Organization the surest means of fulfilling their revived aspirations for German nationalism. Once they realized that they could gain nothing by advocating a policy based on the ability of the West to apply military pressure, many Germans began to feel so frustrated that they decided it would be best to quit the Western military alliance. By doing this they believe they can find an alternative method of attaining unification. The difficulties encountered during the creation of a Federal German army indicates that the people were not over-enthusiastic about strengthening the Atlantic military machine with their own men.

German misgivings became even more apparent when the British and Americans, gambling heavily on nuclear weapons as a deterrent, started reducing the number of troops stationed in West Germany. This fresh conception of Western strategy encouraged the strong anti-militarist tendencies still prevalent

among German youth. All the evidence shows that the desire
for unification is stronger than the resolution to remain in the
Western alliance.

The possibility of another German-Russian *rapprochement*
should never be completely ruled out. German-Russian co-
operation, born in the eighteenth century, might yet be revived
in the twentieth century in spite of all that happened in the two
World Wars. This alliance might now be all the more attractive
to the Russians because they realize that this time Germany
would be the weaker partner. Also, the Germans could be
seduced by the hope that Russia, considerably weakened by the
consequences of the October risings, would now make a less
exacting partner. German confidence is growing as more and
more people come to believe that Communism could not
prevail in Germany. Obviously they think that Communism
could not prevail without Soviet interference in German
affairs. Yet under Soviet pressure combined with economic
promises and other temptations, Communism would undoubtedly spread if Germany were to approach too close to
Russia, while separating herself from the West.

It is not likely that the partnership of the Rapallo agreement
or that of the 1939 pact will be restored. Yet we must recognize
the possibility of Russian-German co-operation becoming one
of the most useful factors in the foreign policy of both Powers.
And it is necessary to bear in mind that pressure towards
German unification might, in some circumstances, invalidate
Germany's membership of the Atlantic alliance.

Even Dr Adenauer realized that he must be more sympathetic in his attitude to fundamental national aspirations
among his countrymen. After his retirement from politics the
situation in Germany will change radically. It will be much
more fluid and far less stable than now. So far economic pros-
perity in West Germany has diverted attention from the drive
for reunification. But economic difficulties, causing unemployment, could trigger off a powerful wave of German nationalism,
and it would be the Russians, not the Western Powers, who

would benefit from this situation. Naturally, they would exploit it too. As long as Germany is divided there is an increasing danger of a revolution in East Germany, or of West Germany leaving the Atlantic alliance in the hope of achieving re-unification through direct negotiations with the Communists.

If the Western Powers, with the co-operation of the Federal Republic, were to succeed in their proposals – unification through free elections and the free choice of a united Germany to decide whether or not it remains a member of either of the major military alliances – it would strengthen the West and encourage the subjected East European nations. But if the Russians were able to enforce their conditions for reunification – direct negotiations between the Federal Republic and the Communist-dominated People's Government, with the pre-servation of 'Socialist achievements' in East Germany – they would be preparing for the establishment in Germany of another 'People's Democracy'. This could only lead to Germany's becoming harassed by the most serious internal conflicts and seriously endanger the world position of the Western Powers.

For the countries of East Central Europe such an agreement on the unification of Germany would be catastrophic. It could only mean the prolonging of their enslavement. This is likely, too, if any further risings among the East Germans were crushed by the Russians.

Although the Western Powers and the Russians remained for so long intransigent in their attitude towards Germany's future, an eventual compromise is inevitable. To reach an agreement with Russia on German reunification will be most difficult. In exchange for the slightest concession from Moscow the Western Powers might be tempted to ignore the misery of the enslaved states of East Central Europe. Indeed, there is fear that to get an agreement on Germany the West might even be willing to accept the accomplished fact of Russia's dominating position in the East and recognize the present position as the future pattern of Europe. Yet this, paradoxically, could danger-ously weaken the West, even though general satisfaction all over the Western world on an agreement about the future of a united Germany would probably blind all concerned to the unpleasant consequences of Russia's triumph. In the same way, after the Munich agreement, the feeling of relief washed away all sense of shame and drowned the warning voice of Churchill. Possibly, remembering this dishonourable experience, Western statesmen will be more provident when facing an agreement with the Russians. But it is vitally necessary to point out all the dangers of a possible extension of the present division of Germany or of a compromise that would, by facilitating re-unification, create a helpless German nation and leave, at the same time, East Central Europe under Soviet domination.

The situation of the enslaved nations will improve or deteriorate according to the conditions in which German reunification is achieved. The position of Germany will be stronger or weaker according to whether the countries of East Central Europe become free or remain under Soviet domination. Not only Germany but East Central Europe occupy important strategic positions in the Cold War. Any compromise that fails to recognize this can only bequeath trouble to the world. Piecemeal tactics (the separation or the attempted separation of one problem from the other) could only benefit Soviet diplomacy and weaken the West. Indeed, no genuine European settlement is possible as long as East Central Europe remains in slavery.

Russia's enormous military power might remain a terrible menace to the free world. By exploiting the general fear of a nuclear war they try to bolster their power. By offensive diplomacy they try to increase their influence on world thought. Their main objective is the destruction of the Atlantic alliance, the ejection of the Americans from European and Asian bases and the decisive weakening of the United States, followed by recognition of the Soviet sphere of influence in the whole of Europe and Asia. In their struggle for world domination East Central Europe is a great asset.

It is idle to attempt a forecast of the future. Unforeseeable incidents often reverse the so-called 'logic of development'.

No impregnable 'iron laws' determine the course of events. Certain forces and influences lead to certain consequences only with a greater or lesser probability. Personalities who have power at a given moment play an important part in spite of their influence being restricted by their surroundings and circumstances. War became probable after the Munich agreement, but it could have been averted or at least shortened to a relatively brief period if, in the months following Munich, France, Britain and Russia had concluded a military alliance. Had Churchill not succeeded Chamberlain in the spring of 1940, Britain would probably, after the fall of France, have made a compromise peace with Germany. Had the attempt on Hitler's life succeeded in 1944, the Russians would not have occupied the centre of Europe. Without de Gaulle, France would not have achieved her equal partnership with the Great Powers. Had the Allies disembarked their D-Day force in the Balkans instead of on the Normandy beaches, the Russians would not have overcome the whole of East Central Europe, and so on. What happened did not have to happen. These examples illustrate the consequences, both realized and unrealized, of certain preceding events.

No one can foresee the outcome of the growing difficulties and sharpening tensions inside the Communist world. But the whole Communist empire is being shaken by conflicting social and national forces – and by powerful spiritual currents. Now the spirit of freedom has been released, anything can happen. But whatever the course of future events that lead to a European settlement, the revolutionary forces in the Soviet empire will not be able to achieve the liberation of the enslaved peoples of East Central Europe without effective political aid from the Western Powers.

The Hungarian experience was significant in this respect. Quite obviously a small nation could not, with its own resources alone, triumph over the overwhelming superiority of the Red Army. But at the same time it became clear that the Russians were able to restore their full supremacy over this small country only because the Western Powers made no effective or practical effort to help. We have studied some of the ways in which the West can put pressure on the Russians. We should realize now that by their indecision during the Hungarian crisis the West have missed their opportunity. This only emphasizes the need for the Western Powers to exploit the continuing Communist crisis by a political offensive against Soviet policy.

A NEW POLITICAL SETTLEMENT

The radical change in the strategic orientation of the United States and Britain, who are concentrating more and more on nuclear weapons, may lead to paradoxical consequences. While the danger of a general nuclear war diminishes to a minimum, the defensive capabilities of Western Europe would be weakened, the more so if the number of American and British forces in Europe were to be drastically reduced. Their military value compared with Russia's strength is not perhaps great, but their political importance is tremendous. Their presence on the Continent is a dependable and perhaps the only guarantee that the Western Powers would automatically repulse a Soviet attack with their nuclear weapons. It is

When writing this chapter the author was already feeling the effects of the illness which led eventually to his death. He was never able to revise it and would probably have added a conclusion to the whole book. The plan he develops in the following pages was conceived immed- after Stalin's death, at a time when it was possible to hope that the Russians might be open to some such suggestion. After the post-Stalin regime was consolidated he continued to put forward his plan, chiefly, as he points out in his book, as a tactical move. But since the writer's death in January 1958 a strengthened France under General de Gaulle's leadership has tightened its links with West Germany and a decisive trend towards an economical and political union of Western Europe has taken shape with the development of the European Economic Community. As the author of this book would certainly have welcomed this development, the question may now be asked whether in view of the changed world situation he would still have upheld his plan.— *Publisher's note*.

understandable that the Russians should strive by every means to destroy NATO, which would mean the withdrawal of American troops from Europe and the closing of American airbases not only on the Continent but also in Britain. Similarly, one can understand why the Russians refuse to link the question of disarmament with that of the political settlement of controversial European issues; they simply want to retain their position in East Germany and in East Central Europe.

This means that the more we depend on preserving peace through the deterrent of American and British nuclear bombs, the stronger and the more favourable the political position of the Russians will become – if they continue to dominate over East Germany and East Central Europe. As long as Germany remains divided and independence is denied to subjugated Communist nations, Western Europe will continue to be susceptible to the dangerous political pressures of Russia, pressures that could only be increased after any reduction in the number of American and British troops stationed on the Continent. Attempts to arrange for general disarmament will fail until the two main European problems, German reunification and liberation of the satellite countries, have been tackled satisfactorily. To experienced negotiators there can be no disarmament without security and no security without a political settlement to satisfy all interested partners.

It is possible to visualize a political settlement that would make a new system of European security practicable. The Western Governments, including Dr Adenauer's Federal Republic, will not accept any Soviet proposals intended to extend Soviet influence throughout Germany. On the other hand, Moscow will reject any proposals for reunification unless they include guarantees against a united Germany becoming a member of the Atlantic Alliance. A settlement can only be envisaged if Germany becomes united through free elections but gives a pledge to refuse the blandishments of military blocks for a considerable time. In all other things Germany could be a truly sovereign power with an army of her own.

This could be subjected to restrictions similar to those imposed on other states by a general disarmament agreement.

The men in the Kremlin will not withdraw from East Central Europe unless they are assured that this region will not be used as an assault beachhead for an attack on Russia. A settlement could be based on an undertaking by each Government created in these territories by free elections, to remain neutral. Such a pledge could be internationally guaranteed. On the whole, in their foreign policy, these subjected nations would follow the example of Austria. It would also be desirable if Germany, on the one hand, and Poland and Czechoslovakia, on the other, were to promise to try to solve some disputes and controversies by peaceful means. The countries of East Central Europe might accept the same obligations towards any controversial issues that might arise among them.

Such a settlement would be completed by the simultaneous withdrawal of Western soldiers from West Germany and Soviet troops from East Germany and East Central Europe. The reduction of American and British forces in other West European countries should depend on the progress of general disarmament. Even after a settlement on these lines, Russia would remain the strongest military power on the Continent. Complete withdrawal of Western troops from the Continent would give an incalculable advantage to the Russians. Not even their withdrawal from East Central Europe would right the balance.[1]

Agreement on all these proposals could be embodied in a new European security system or at least could become a basis for such a system, guaranteed by everybody concerned, including the United States and the Soviet Union and possibly even the United Nations. This security system could be linked, at the same time, with a disarmament agreement.

[1] Hugh Gaitskell, discussing similar proposals in his book, *The Challenge of Co-existence*, London, Methuen, 1957, says: 'I must underline that in any plan of this kind American troops should stay in Europe – in the Low Countries, in France and in Britain. In short, NATO should not retreat further back than the frontiers of Germany.'

In advocating these proposals since 1953,[1] I have constantly in mind two fundamental ideas:

To achieve the liberation of the countries of East Central Europe through neutralization and free elections;

To facilitate the reunification of Germany through her pledge not to enter into any military alliance with another state for a period of some 10–20 years.

After the October risings, the Hungarians especially asked for the neutralization of their country.[2]

[1] The author conceived this plan as early as 1953. He wrote several memoranda and articles and made numerous statements containing this plan for a European settlement. The first memorandum is dated September 8, 1953; he made the last statement in New York in October 1957. One of his articles on the subject was published by the *Manchester Guardian* of May 9, 1956.

[2] Different suggestions and plans, analogous to the proposals we have specified, were submitted by several distinguished Western politicians and some exiles from Western Europe. Dr V. V. Tilea, a former Rumanian Ambassador in London, has eloquently defended the neutralization of East Central Europe since 1954. Adam Ciolkosz, chairman of the Executive Committee of the Polish Council of National Unity in London, has spoken in support of the idea of a neutral zone in several occasions. The Polish liberal, Dr Stanislav Olszewski, has also discussed the proposals in great detail. Mr Gaitskell has spoken in this way on many occasions, including one in the House of Commons at the end of March 1957, when he said: 'It seems to me apart from anything else that we owe it to the peoples of the satellite countries, at least to examine what can be done to win freedom for them by diplomatic means.' Elsewhere, Gaitskell explained his ideas in this way: 'The path to be followed seems to me an extension of the Eden plan put forward in 1955. It was at that time proposed that there should be a withdrawal of forces from the frontiers between East and West Germany, leaving within Germany itself a zone in which there were no foreign troops. Would it not be possible to extend the area of such a zone until it covered, say, the whole of Germany, Poland, Czechoslovakia and Hungary – and, if possible, Rumania and Bulgaria?

The withdrawal could be a gradual one, taking place over a period of time. It would have to be subject to control, as would also the size and character of whatever national forces it was agreed that the countries in question should possess.

But here the latest proposals of the Russians themselves for a zone in

Because this plan for Europe's future means taking a calculated risk, it has been rejected by many experts, especially those in official Western circles and, also, by a great many exiles from the subjected countries. The proposals are said to endanger the North Atlantic Treaty Organization which has vital need of West Germany. Yet the West German contribution to the military power of NATO has so far been surprisingly small. And it is possible that after the retirement of Chancellor

which there would be both aerial and ground controls might be appropriately introduced. Indeed, one could envisage the whole plan as forming a part of a wider move towards a comprehensive disarmament agreement between the Great Powers.

In the early stages it might be advisable to leave the alliance unchanged. To begin with, both NATO and the Warsaw Pact might continue. But if foreign troops withdrew, it is doubtful whether this situation could last long. Indeed, the Russians might refuse to contemplate the plan without neutralization on both sides from the start. They would assume, no doubt, that the satellite countries would prefer to be neutral, and they would therefore wish to ensure that Germany was neutral as well. I believe that this is a risk which we ought to take. Finally, together with the permanent control on arms in these territories, there should be a multilateral European security plan, in which the various states in the neutral zone would have their territories guaranteed by the Great Powers as well as by each other.'

A Conservative, Lord St. Oswald, speaking in the same way during a debate on Eastern Europe in the House of Lords on July 4, 1957, said: 'I should like to see the Western Powers laying on the table definite terms for a neutralized belt across Europe. The initial requirements of those terms would be the withdrawal of Russian troops from the captive lands, followed by free elections under United Nations supervision. If that could be brought about, as I believe it can, it would enact the uncompleted provisions of the Yalta Agreement, and at long last vindicate our signatures on that agreement. . . .

Even if such a plan, put forward in good faith by the Western Powers, were rejected, ultimately or out of hand, by the Soviet leaders, it would still be of benefit to put it forward. Because the peoples of the slave nations would know that the proposal had been made, they would draw courage from it, and the position of their Russian persecutors would be even harder than it is today.'

Similar sentiments have also been expressed in talks broadcast by the B.B.C.

Adenauer the efforts to prevent Germany from ending the Western military alliance may not be successful.

Concern has also been expressed about the possibility of American withdrawal, not only from West Germany but from the whole of Western Europe. It is difficult to understand why the American troops could not stay – as Mr Gaitskell thinks necessary, for instance – in France, the Benelux Countries and Britain. Also, we should realize that under the new defence strategy of the Atlantic Alliance, the size of the American forces on the Continent will be reduced, even if the Russians retain their present domination over the centre of Europe. Britain has already cut her force in West Germany.[1]

Would the Americans lose interest in the defence of Europe if Germany were to leave NATO of her own accord? Surely this would be one more reason for their becoming even more active in the defence of Europe.

Another objection made against the plan is that it lacks any guarantee that the Soviet armies would not return to the countries they have left, especially after the withdrawal of the Americans. This fear is not unfounded. It would be necessary to insist on the United States and the other Western Powers giving an explicit warning that they would answer such Soviet aggression with a nuclear counter-attack. It would be necessary, too, to guarantee, in the kind of agreement we have in mind, free elections in the countries of East Central Europe. As long

[1] A Polish military expert, Captain E. Hinterhoff, in his remarkable study, '*Une chance pour l'Europe*', in the French review *L'armee – La Nation*, in April 1957, drawing attention to the Soviet infiltration in the Near East, explained that this meant the Americans should concentrate on this region instead of on Europe. Having analysed in detail all the changes in American strategic planning (leading to the formation of numerically small units, equipped with tactical atomic weapons), the author decides: 'It is necessary to reckon with considerable reductions of American land forces in Europe, if not with their gradual withdrawal.' For this reason he recommends a simultaneous withdrawal of American and Russian troops, the formation of a wide 'belt' of neutral states – United Germany, Hungary, Rumania, Czechoslovakia and Poland – and the demilitarization of this zone.

as the present Communist regimes remain in power, there will always be the danger that a Moscow stooge will 'ask' the Kremlin for 'help'.

It is true that after a plan of this kind had been accepted, the Russians would retain their military superiority on the Continent. But even if we do not take into account that a united Germany and the liberated countries of East Central Europe would have their own armies, ready to defend their national independence, we feel that Mr V. V. Tilea is right in saying: 'Is it not better for the West to let Soviet Russia start a war from her own frontiers – through a buffer belt rather than from the Elbe?'

Misgivings are expressed whether the neutralization of Germany and East Central Europe would not strengthen similar tendencies in the Western countries. This is possible. But it is the responsibility of leading statesmen, publicists and diplomatists always to fight those tendencies that are judged to endanger the security and defence of their countries. Anyway, if British and American forces in Europe are reduced, in due time steps will have to be taken to anticipate neutralist and other defeatist movements, all the more so if the Russians remain on the Elbe and the Vltava.

It would be idle to contend that the objections and misgivings mentioned are unfounded. But it is worth while to consider instead the superior advantages of the suggested plan. They seem to outweigh, to a great extent, any of the risks that must be taken in putting the proposals into practice.

The main advantage of the plan rests in the fact that, while the menacing superiority of Soviet power in Europe would be greatly reduced, the security of Russia itself would be in no way endangered. This alone would provide truly favourable conditions for peaceful co-existence or friendly trade competition between the East and West. The tension that now exists in Western Europe would be reduced if the Russians would withdraw behind their own frontiers. Germany would be re-united. The nations of East Central Europe would be free.

The balance of power would swing to the benefit of the West in spite of Russia's still remaining the strongest Power on the Continent. Western civilization could once more influence the whole of East Central Europe without hindrance. At the same time, the influence of the Russian civilization could also be felt where it was genuinely appreciated. In some ways Russian security would even be enhanced. The Russians would have no further need to fear the aggressive intentions of the Germans. Yet this fear would exist, no matter whether the Germans remained members of the Atlantic Alliance or made their own way towards unity. Only a plan that involved Germany in the general scheme of European peace could bring comfort to the Russians. True enough, the Russians would lose their supremacy over their satellites, but even so they would gain. They would no longer need to watch for rebellious tendencies. Instead of being enslaved, these countries would become their partners and neighbours. Instead of being rebels, they would be cash customers. Russia's economic co-operation with these nations (which cannot be severed, because of the changes in East Central Europe since 1945) would bring them more benefit than is possible now when they are obliged to maintain an enforced domination over these countries. The enslaved peoples now have a profound hatred of Soviet tyranny. Once free, they will desire nothing more sincerely than peace and friendly co-operation with everybody, Russia included. Hungarian rebels were expressing this belief even during the fierce fighting against Soviet soldiers.

The political settlement we have advocated, if backed by international guarantees from all the Great Powers, would substantially enhance European security and could contribute to an easier solution of the controversial issues in the Near East and Asia. In this way realistic provisions for disarmament would be secured.

The advantages of such a settlement of European problems are sufficient to explain why we suggest the Western Powers should take the initiative in making the necessary preliminary

moves towards negotiations. Of coarse, it is not likely that the
Soviet Government would accept this plan in the present
situation. The Russians have not yet relinquished the hope of
realizing their expansive aims, especially because some tendencies in Germany and in the other Western countries are,
involuntarily, helping them. But I am convinced that the
Western Powers, in presenting these proposals to the Russians,
would strengthen their moral and political position without
losing anything. Their initiative could drive the Soviets into a
precarious defensive. If Moscow were to refuse such a proposal, it would incite the whole German nation against Russia
and drive it into the embrace of the West. The enslaved nations,
eagerly hoping to attain the neutral status enjoyed by Austria,
would grow dangerously restive. Many reports from the enslaved countries, especially since the October rising, confirm
that this desire is shared even by disillusioned Communists.

Moscow would lose much of the sympathy of the Asian
democratic nations, who would realize even more clearly than
during the Hungarian Revolution that this negative attitude of
the Russians to the plan was further proof of the Kremlin's
imperialistic aims and intentions. Moscow's attitude would
obviously be criticized in Europe, North and South America
and in the African countries. This could only lead to new and
serious frictions among the Soviet leaders. If the Western
statesmen would indicate, at the same time, their readiness for a
satisfactory settlement of the problems in the Middle East and
the Far East, it is even possible that Peking might eventually
advise Moscow to relinquish its intransigency. At any rate, the
Kremlin rulers would be under such strong pressure, both
international and internal, that they could hardly continue to
resist.

Bold initiative from the Western democracies would forestall
similar initiative from Moscow. The resources of the Russians
are overstrained and since the October rising they have encountered serious difficulties in the satellite countries.
Khrushchev has involuntarily exposed Russian vulnerability by

discussing the satellite countries since October 1956 more often and more carefully than before, stressing repeatedly and with noticeable irritation that these countries will remain in 'the Socialist camp'.

The Soviets may try, in certain circumstances, to escape from their predicament by granting further autonomy to the enslaved countries, even at the price of a considerable diminishing of the influence of the Communist parties. They might, at the same time, revise their attitude to the German question. If they were to decide, because of the growing opposition of the enslaved nations, to content themselves with having a decisive influence over them, instead of the present exploiting domination, they could gradually bring about a state in which these nations might become resigned to enjoying considerable autonomy in the administration of their own internal affairs. The Russians could even gain the sympathy of the Germans if they were to facilitate their reunification. Through similar adjustments, Communist leaders could stabilize their influence in East Central Europe and probably extend it to the Rhine. This would mean they became even more dangerous rivals to the West than before. At present the Western Powers are protected against this danger mainly by the intractability of Moscow itself. Quite understandably the Russians do not want to forfeit this direct domination over East Central Europe, fearing that any relaxation of their tyranny might put the whole regime in jeopardy. Inner pressures may force the Soviet leaders to realize that Stalin's empire cannot be preserved intact for ever.

Necessity may press Moscow's new leaders to try to transform their empire into a Commonwealth under Russian leadership. If this happened, the Russian 'sphere of influence' would probably spread even over the rest of Western Europe.[1]

[1] It is, as Mr Tilea said in *The Times*, in May 1957: 'The great danger for the West if it does not launch this plan [proposing a neutral belt], lies in the possibility of Russia not only proposing it but actually accomplishing it. She would thus, by giving full freedom to the satellites, gain with a

If the West does not want or cannot use 'a policy of strength' against the Soviet Government, it can only prevent the danger of Moscow's influence growing by boldly achieving a political settlement that would lead to the withdrawal of the Red Army from the centre of Europe to beyond the Russian frontiers. This could only be done through a compromise agreement with Moscow, that in its turn would bring counter-balanced benefits to everybody, including the nations of East Central Europe.

THE NEED OF AN ACTIVE POLICY AND DIPLOMACY OF THE WESTERN POWERS

Soviet rulers, dizzy with the cult of power and the merciless application of force, would abandon their positions in East Central Europe only under pressure of necessity. The Western Powers can bring about Soviet compliance by firm policy, elastic, imaginative diplomacy and thoughtful propaganda.

Firm policy should be based above all on a resolute determination to preserve and strengthen the Atlantic Alliance. Whatever weakens this, strengthens Russia. Any effective negotiations with Moscow presuppose unbreakable solidarity of the Western Powers, based on the military power of NATO. Until a settlement about the main controversial issues in Europe and Asia is reached, the existence of a strong Western bloc remains vital for the whole free world, as well as for all those behind the Iron Curtain who yearn for freedom. That is why it would be very dangerous to consider any withdrawal of American and British troops from Europe before a settlement of the main causes of tension between the free world and the Communist world.

It is also necessary to build a united Europe. The Russians consider all moves towards the unification of Europe as serious

single stroke the lost sympathy of all those 100 million people and turn the existing relative sympathy for the Western Powers into direct contempt and hatred. Russia would not have to worry for two generations about the leaning of Central Europe towards the West, especially as the trade links of that part of Europe will in any event have to be for a long time mainly with the East.'

threats to their aims towards expansion. The Kremlin has systematically thwarted all attempts at closer co-operation among the nations of East Central Europe. Even now they do not allow their puppet Communist Governments to mix freely, but strive instead to integrate these countries into a general 'Socialist camp', where they remain directly under Russian domination.

Expansionist ambitions cause the men in the Kremlin to oppose the unification of Europe. They stormed against the European army, denounced the Common Market. They claimed that these were the devices of capitalism and imperialism. The more united Western Europe becomes, the more able the countries concerned will become in their resistance to the machinations of the Russian tactics of setting one country against another and gradually weakening each in turn. It is particularly important to remember that the more wholeheartedly Germany takes part in European institutions, the more difficult it will be for Moscow to persuade Germany to play her party game. Only a united Europe could effectively propagate 'the European message' behind the Iron Curtain. It is significant that Western Europe, shocked by Soviet brutality in Hungary, spoke with more convincing emphasis and deeper understanding than the voice of the world did when the United Nations discussed liberation and the needs of the enslaved nations.

The firm policy of the West – as far as Europe is concerned – should manifest itself in an emphatic declaration that the Atlantic Powers consider both German reunification and the restoration of the freedom and independence of the nations of East Central Europe fundamental conditions of any political settlement or agreement with Russia. In spite of numerous declarations (some of an official or semi-official nature), the Western Powers have had difficulty in proclaiming, in any statement worthy of being called a pledge, that the peaceful liberation of the nations of East Central Europe was a basic principle of their foreign policy.

Because the so-called liberation policy was restricted mainly to the field of propaganda, the Russians felt justified in ignoring it. If the peaceful liberation of the Central European nations were officially proclaimed a definite aim of the Western Powers, the Soviet Government would be forced to give serious consideration to what was being said, especially as any such declaration would encourage all the enslaved nations living in a state of latent revolt against Soviet domination.

The effect of such a declaration could be even stronger if the Western Powers proclaimed at the same time that they would consider the neutral status of the liberated nations of East Central Europe as a suitable and desirable part of a new system of Continental security. They would clearly prove in this way that they have no intention of exploiting the liberation of these nations to embarrass Russia. They should emphasize that they wish to liberate the satellites merely in accordance with internationally recognized principles governing the right of every nation to freedom and independence.

Their readiness to guarantee the neutrality of Central European nations would also prove their belief that the wide strip between the Baltic and the Mediterranean, in the past so often an excuse for discord and conflicting ambitions among the Great Powers, should become a region of peaceful and friendly co-operation.

Such a declaration of the Western Powers could profoundly embarrass the Russians, especially if it were stressed at the same time that the proposed political settlement would open the way to real and substantial disarmament. On this basis it would be possible to mobilize world opinion against Russian inflexibility and greatly stimulate the hopes of the enslaved countries, and of many Russians, too, that the days of Communist dictatorship were numbered.

The plan I have outlined should be accompanied by wide propaganda. People on both sides of the Iron Curtain should be told of the purely peaceful aims of the plan.

Public opinion in Russia cannot exist in the same sense or even to the same extent as in the free countries. Yet it exists, especially among the Soviet intelligentsia and bureaucracy. These people have limited opportunities at least of listening from time to time to foreign broadcasts. So the Western Powers should repeat on every appropriate occasion that they have no hostile intentions towards Russia or her people. It should be emphasized that they sincerely wish to co-operate with them. It should also be frequently stressed that the Western Powers have no intention of interfering with any attempts made by the Russians to reach a political agreement with the now enslaved nations. This answers Soviet propaganda repeatedly asserting that 'the Western imperialists' aim at the destruction of Russian administration and the disintegration of the United States of Soviet Russia.

The Western Powers should constantly reaffirm that they have no intention of supporting any attempt to restore any of the regimes that existed in Eastern Europe before they came under the influence of the Red Army's Commissars or of enforcing their own political and social systems on the peoples in Communist-dominated territories. The Western Powers should merely reiterate that they are ready to recognize and to respect any regimes that emerge from free elections. Let us not forget the impact of the Communist propaganda that continues to repeat to the workers in Russia and the enslaved countries that the fall of Communism would bring not only a return of capitalism but also unemployment. Russian broadcasts constantly warn the peasants in Central Europe of the danger of restoring the large private estates. It is taken for granted that this is the ultimate aim of the Western Powers.[1]

[1] Dr A. Berle Jr, the Liberal leader who is a former American Under-Secretary of State, said in an address at the Free Europe College in Strasbourg before the October risings: 'It is a matter of indifference whether a Poland or a Czechoslovakia whose Government offers liberty of thought, opportunity for spiritual development and the ready possibility of a prosperous economic life for all, choses to operate its railroads or factories by private corporations or by Socialist committees. Our insistence is that underlying values shall be realized and that under either system men and women must have a ready and available avenue towards a freer, larger life.'

The Polish and Hungarian risings clearly revealed the aspirations of all enslaved nations. This helped the Western democracies in preparing a new policy (and the propaganda to go with it). Their last doubts, if they existed at all, were dispersed. It was all too obvious that all the nations of East Central Europe passionately desired liberation, not only from Soviet domination but from local Communist tyranny as well. Hungarian revolutionaries expressed the wishes of all these nations when they asked for neutral status and free and peaceful co-operation with all other nations, including Russia. Polish and Hungarian rebels proved that they wished neither to return to capitalism nor to retain Communism. They desired instead a new liberal and Socialist democratic order. Voices from the other captive countries make a similar plea whenever they have an opportunity for making themselves heard. The West would greatly help the people behind the Iron Curtain if, through its policy, diplomacy and propaganda, it would support these desires.

Western Governments constantly fail to recognize the dynamic force which the ideas of freedom, the rule of law, social justice and respect for the individual have on the minds of the people behind the Iron Curtain. This includes the Russians. Communism has lost its old appeal. No longer does it fill people with overwhelming, impetuous zeal. Its influence is waning. But behind the Iron Curtain there is a renaissance of liberal Socialism, characterized by a renewed respect for spiritual and religious values. Marxist materialism is being superseded by a new spiritualism or humanism, conceived socially.[1]

---

[1] Ion Ratiu, a young Rumanian, vividly stated the case when he wrote in his *Policy for the West*: 'The West has a defensive policy; its whole structure is fundamentally based on fear. How to stop Communism? This is the question which seems to be the permanent pre-occupation of Western statesmen. The West must find a positive policy with such a powerful appeal throughout the world that it would force Communists into the position of looking for means to prevent the further spread of democracy. Western democracy is in duty bound before history to grasp

Eastern Europe in the Post-War World

Since the October risings, the situation has changed radically: today there is a real possibility of the Western democracies passing from the defensive to the offensive. As long as the West is able to preserve a strong Atlantic Alliance, it can prevent further Russian military expansion. But because it tried – and rightly so – to save the world from another catastrophic war, it cannot use military means against all-powerful Red armies. In this way Western policy remains defensive. Yet the political and ideological potential of the Western democracies is far stronger than that of the Communists. The West could tighten the crisis of Communism through a political offensive exploiting all the forces in revolt behind the Iron Curtain, against the despotism of the Kremlin and Communist dictatorships.

A political offensive means above all timely political and diplomatic action. Astute Western diplomacy could deprive the Russians of the initiative that they have held for so long. Whenever it is possible to anticipate events, it is best to try to influence them in favour of the cause of freedom. Vigorous propaganda, truthfully interpreting the crisis of the Communist world, could sharpen inner tension and help the forces of liberalization. The fundamental demands, postulated by the Hungarian Revolution, provided safe directives for propaganda to pierce the Iron Curtain. Every suitable expedient should be used. It should be made possible for great numbers of people from Russia and other Communist countries to travel to the free world. Visits of Western individuals and groups to Communist countries should be organized. Democracies cannot control their tourists as effectively as Communist Governments control their own people who are allowed to visit the West, but it would be possible to instruct at least some of them to consider themselves as envoys behind the Iron Curtain – envoys of the free world.

It seems expedient to develop as much as possible the

the opportunity and to accept the responsibility of championing the free institutions which it treasures.' Ion Ratiu, *Policy for the West*, London, The Harvill Press, 1957, pp. 162–163.

cultural relations between West and East in order to strengthen those in the East who long for freedom of spirit. In some circumstances even economic or financial aid granted by the Americans and other Western countries could strengthen the liberation movements.

When the danger of a general war diminishes, the task of diplomacy and propaganda must increase. In the eyes of the Russians 'peaceful co-existence' does not mean the end of the struggle between capitalism and Communism, but a permanent, ruthless war waged by political and economic weapons. Communists engage in this all the more stubbornly and mercilessly when faced by a domestic crisis. The Western democracies would need now, even more than in the past, a central staff for an intensive political and ideological war against the Communist world.

The political, diplomatic, propaganda and cultural weapons used systematically in a combined operation by the West could strengthen and encourage the forces of liberalization that need sustaining in the struggle for freedom behind the Iron Curtain.

Combined internal and external pressure could eventually persuade the Russians seriously to negotiate with the West about a new political settlement in Europe. This would inevitably lead to their leaving the dominating positions that they have occupied in the centre of Europe since the end of the war.

Index

Index